Best Of Times, Worst Of Times

Bomber Command – Two Men – One War

Jeff Steel

Joe Shuttleworth

16pt

9780369374059

Read How You Want
LARGE PRINT BOOKS, BRAILLE & DAISY

Copyright Page from the Original Book

Big Sky Publishing Pty Ltd
PO Box 303, Newport, NSW 2106, Australia
Phone: 1300 364 611
Fax: (61 2) 9918 2396
Email: info@bigskypublishing.com.au
Web: www.bigskypublishing.com.au

Cover design and typesetting: Think Productions

A catalogue record for this book is available from the National Library of Australia

Title: Best of Times, Worst of Times: Bomber Command - Two Men - One War

TABLE OF CONTENTS

Dedication

Flight Lieutenant TH. Blackham DFC—124922—Pilot
Pilot Officer C.R.E. Walton—174051—Flight engineer
Flying Officer D.G. Jones—144926—Navigator
Flight Sergeant S.J. Godfrey—175487—Bomb aimer
Sergeant S.C. Wilkins—1396525—Wireless operator
Sergeant H.G. Ridd—1003849—Mid-upper gunner

Prologue

It was the best of times, it was the worst of times, it was the age of wisdom, it was the age of foolishness, it was the epoch of belief, it was the epoch of incredulity, it was the season of Light, it was the season of Darkness ... we were all going direct to Heaven, we were all going direct the other way.

Charles Dickens wrote those opening words to *A Tale of Two Cities* in 1859. He was writing about the French Revolution. His words – 'best of times' and 'worst of times' – are also perfect to describe the very different experiences of two men who were caught up in the cataclysm of World War II: rear gunner Joe Shuttleworth and his pilot, Tom Blackham. In the maelstrom of the Hitler war, one would, indeed, have the best of times; the other would have the worst of times.

On the night of the last big Berlin raid in 1944, a team of Luftwaffe men in a nightfighter had set out from Rostock after Joe and Tom. The Luftwaffe men did not know who the Royal Air Force men were – only that they wanted to kill them.

The German crew were a whisker away from success. With Joe's injury, the war was over for him. After five terrifying, life threatening trips over the heavily guarded German capital of Berlin, he had more than done his bit for the war effort. Later, other Luftwaffe men would try to kill Tom, but then, curiously, they would go beyond the call of any imaginable duty to save his life.

World War II was a vicious, pitiless business. It is surprising, but also heartening, that there was still some honour, decency and humanity alive in isolated pockets.

For Joe, the war would give him comradeship, the crucial feeling of having 'done your bit' and a wife. He travelled the world and saw wonderful things that he would not otherwise have seen. There was no airman who would have 'the best of times' more than Joe Shuttleworth.

Without a doubt, though, there was no airman who would suffer 'the worst of times' more than Tom Blackham. He was destined to find out why dropping bombs on Hitler's Reich was a good idea. He would experience the full septic horror of what Nazidom had to offer.

The men who flew in Bomber Command, such as Joe and Tom, had a particular self-image. They saw themselves as ordinary blokes faced with a job that had to be done. It was a simple proposition of cause and effect; they had merely, in a very routine way, volunteered to go and do it. It was poor etiquette after the war for 'civvies' (civilians) to call them 'heroes', as this would only invite a cocktail of embarrassment, irritation and scorn.

Those of us in later generations cannot accept this view of the world. To us, who they helped save from Hitler's dystopian nightmare, the risks that the Royal Air Force crews faced preclude them from the name 'ordinary blokes'. Ordinary blokes do not cheerfully accept the risk of being shot down in flames. Ordinary blokes do not accept the risk of being dead by tomorrow morning. Ordinary blokes do not run the risk of being hideously disfigured, but left suffering for decades.

Many of these men would protest, 'It was always the other bloke who was going to be shot!' But still, every raid offered a substantial chance of death, or worse. In their hearts, they knew this, even if their minds suppressed it.

No fewer than 125,000 of them flew on Royal Air Force operations. Of these, 75,000 were killed, wounded, or taken prisoner. It is sad to think that almost all of their stories were lost ... this book contains two that were not.

Lest we forget!

Jeff Steel
Melbourne, Australia – 2021

PART 1

JOE'S STORY

1

Over the Baltic Sea (16 February 1944 – 0100 hours)

'Enemy coast ahead, skipper.'

'Thanks, bomb aimer. What's our position, navigator?'

'Five minutes from the coast of Germany, skipper. We'll pass Rostock to the west.'

The four Merlin engines droned on over the Baltic Sea with a deafening roar, making it difficult to hear the skipper's orders, even through earphones.

An order crackled down the intercom in Blackie's Scottish lilt. 'Gunners, keep your wits about you. The Herrenvolk are bound to be gunning for us.'

Hitler's Reich was creaking and crumbling but was by no means defeated. At this stage, his empire was no longer the roaring lion of 1940, but more a wounded, desperate, yet still very deadly snake.

In my fifth operation over Germany, we were on our way to Berlin in a Lancaster heavy bomber. Berlin was guarded with a 50 kilometre cordon of deadly 88-mm flak guns and countless nightfighters. Berlin – the 'Big City', as we called it – was infamous for being the worst trip the Royal Air Force could take on. Since all of my trips had been to Berlin, my life expectancy was less than most. Still, 'most' did not have a good life expectancy either, so there were no complaints. There was a war on and a job to be done. Anyway, it was always the other chap who was going to get 'the chop'. That's what we told ourselves.

'Any sign of activity, gunners?'

'Not a thing, skipper,' said Ridd, running his mid-upper guns left and right.

I swung my own rear turret with its four Browning .303 machine guns left and right, then left again. The sight of the huge armada in the sky was a stirring sight. I could not count the bombers, but there were so many that it seemed that you could walk from one aircraft to the other, as far as the furthest horizon in the moonlight. We learned later that there were 891 bombers heading for Berlin that night. I did not know it at the time, but that raid carried the heaviest load of bombs in military history up to that point.

Below us was a thick carpet of cloud. We had the skies to ourselves, or so it seemed.

It was my turn to give a report to the skipper.

'Rear gunner to skipper. Nothing here either, Blackie.'

'Well, keep your eyes...'

***

Without warning the world went suddenly dark and my head hurt. At least, my head was trying to hurt, but there was a lot of confusion.

Why did it suddenly go dark? It had been light. Now, it was light. There was light everywhere. You couldn't have light in a Lancaster bomber, or the nightfighters would see you from miles away.

Oh, God! My head really hurt now. I could get my left eye open, but not the right. That must have been something to do with the confusion.

I felt like I should have been hurting, but instead, there was a warmth. They must have given me something. Had they given me morphine? Who were they? Why was I suddenly in the light?

'Bed eight is waking up,' said a female voice. This made no sense. You couldn't have female voices in a bomber over Germany.

'Let's have a look at him,' said a comforting and caring male voice.

There was a white coat. People were speaking English, but only a second ago, I was over Germany.

'What?'

'OK, old chap, just relax. We'll look after you.'

He checked my pulse. I was in and out of consciousness, but he probably did some other checks.

'Move him out in the morning, first thing.'

I must have fallen back asleep, or into that half-awake, half-asleep state that I had originally found myself in.

I did not know what was happening. It was clear that a catastrophe of some kind had happened, but where were Blackie and the crew? I was on my own in a hospital bed.

A nurse told me I was back at my home base of Skellingthorpe Bomber Station in the English Midlands. How had that happened? How the heck could I be back in Lincolnshire? It was only seconds ago that we were flying over the German coast and lining up for a bombing run to Berlin. I could not understand what was happening.

***

Perhaps I should start at the beginning.

I had always been keen on flying. It thrilled me from my earliest days, growing up in Queensland. The skies were so blue there – nothing like the thin grey light and carpets of cloud that hung over Britain, Holland and Germany.

My family home at Sherwood was close to Archerfield Airport, some ten kilometres south of the city of Brisbane. There was another big house just outside Sherwood, which served as a navigation point for aircraft coming into the airport. Pilots would use it as a landmark to line up their final approach on the runway. To young boys of the area, that big house was like a Christmas gift. We all grew up watching aircraft turning as they flew over it and landed. This was followed by other aircraft taking off. Aviation, then, was more of an art than the science that it has become. There was a sense of romance about it. It was spellbinding.

The regular passenger flights in and out of Brisbane were enough to whet the appetite of a young man's fancy. Still, whether it was an obsession, compulsion, or vocation, an inner voice spoke to me loudly and clearly. If it seemed like a slice of good fortune that some people actually got to fly in those propeller-driven aircraft, it must be pure heaven to actually fly them and I wanted to be a part of it.

***

In 1934 came the seminal event: the MacRobertson Air Race. This event was not just big, it was huge in its conception, operation and public enthusiasm. The idea had come from the Lord Mayor of Melbourne Sir Harold Gengoult Smith, who had proposed it as a celebration to mark the centenary of the founding of the city of Melbourne. Sir MacPherson Robertson had donated a prize of £10,000, on the condition that the race bore the name of his confectionary company.

Some 20 competitors left the Royal Air Force base at Mildenhall in Suffolk, in the Eastern counties of the United Kingdom. The first to fly over Flemington Racecourse in Melbourne would be the winner. The aircraft were typically British in the uncanny mixture of excellence and eccentricity in their design, with Granville R6s, Fairey Puss Moths and Lambert Monocoupes being some of the entries. Relative to later progress, this represents aviation back in Saxon or Norman times, but in the mid-thirties, this was the cutting edge of the most exciting technology of the age.

For us in Brisbane, the interest rose to extreme heights as we tracked their progress on Movietone News at the cinema. The intrepid aviators passed through Baghdad in the British Mandated Territory of Iraq. Then, they progressed to Allahabad in the northern part of British India. The next stop was Singapore in the Federated Malay States. The final leg was through Darwin and Charleville in Australia. Every stop was within British territory. This gave ample evidence that the British Empire was one on which the sun never set—not that we needed evidence in those days.

Eventually, the strange but impressive squadrons of aircraft came to Archerfield. I actually saw them as they arrived and departed. It was a breath-taking moment; one I will never forget! There was just no doubt about it. Aviation was beguiling in the extreme. *Nothing on earth was that exciting.*

Movietone News completed the story for us in the cinema, showing the squadrons in glorious black-and-white moving pictures with sound as they passed over Flemington Racecourse, landed at Laverton, then followed the triumphant parade down Bourke Street in Melbourne. Scott and Black, who piloted the winning De Havilland DH88 Comet Racer, had reduced the flight time from London to Melbourne from 162 hours to 71 hours. Their aircraft still exists in a collection in Bedford in the midlands of the UK. By a resonance of fate, it is called the Shuttleworth Collection – maybe some anthropologist can find some aviation thing in the Shuttleworth DNA. The complete record of the aircraft in this dramatic air race is given in Appendix 1 of this book.

***

The memory of that day even eclipsed that fabulous, epoch-making day when Amy Johnson, who was world famous as a female pilot, arrived in Brisbane in a De Havilland Moth, having flown all the way from England. A woman flying from England to Australia – this bordered on science fiction. The world of aviation was just endlessly fascinating and exciting.

Shortly afterwards, a big day in my early life dawned with excitement, adrenaline and heart-thumping anticipation. I got my first flight – a joyride around Brisbane. It was brilliant ... breath-taking.... seductive! The speed down the runway. That lighter than air feeling at take-off. The sight of Brisbane and the sea from 4000 feet. We even banked around that big house that they used for navigation. It was so tiny from the air!

Then, my father had an unusual experience on a flight up to Townsville in a Stinson, an American passenger aircraft of the day. The memorable part of this trip was that the pilot, presumably running out of fuel, actually landed on the beach just outside of Townsville. There was no great drama about it. The pilot said, 'You'd better all get out quick – the tide's coming in!'

My dad and the other passengers filed down the stairway and onto the sand in good order. The pilot taxied the aircraft out of the reach of the incoming tide. If that happened these days, there would be a huge fuss in the media, the pilot would probably be investigated for months and we would all receive counselling for post-traumatic stress disorder. But in those days, they just got off the beach, took a bus into Townsville, and went about their business.

***

Amusing though this was, there was a darker side to the world, which no-one could avoid. In those days of the mid to late thirties, everyone in Brisbane was increasingly talking 'war'. At the cinema, Movietone News now showed German tanks rolling into Czechoslovakia. The footage of the evil opera of Hitler's Nuremberg rallies was terrifying. It seemed that every radio news bulletin and newspaper headline had to do with Hitler and his endless posturing, ranting and screaming.

When 'the balloon went up', it was not even a surprise. Neville Chamberlain declared war on Germany on Sunday 3 September 1939, at 1115 British Standard Time.

It was evening in Sherwood. We had been alerted that the Australian Prime Minister, Robert Menzies, was to make an important announcement in the late evening. There was tension in the air as a voice-over paved the way for the Prime Minister. My family all gathered together and sighed in resignation along with every other family across Australia at what we knew was coming.

Over the radio, we heard a rustle of papers.

'Fellow Australians, it is my melancholy duty to inform you officially that in consequence of a persistence by Germany in her invasion of Poland, Great Britain has declared war upon her and that, as a result, Australia is also at war.'

And with no formal cabinet discussion or resolution, the whole bloody catastrophe that had been waiting to drop onto the world for years did so, quietly, quickly and irrevocably.

***

What happened next was quite strange. Years of priming over the radio and cinema meant that everyone was psychologically prepared for war. Young men across Australia volunteered for the armed forces in a tidal wave of slouch hats and impeccably pressed uniforms. That irresistible tidal wave was made up of patriotic fervour, a hate for Hitler and the Nazis and a feeling that 'we're in a war and in a war, young men join up'. I don't think there was any soul searching. You just joined up like all of your friends did. In my case, I resolved that I would when I was old enough. At that time, to my frustration, I was still two years too young.

The immediate fear was that this new war would be another dreadful trench war, as World War I had been. This was a fear that everyone knew only too well. Throughout the twenties and thirties, everyday life in Australia had been scarred by the memories of the thousands who never came back from Gallipoli, the Somme and the other obscene killing fields in Europe. The depraved butchery of trench warfare had scarred the psyche of a generation. Mind you, this still did not stop young men volunteering for more of the same! It might be something to do with testosterone and an appalling lack of risk-awareness.

And then, all that happened was nothing. Absolutely nothing happened. Not for seven months from September 1939. Hitler and Stalin had both invaded Poland and the Baltic states, wherever they may be, but in Brisbane, we had no idea about any of that.

***

Then, in May of the next year, it all started. The Germans defeated the British and French in devastating form in 1940. They were booted out of Europe via Dunkirk. Then, the Battle of Britain began.

We followed it in Australia through radio, the newspapers and Movietone News at the cinema. Australia was certainly on Britain's side, but it was all a long way away. It is crucial to this story to understand that Australians still felt a loyalty and kinship to the mother country. It is true that my generation no longer referred to the UK as 'home', but the affinity for King and Country was still very much there. *Forty Thousand Horsemen,* a famous propaganda film of the day, said, 'The Tommies' fight is our fight.' Most Australians would have agreed with that. A more authentic word might have been 'Pommies', rather than 'Tommies', as even in 1940, the ravage of political correctness was rearing its ugly head.

Several of my friends had applied to join the Air Force. In a blaze of sheer envy, I wanted the same. The feeling, which was very positive within me, only became more deep-rooted and all-pervasive as time wore on. To make my envy scream like an aero-engine on take-off, my friend Roger had a pilot's licence. He would take an aircraft out and buzz down in a power dive over his family home in a spirit of unbridled exuberance. After each of these exploits, his mother would drive over to the airfield and pick him up in the car. Roger was typical of many young men of the day: he had a pilot's licence but could not drive a car.

***

Then came February 1941. Australian troops were in North Africa. The Luftwaffe was bombing London every night. The Italians were attacking Greece and the British and Australians were going to sort them out. This was just not something you could stay out of. There was a problem.

I was 19 years old, so needed my parents' consent to join up. They were dead against me volunteering, presumably because they did not want me killed, gassed, or worse as per the war of 1914 to 1918. Still, I had an ace up my sleeve and played it.

'If I volunteer for the Air Force, I won't have to fight in the trenches.'

You beauty! It took some lobbying and deft diplomatic footwork, but they eventually agreed! I duly sent off the application form, complete with that vital parental countersignature.

***

Then, once again, nothing happened. Singapore fell in February of 1942 and the war did not seem so far away. But still, nothing happened.

I had now waited months without hearing anything. This was due to the deluge of volunteers to join the forces, as well as the fact that the military command could only process the queue 'in due course', as officialdom is fond of putting it.

Here I was, actually volunteering to help King and Country, but Mr Menzies was ignoring me and Mr Churchill presumably had other things to worry about.

My real agenda was to pilot an aircraft. This was my once-in-a-lifetime chance to learn how to do it, whilst a grateful government footed the bill. But for the time being, I was just kicking my heels and achieving nothing in particular.

***

But then, the golden morning dawned and the letter came! Out of the blue in May 1942, I was told to report to Initial Training School.

I was quite clear in my mind: I wanted to join the aircrew. Like everyone who volunteered for aircrew, I wanted to be a pilot. I could see myself with that blue uniform with the wings attached to it. The thought of moving a flying machine through the clouds and over the countryside was thrilling. It was attractive – no, more than that, *it was captivating.* It transported you to another state of being.

It is also worth remembering that the pilot brevet on the uniform was not just a badge of technical proficiency, but an enormous status symbol as well. The way girls flocked to men with that pilot brevet was wonderful to behold! Indeed, that whole testosterone issue was one that had many facets.

I would have been quite happy for a posting to Europe, because that offered a lot of excitement and adventure, but at this stage, I had really not decided where my future as a pilot would take me.

***

We spent three months at Initial Training School in Sandgate, Queensland. We learned all about doing drills (which were not immediately useful to aircrew) and aeronautics (which were). They also drilled us in all the other basic skills, attitudes and acceptance of military discipline required by servicemen.

I was, at least, now in the Royal Australian Air Force and wearing the blue uniform.

One sad episode will always remain in my mind, though. We had an American pilot on the base, who impressed us hugely with his aerobatics. One day, he was flying his Aerocobra just metres above the waves, to the admiration of those of us who were watching him. We were transported with his sheer brilliance, bravado and wonderful control over the aircraft. But then, the water caught his wingtip. It was just a small splash at first. Then, we saw a sickening bigger splash. The laws of dynamics took over and the aircraft cart-wheeled. In a second, it was reduced to a pile of scrap. The water was shallow, so we all swam out to try to help him, but the violence of the crash had snapped his spinal cord and killed him outright.

From then on, the commanding officer issued an order forbidding aerobatics, with survivors who tried it to face a serious charge.

The main reason for the Initial Training School curriculum was evaluation. Was a man fit and keen enough to join the aircrews, or was he not? I really wanted to be. I yearned for it.

We were tested on all the various aptitudes that a pilot might need. The evaluation also included a medical evaluation, which I passed easily enough.

Then came the bad news.

'Sorry, old chap. Your eyesight is just not up to scratch for a pilot. Sorry and all that. Next!'

That was a disappointment. At breakfast that morning, my hopes and aspirations had been as high as the new Sydney Harbour Bridge, but by lunchtime, they more resembled the ruins of Pompeii.

I knew I also could not be a navigator, because those jobs went to people who were good at maths, as did the bomb aimer jobs. Nevertheless, there were consolation prizes available.

***

After a short time though, my posting came through. It was not a great thrill, but it was not too bad either.

I was sent up to Maryborough to Number 3 Wireless and Air Gunners' School. I would train both as a wireless operator and air gunner.

In the early part of the war, from 1939 to 1942, the Royal Air Force had relied on twin engine bombers, such as Wellingtons, Whitleys and Hampdens, with their five or six-man crews. However, in the white heat of the bomber war, these passed quickly into obsolescence, as the 'heavies' replaced them: the four engine Stirlings, Lancasters and Halifaxes, with seven-man crews. This increased the Royal Air Force's strike capability enormously, but also created a severe shortage of crew skills. To bridge the changeover, they needed lots of men with dual qualifications, who could act either as wireless operators or air gunners. These men would wear a 'WAG' (wireless operator and air gunner) half brevet on their uniform.

The Morse tests began. Initially, we had to send messages at four words per minute. The trainer allowed us just one mistake. Then, we had to increase our speed. You would pass the course when you got to ten words a minute with one mistake.

Darn! I just missed it. It was another blow, but not a devastating one. The overall failure rate for students of Morse code in the Royal Air Force was 60%, so at least I was in good company!

It was then decreed that I would instead be a gunner and wear the 'AG' (air gunner) half brevet. It wasn't as prestigious as pilot's wings, but any aircrew brevet was still very acceptable. It set you apart from the 'penguins': airmen who didn't fly. I would still achieve part of my ambition to fly and be 'doing my bit' for the war effort, which was extremely important during those dark days.

***

The British base of Singapore, which was such a redoubt of the British Empire in the MacRobertson Air Race days, had fallen to the Japanese. Japanese armies were working their way across the Pacific to invade Australia. Terrible things had happened and were still happening somewhere about Australia's northern horizons. The Japs were known to be cruel, vicious, and heartless, and were to be thrown back by any means – fair or foul.

Meanwhile, the Air Force moved me to Evans Head in New South Wales, and life went on more or less as before, Japanese threat or not. On the home front, the war was starting to have its inevitable effect. The

Australian Government had imposed rationing on beef and pork, although you could still buy offal, such as kidneys or lambs fries.

As a gunner, I learned how to set up, assemble and fire a 'go-gun', as we called them. Officially, these were known as Vickers K .303 machine guns.

The aircraft that we trained on were three-man light bombers, Fairey Battles. These Battles had a number of honours to their name. A Battle had had the first aerial victory in World War II and our instructors were proud to tell us that the first Royal Air Force Victoria Crosses of the war were awarded to a Fairey Battle crew (though they forgot to mention that they were posthumous). The Battle was also the first aircraft to be equipped with the Rolls-Royce Merlin engine, a wonderful engine with which I would renew my acquaintanceship later in Lancasters.

The Fairey Battle, however, had proved to be a death trap in combat, when put up against the Germans' Messerschmitts and Focke Wulfs. It had also performed appallingly during the Battle of France. Mercifully, it was retired from combat operations before any more plunged to earth in flames, taking their three-man crew screaming to earth with them.

Still, for us training in the New South Wales sunshine, where there were no Luftwaffe pilots after us, the Fairey Battles were wonderful! I sat at the back of the long cockpit, open to the elements, with the 'go-gun' pointing upwards and backwards. The pilot would take off in conjunction with another Fairey Battle, which acted as a target tug. The target was a long fabric sleeve called a drogue, which was pulled through the air using an extremely long cable. My job was to fire at the drogue and register as many hits as possible, whilst preferably missing the tug. The bullets contained a payload of paint, so that hits could be identified back on the ground and analysed.

Candidate air gunners had to achieve very high hit rates to be accepted for aircrew. This was now my last chance. I had to pass, or I would not make it into the aircrew.

I bettered the standard with relative ease, which was rather odd. Hitting the target with a high hit rate required excellent eyesight – if anything, greater than that required by a pilot. I am sure the Royal Australian Air Force's opticians knew what they were doing, but it does make me wonder why I could not be a pilot.

Throughout it all, we were young men going through an adventure and rather enjoying the experience. Whilst you knew that, in a general sense, war could be a risky business, you always thought that anything life-threatening or otherwise unpleasant was always going to happen to someone else.

***

After a couple of months, my posting came through. Yes! I was accepted for aircrew as a gunner. That was good.

I got my 'AG' half brevet to sew onto my uniform, which was even better.

Best of all, I was posted to the United Kingdom and was to report for transport by ship in a few days' time. The adventure was beginning!

2

The Klipfontein and Union Pacific Railroad

The *Klipfontein* was a 10,000 ton armed freighter of the Holland Afrika Line. It had been commandeered by the United States War Shipping Administration and converted for use as a troop ship.

We were trained aircrews, on our way and heading for the war zone. This was immediately obvious! On the quayside in Brisbane, it came to our notice that the ship was armed with twin 120 millimetre guns. Quite how much of a fight we would have put up against a Japanese battleship remains unclear. What were our chances of hitting a Jap aircraft if it attacked us? Probably, no-one asked the question because they didn't want to hear the answer. As always, we believed it was someone else who was going to shot, bombed, or torpedoed, so I do not recall us dwelling on it unduly.

We put to sea late on a lovely Queensland afternoon. We had all seen the newsreels of ships departing with Imperial pomp and ceremony for the abattoirs of World War I, with weeping mothers, streamers and merry choruses of 'Waltzing Matilda'.

This time though, sadly, there were no brass bands or distressed but proud relatives to see us off. Perhaps the awful realities of World War I had dampened any enthusiasm for jollities in the second lot. Also, there was a war on, meaning our departure had to be discreet – secret, in fact. We could not tip off any sinister German or Japanese agents that we were on our way.

***

Brisbane was soon behind us. Queensland too was behind us after some days, as we found our way into the Pacific Ocean. It took us 19 days to travel from Brisbane to San Francisco. We didn't see land in all that time.

The officers didn't organise anything for us. I was to discover that this was how the Air Force worked with its aircrews. If you were not 'on ops', you were often just left to fend for yourself. This suited me – in fact, all of us – wonderfully.

We spent some of our time chatting with the American troops on board, who were very nice blokes. Hearing them talk about their world, it all sounded very glamorous to us from rural Queensland. It's interesting though how, in later life, you remember the small things – for example, that the Americans gave us some of their soap. Our soap was like a block of wood, with a lather to match, whereas theirs was actually formulated for use in salt water, so was much better. They were very happy to share it with us.

There were also lots of copies of a great American magazine called the *Saturday Evening Post* to read. This had fiction, non-fiction, cartoons and features. The artwork on the covers was wonderful and to this day, it remains one of the best magazines that I ever came across.

Some of the airmen would play cards. Games such as poker and blackjack were popular. Others would do physical jerks. We also spent a lot of time sun-baking and I got a fabulous tan.

On board the *Klipfontein,* the officers received first and second-class cabins, which were very civilised, if not a little cramped. However, the accommodation was not so civilised for the rest of us. There were probably 500 or 600 testosterone-fuelled young men of 'other ranks' (non-officers) on the ship. We were billeted in hammocks down in the hold of the ship, which was like living in an overfilled sardine can. The hammocks were arranged three high, within a dark, dingy hold that stank with the perfume of unwashed bodies, cigarette smoke and occasional seasickness.

As we moved into tropical areas, it wasn't just uncomfortable, but also stiflingly hot and humid. Like many others, I gave up on the official accommodation and took my bedroll to sleep on the deck. Sometimes, I was splattered by the green Pacific Ocean blasting over the deck but on the whole, it was very pleasant.

This was also a good idea, because if we were hit by a Japanese torpedo, those of us on deck would be first into the lifeboats.

Also, in the middle of the night on deck, I caught occasional sight of some mythical creatures who were rumoured to be aboard the ship. They were American nurses, who were very distinctive in their crisp, white uniforms. The skipper had clearly ordered them to stay in their quarters, since a bevy of a dozen or so females in a ship full of testosterone-charged young men constituted a threat. The skipper had doubtlessly seen the popular pre-war movie *Mutiny on the Bounty,* where Captain Bligh's crew mutinied due to their attachment to members of the other sex. Our skipper was not going to let that sort of thing bring his ship to grief, thank you very much!

For the majority of the trip, the weather was lovely. We really enjoyed the blue Pacific, gorgeous sunny weather and whole adventure of being together as a band of young men heading out to exciting times.

As with any body of servicemen though, there was a lot of griping. In our case, it usually had to do with the food. This mainly consisted of canned beans or spaghetti and canned fruit, when many of the lads were used to steak and eggs for breakfast. They were very vocal when it was not served up!

***

After 19 days, we saw land on the horizon. That was a relief, because it was starting to feel as if we would never see land again. Also, for the last two days, the weather turned against us and we experienced what it was like to be thrown around an ocean.

As we hurried to the rails on deck and searched the horizon, there it was – land! First, we saw a long line of dark woods to port, then a lot of colourful houses on the coast to starboard.

At night, the coast disappeared as we sailed along the California coast. Due to wartime conditions, the American authorities had imposed a 'brown-out' to make the coastline invisible to any marauding Japanese warships. The lesson of Pearl Harbour had been a hard way to learn but was not forgotten.

Next morning found us sailing into the wide approaches of San Francisco Bay. We saw several American troop carriers sailing out and heading into the South Pacific. The ships were huge and seemed to have thousands of men on board. I suppose they were going to the Philippines and New Guinea and all the other places to which General MacArthur was going in order to sort out the Japs. Such was the reputation of Japanese bestiality that we just hoped they would kill as many of the evil little sods as possible.

Then, as we came closer to the city of San Francisco itself, we were all so impressed with the sight. It was a lovely looking place. As we got closer, we saw that the trees in the woods were absolutely massive. The houses, as we came closer, looked more and more charming. Then, we came around the headland and saw the Golden Gate Bridge. We were going to sail right under it. As we came around the point, we saw the city to starboard.

As we pulled slowly down the harbour, we lined the rails and looked forward to the time we would spend in that wonderful city. Imagine, the sights to see, people to meet and the girls! *The girls!*

Someone pointed out an island with a large building on it that looked like a castle. This was Alcatraz Island, which was still a working prison at that time. Al Capone had been a resident, though had, by this time, moved on. The people in the prison must have looked down on our ship with terrible envy. I can actually claim to have been looked at by Machine Gun Kelly and also Robert Stroud, the Birdman of Alcatraz, whose story would later be made into a film starring Burt Lancaster. Thankfully, there were bars between us, so I didn't meet any of them in the flesh.

The ship stopped right underneath the stern gaze of Alcatraz, with its fortress-like buildings and distinctive water tower. The engines stopped. We anchored. Nothing happened. We just sat there, looking at the wonderful skyline of San Francisco and wishing we could be there. And that, of course, was part of the mental torture of Alcatraz. A man could be in there for 30 years, looking at San Francisco just a few hundred metres away, but not be able to go there. For us, a 24 hour delay was bad enough.

***

Eventually, the engines started with a cough and a rumble! At last!

Then came the bombshell. We would not be stopping at San Francisco. We were to proceed to Oakland on the north of San Francisco Bay, where a train was waiting for us.

So, we bid goodbye to the *Klipfontein,* which had been our home for three weeks. Taking one last fond look across the bay to San Francisco, we embarked on a Union Pacific special troop train to take us across the United States.

***

Compared to the small trains in Queensland, this train was enormous! At the front was a huge black locomotive, which looked twice the size of the railway locomotives that we saw back home.

After the *Klipfontein,* the accommodation seemed luxurious. The carriages were enormous too, and very comfortable, with bunks for us to sleep on. This was just as well, because the journey was going to take a week or so. We even had attendants who would come around the sleeping cars to let the bunks down and arrange the bedding when it was time to turn in.

Leaving the Bay Area behind, we headed up through the high sierras towards Sacramento. Someone pointed out that that was where the Pony Express used to go before the railways were built. We had seen it in the pictures and now, we were in that country ourselves. We were in America – the America of Hollywood, cowboy films and film stars.

The scenery was breathtaking, with mountains all around, clear fast-running rivers and miles and miles of forest. The forest was very different to what we had seen in Australia. We were used to gum trees, but these were pines and redwoods – millions of them. And there, to cap it all off, were the snowcapped peaks of the even higher sierras. They were so high and so beautiful with their snowy caps, even though it was May. It was the first time I had seen snow.

As we got higher, we saw snow along the side of the railway track. For someone from a sub-tropical climate, this was a thrill! Like the Pony Express, skyscrapers and the *Saturday Evening Post,* that was something that we did not have back home in Queensland. It was all so fascinating!

So far, Adolf Hitler's war had given me a privileged existence, got me into flying and brought me to this beautiful land. And, to top it all off, I had my 'AG' brevet on my tunic! I knew – we all knew – that the war was going to be a serious – and probably deadly – business, but so far, it had really been an enjoyable experience.

***

The first main stop was at Sacramento to change locomotives. To our surprise and delight, there was a welcoming party of several dozen people waiting for us, who came down to wish us well. They gave us books to read, food parcels and any other bits and pieces that they could think of. Others felt that as we were going to Britain, which was a major war zone at the time, they would just let us know that they supported us.

Once again, we all felt that the Americans were capable of a lot of kindness. As on the *Klipfontein,* there seemed to be no limit to the feeling of friendship and generosity between allies.

I thought America was a lovely country. The people were very good to us and made us feel very welcome. There were a surprising number of people that we met at the railway stations, who had sons and daughters in Australia and they couldn't do enough for us. Someone or other did note, with a curious smile, that the goodhearted Americans made such a fuss of us that any secrecy that we wanted to maintain was heroically compromised. Any sinister German or Japanese agent within a hundred miles would have been aware of our presence and would send a message home that we were on our way.

There was no rationing in America either, which was wonderful! You could get hold of anything you wanted.

There was no blackout either, although we would encounter this soon enough.

***

The stop at Salt Lake City was also memorable. We were only there for an hour, but the engine driver (or 'engineer', in American-speak) let us climb up into the cab and have a look around at all the gauges, pipes, levers, handles and valves necessary to bring one of these huge beasts into motion. A cynic might have wondered if the eyesight requirements to drive such a huge locomotive were as stringent as those to pilot one of the Royal Air Force's warplanes.

As an extra treat, we got ice cream. Then, we piled back onto the train and off we went.

***

We passed through the endless flat expanse of the prairies. We had seen this on cowboy and Indian films, though it never occurred to us as possible that we would ever get to be there.

'What state are we in?' was a frequent question. The answer might be 'Wyoming'. 'But we were in Wyoming yesterday as well!' The United States was a big country.

Crossing the stupendous width of the Mississippi River brought back memories of reading *Tom Sawyer* and *Huckleberry Finn.* The country did not seem to have changed much since Mark Twain's day, either. Some of the rural areas of the United States had living standards that were very bad by Australian standards, which was quite surprising given the 'land of milk and honey' propaganda that Hollywood poured out week by week.

**

Our journey took us through Chicago. I would imagine that we looked out for gangsters, but really, that era had passed by the time our train chugged through.

New York was coming closer now. Passing down the Hudson River, we marvelled once again at the scenery. We saw the hideous castellated shape of Sing-Sing Prison, which we had heard of in the gangster movies.

Shortly after, we passed under the George Washington Bridge. There, in all its glory, was New York City on the left-hand side of the train.

We learned that we were not to stop off here either. Instead, we carried on to a timber barracked camp outside Boston, which was called Stanmore Park.

**

Then came the good news! We were to get a week's leave, which meant trips into New York for sightseeing.

I had seen a lot of photographs and film clips of the Empire State Building, Chrysler Building and all the other skyscrapers. In real life though, they were much more dramatic, more real, more imposing: they took your breath away.

Times Square was sensational in daylight, but we looked forward to seeing the dazzling light show at night. Then came the surprise! New York was actually blacked out at night. The war was coming closer – or, more accurately, we were coming closer to the war.

The blackout in New York was not as protection against bombers, which did not have the range for an attack. Rather, there had been many reports of German U-boats off the coast of the United States. A lit-up New York offered a great aid to the German Navy's navigation. Therefore, it was kept dark.

3

The Queen Elizabeth

Some days later, back in New York, we found our ship to take us to the United Kingdom.

You could have knocked us down with a proverbial feather. It was the *Queen Elizabeth,* the world's biggest liner. It sailed without escort. Its top speed of 28 knots meant that any U-boat had very little chance of sinking it, since these smaller boats had a top surface speed of barely half of that of the *Queen Elizabeth.*

Still, had we come under the gaze of the German battleship *Tirpitz,* or the 'three ugly sisters' – the battle cruisers *Scharnhorst, Gneisenau and Prinz Eugen* – we would have been a sitting duck. We could only hope that someone in the Admiralty knew where these monsters lurked and that they were not within a hundred – or a thousand – miles of us. The other German naval behemoth, the *Bismarck,* was at the bottom of the ocean where it belonged by now. In fact, we would pass just a couple of hundred metres above its final resting place.

The *Queen Elizabeth* was decked out in wartime grey paint, to hide it on the seas from the eyes of the Germans' long range Condor reconnaissance aircraft.

These would pass our location and bearing on to the U-boat captains, every one of which would love to go down in history as having sunk us. In this drab get-up, she wasn't at her best, but she was still a very, very impressive ship.

We filed up the gangplank onto this huge monster of a ship. It was truly awe-inspiring.

Things got even better! Some of us were selected by some unknown military process to do watches. A petty officer took me to my position high above the bridge, where we had to watch out for any German U-boat activity, unidentified aircraft (especially those Condors) and anything else that might be a danger to the thousands of men who were on board.

Orders were precise. If we saw the slightest thing – be it a convoy, ship, aircraft, bank of fog, smoke on the horizon, lights at night, or something else that we could not quite identify – we were to report it immediately to the officer of the watch. There was not yet any onboard radar on ships, meaning our eyes were the sole guarantee of the ship's safety.

The watch system worked as follows:

First watch:	2000 to 0000
Middle watch:	0000 to 0400
Morning watch:	0400 to 0800
Forenoon watch:	0800 to 1200
Afternoon watch:	1200 to 1600
First dog watch:	1600 to 1800

Last dog watch:	1800 to 2000

The system worked so that each day, you were on an earlier watch than the day before. A vital part of the whole system was that the people involved in it had to be guaranteed sleep. A tired man dropping off to sleep on his watch could jeopardise the whole ship and everyone on it. We were reminded that in World War I, men who fell asleep on watch were sentenced to death. 'Rubbish!' said one of the old hands. Still, we did not want to test this out.

Someone said there were 20,000 American troops on board. I don't know if that was true, but it certainly felt like it. They were sleeping in bunks in the holds, in the ballrooms, in bars and in cafes and restaurants. In peacetime, there would be lots of alcohol in those areas, but if there was on this trip, we never saw any of it. There were even men sleeping in the cinema, in recreational areas and in the passageways – in fact, anywhere that a man could physically doss down. Only a lucky few had permanent hammocks. Otherwise, a man might be allocated a hammock for a 24 hour period, after which he would be turfed out and he would have to find space in a corridor again.

Down there, the majority of the American soldiers smoked. The smell of the Lucky Strikes and Camels mixed into a cocktail with the fragrance of rancid feet and coloured the atmosphere blue. Still, it was all very close and friendly.

The lucky few of us on watch were allocated single cabins. This was so very much better than the *Klipfontein!* There were to be no sweaty hammocks, smoky bilges, or stale body smells for us. It is also worth bearing in mind that it was not possible for us to sleep on deck on the Atlantic – we would have frozen to death! It's also hardly surprising that we did not volunteer to change places.

As with the Pacific, our luck held over the Atlantic. It was very smooth. That also meant that we could travel faster and keep even further away from any U-boats that might have spotted us.

***

We had been some days out – I can't remember how many-when there was some excitement on deck.

The lookouts had spotted an aircraft in the distance. It was low, large and not moving very fast.

'Oh God! Don't let it be a Condor!' said someone.

Our blood ran cold. If a Luftwaffe Condor saw us and reported our location, our remaining lives might be very short in duration. As the grey shadow moved towards us, we strained through the sea mist to see the outline.

'Has anyone actually seen a Condor before?'

No-one had. We waited for someone to say with some authority what it might be.

Finally, the word came from the lookout at the masthead. 'It's a Sunderland flying boat!'

Phew! It was the Royal Air Force's Coastal Command keeping an eye on us and reporting back our position to the Admiralty. If we were within range of a Sunderland, it meant that we were now only a day or two from our final destination. The trip had been very enjoyable and in one way, it would be sad that it was over. On the other hand, this was wartime and, even though we were much faster than any U-boat, you never quite knew if one would get lucky.

The Sunderland flew around us once. A few on deck waved, though its crew could probably not see. The pilot waggled his wings and the aircraft disappeared in the direction from which it had appeared.

***

On the ship, we fell back into the old routine. Some played cards for money and lost. Some took walks around the huge decks and admired the Atlantic. Others read magazines and wrote letters home to be posted when we got to the UK.

In the time-honoured air force manner, we were left to our own devices when we were not on watch. The most important time of day was when you were allocated on watch. The easy discipline regime would suddenly come to a crashing end. You had to be on time, or there would be trouble! I don't think we ever found out what 'trouble' meant, but those eagle-eyed naval petty officers were not men that you would provoke in any way whatsoever.

One day, as we passed along the coast of Southern Ireland, someone pointed out the spot where the German Navy got the *Lusitania* in World War I.

'Yes, but we are too fast to be caught.'

'So was she!'

We went back to playing cards.

***

Five days after leaving New York, there was a commotion, as the lookout sighted land on the starboard bow. It was Land's End!

We had reached our destination without any bother from Condors, battleships, or German U-boats. We had rather expected an escort of destroyers or corvettes, but none turned up. Apparently, the Admiralty thought our speed rendered us safe.

We lined the railings. On the right was a long dark finger of land, which was Pembrokeshire in Wales. After dark, this became a total blackout. Someone mentioned that this was probably where the Sunderland flying boat had come from. On the left was a similar long dark finger of land, which was County Wexford in Ireland. On that side, there was not a blackout after dark. This was odd when you thought about it. To the right, World War II was going on, but to the left, it was not. The Irish government remained neutral throughout the war.

At first light, the sky was clear and sunny as we passed through the narrow gap between Stranraer in Scotland and Bangor in Northern Ireland. The scenery on both sides was glorious in the May morning sunshine. We slid past the Isle of Arran to port and looked at the beautiful sight of the hills on the left-hand side. Then, we passed the Isles of Bute and made a sharp turn to starboard at Dunoon, into the Clyde estuary. Someone from Dunoon was to play a major part in my story, but that is for later.

With a depressing speed, the intense beauty of the Scottish countryside gave way to an endless industrial landscape of dockside cranes, which led for miles down the Clyde to Glasgow.

4

On to Brighton

Early in the morning, we disembarked at Greenock. This was to be the first of two historical resonances that day.

A century earlier, Greenock had been a major port for people who migrated to Australia. The journey took four months, going via Rio de Janeiro and Cape Town. I would have to say that my journey back to the mother country was a huge improvement on that!

So, this was it then – we were in Britain. Like all the other servicemen, I had looked forward to arriving there enormously. Now, at last, I was within reach of the things that I had looked forward to – meeting people, seeing the sights and experiencing a different kind of country. I had eagerly looked forward to seeing some of the well-known sights: Canterbury Cathedral, Westminster Abbey, Buckingham Palace, Windsor Castle and the Houses of Parliament – well, if they were still there, that is, and not bombed out of existence.

Canterbury had been bombed the previous year. Buckingham Palace had also suffered bomb damage and Westminster Abbey and the Houses of Parliament were at risk, like everything else in central London. On disembarkation, we formed into ranks and were put on yet another special troop train. This time, we were headed for Brighton, on the south coast of England.

This was a very different experience to the train trip across America. On this train, no-one knew we were coming and there was to be no welcome waiting for us. Still, it was so good to be living in a constant state of adventure that I do not recall this being too devastating at the time.

***

As we travelled down through lovely scenery in the English Lake District and through Wigan North Western station, a second resonance with history occurred.

Although it was lost on me at the time, as the train hurried through the industrial heartlands of Lancashire and the West Midlands, this was curiously significant. Henry de Shuttleworth of Shuttleworth Hall had lived in nearby Whalley and died in 1329. Ughtred, his son, lived a short distance away at Burnley. They were, presumably, my ancestors. This was during the reign of King Henry III, at the time of the Black Death.

One very important aspect of a British serviceman's life, which I was to discover on the journey, was that of the NAAFI (the Navy, Army and Air Force Institutes). This was the staff canteen for the armed forces. I was to discover that every air base, training establishment and even every large railway station had one. This was the place where you got your food, heard the latest (usually unreliable) rumours and met your friends socially. It was in these canteens at the various large railway stations between Greenock and Brighton that we were fed, usually as the steam locomotives were being changed.

***

One noteworthy junction was that at Crewe to the south of Manchester. The station was huge, with trains arriving and departing every few minutes. There were trains for London, Manchester, Liverpool, Glasgow and endless other places. Many of the trains were special troop trains going to unspecified places, which were designated only by numbers. Life was so much more exciting here than it had been in the suburbs of sleepy Brisbane.

The clearest memory I have is that of the thousands of people who passed through. A huge proportion – perhaps three quarters – were wearing service uniforms. Some were recognisable as navy, army and air force servicemen, though there were many others that were unidentifiable. To see these thousands of mainly young men in so many uniforms told you there was a war on, even if you had not known it beforehand.

Every station had its collection of admonishing posters –'Is your journey really necessary?' The authorities wanted to discourage civilians from travelling by rail to make more room for servicemen.

Others read 'Careless talk costs lives' and reminded us not to discuss any sensitive matters that could be overheard by German spies. In some weeks' time, posters reading 'Join the Women's Land Army' would join them, as Britain mobilised its women into an agricultural work force to replace the men who had been called up into the forces.

Around 90 minutes after leaving Crewe, had we been very vigilant, we would have caught a glimpse of a rather eccentric, gabled stately home off to the right. At the time, we most certainly did not see it. Likewise, the next station meant nothing to us: Bletchley. We would not discover what had happened there until 40 years later.

***

Australians had always said what a small country Britain was. It didn't feel like it. That railway journey took 14 hours!

We arrived at Brighton at 2000. We were to stay there until a place could be found for us at an Operational Training Unit. We were billeted immediately. My billet was a single room at the exclusive Grand Hotel, where the IRA would attempt to murder Margaret Thatcher some decades later. It was very luxurious, but it was greatly disappointing that the bar was closed for the duration of the war. Not only this, but there was no lift, meaning I had to lug my huge Royal Australian Air Force kitbag, gasping, up six flights of stairs. Yes, I was indeed learning about the privations and strictures of war!

The whole episode was so typical of air force life. On the one hand, the organisation of the train and billeting was exemplary. On the other hand, no-one had any plans for us. In particular, the organisation of our passage to the Operational Training Unit seemed very haphazard. After a week, there was no word about where we might be sent. Two weeks was to extend to three and then to four. As ever, we were left to our own devices and had to organise our own form of practical war effort to defeat the evil Germans. This involved spending a lot of time in pubs, talking to lots of the locals – especially to girls.

I was to discover that the distinctive light blue of the Royal Australian Air Force uniform, the 'AG' brevet and the Australia shoulder flash catapulted me to a new level of 'desirable boyfriend', which, if not quite at Hollywood levels, was not that far beneath it either.

The room temperature English beer was another privation of war that I never really got used to. They just kept bottles of beer on the shelf and opened them up when you bought them. To Australian eyes, this was very uncivilised. However, there was no time to waste on the horrors of the British brewing industry. The atmosphere, the rumours and the expectation was that the whole place – in fact, the whole south coast of England – was just beginning to gear up for the invasion of France, although no-one knew when it would be. There was a great sense that the defeat of Hitler was to be a vast national project in which every single person took part.

***

There were many indicators that Britain was a country totally and completely at war. No-one had seen an orange or banana for three years and civilians needed a ration book to buy food, clothes, or household goods. No ration book: no purchase!

As you travelled by train, most houses had the same corrugated-iron structure in the back garden. Known as Anderson shelters, these were uncomfortable and quite primitive, but would keep a family safe from dropping bombs unless there was a direct hit, in which case they would die.

All over built-up areas, there were signs – 'Air Raid Shelter This Way'. These were purpose-built shelters that were proofed from all bombings, many of which were underground.

In the streets, 'EWS' was written in large yellow letters. This stood for emergency water supply, which signified the place that you went to if your house was hit and you needed water urgently.

The blackout was rigidly enforced. If anyone was careless enough to let a light be shown after dark, there were consequences. A very unpleasant man in a military style helmet bearing the letters 'ARP' (air raid protection) would beat on the door. The shout of 'Turn that bloody light off!' was a recurring memory of World War II to people in the UK.

There were virtually no private cars on the road. Petrol was available to doctors, but very few other civilians.

All of this was the reality of life in Britain at the time. It was with you every moment of your waking life and even when you were asleep. There was always the possibility that the sirens would blare out their 'moaning Minnie' sound and you would have to run down into an air raid shelter in your pyjamas. Even your pyjamas bore the austerity mark that announced how many coupons from your ration book were required to make the purchase.

Despite all the privations, shortages, blackouts and ration books, it was very clear that everyone expected to be on the winning side. If there was anyone who thought that Britain was not going to be on the winning side, I never met them, or even heard about them.

***

In the Grand Hotel, they served us up breakfast, lunch and dinner – no NAAFI for us in Brighton!

One of the perks of wartime was an endless supply of free cigarettes and cigars. The Australian Comfort Fund supplied such brands as Players Navy Cut, Woodbines and the utterly deadly Capstans. The latter were so loaded with carcinogens that they were only slightly less dangerous than Luftwaffe nightfighters. I didn't smoke, so my allowance found its way onto the shelves of a local tobacconist. This was a win-win, as it gave the tobacconist a way of beating the inevitable restrictions on supply and me, a welcome supplement to my meagre pay.

There were thousands of British, Australian and New Zealand troops around the town. There were endless patrols of fighter aircraft, with deadly Spitfires, Hurricanes and the even more powerful Typhoons and Mosquitoes passing overhead and going out into the channel to look for German intruders to chase off or, preferably, kill. In all directions, there was vast amounts of traffic, moving men, machinery and armaments. There were also lots of barrage balloons to hamper the attempts of enemy aircraft to bomb us or rake us with cannon fire, by forcing them to fly higher.

From memory, I don't recall seeing any Luftwaffe reconnaissance aircraft during daylight hours. The Royal Air Force had got the upper hand over the channel, to the point where the Germans couldn't get an aircraft to have a look at the invasion preparations and expect it to get back to France in one piece. There were, however, incursions by small numbers of German aircraft almost every night. Late at night, there would be fireworks as anti-aircraft batteries opened up with a deafening crash all along the coast. Tracers would lacerate the sky and shells would burst with a sudden dull, red glow. Searchlights pencilled their way in cones, looking for victims. Presumably, the Luftwaffe was testing the air defences. I learned that the bombing raids on London had been finished for almost two years already.

In the mornings, we would regularly see American B17s and B24s in their hundreds, going out on daylight raids over Northern France and Germany in very tight, precise formations. In the late afternoon, we would see them return and hope that they all made it back. One of the curious points was that Americans were transitioning their bombers from silvery paint to dull bottle green. According to rumours, that saved £70 when building each aircraft. Money was tight!

During peacetime, the seafront at Brighton had been one of the great attractions. Now, it was sealed off. The three piers were closed 'for the duration' and the beaches quarantined with coils of barbed wire, except for a narrow portion in front of the Grand Hotel. The beach was, in any case, hostile to the feet, as it was made up of millions of flat, smooth stones – not like the lovely sandy beaches of Australia, with their blue water and palm trees. Not to mention, the water was as cold as buggery! Eastbourne was a much better beach than Brighton, so I took a bus trip with some friends there. However, we were still thwarted! You couldn't get onto it, because it was surrounded by even more barbed wire and army patrols to make sure you didn't try to bypass it.

The oriental palace of the Brighton Pavilion was spectacular in its opulence and decadence and fortunately was still open – war or no war. It dated from the early 1800s and to Australian eyes, was fascinating. In our own country, we had very little at all that went back that far.

Overall, Brighton seethed with activity, but for us, waiting to go on to Operational Training Units, it was as if we were frozen in a bubble of bleak inactivity. As we used to say, 'They also serve who stand and wait.' We did a lot of waiting.

Winston Churchill was on the radio frequently and his broadcasts were eagerly listened to. Churchill had the confidence of the British people during the war, to the extent that I do not think I have since seen a Prime Minister with so much support, as there was in that time. Listening to the radio news was a major part of life in World War II, as it was where everyone first heard what was going on – the progress of the Russians on the Eastern Front, the Bomber Command raids on German territory (always very popular) and news on the convoys carrying materials and food that were the lifeline of men across the Atlantic.

The local people were very welcoming to us servicemen. Talking with the locals, I discovered that during the Battle of Britain in 1940, people had been really frightened of a German invasion. Once Hitler had slackened off the air attacks and put his dark intentions towards Russia, fears of a German attack had largely subsided. It was also important to the local people that King George VI and Queen Elizabeth stayed in London. Reports said that courtiers at Buckingham Palace had advised them to go to Canada for the duration of the war, but Queen Elizabeth (who allegedly wore the trousers!) said 'no'.

During the war, there was a dance on every night, although Saturday night was the big one of each week. Dances were a popular form of entertainment and many – or indeed, most – adults would go along to them and show their skills in waltzes, quick-steps and two-steps. One very popular dance in the England of the day was the Lambeth Walk, which everyone had to know. In the hotel, we had the British Forces Broadcasting Network, which introduced us to a new form of music – swing, played by Glenn Miller, Benny Goodman and Count Basie. Now, that was something really different, as it was incredibly new world and threatening to the British traditionalists, of which there were many. Unfortunately, at this time, the Americans had not yet showed us how to dance to it.

During this time, many servicemen met and formed friendships with girls at these dances. Many of these progressed within a few weeks, or even days, to marriage. Whirlwind romance was the spirit of the age. You did not want to dwell on it, but you knew that you could be dead in few weeks, so it was best to enjoy life while you could. In Brighton, I met a lot of girls, but did not form any deep relationships myself.

My cousin Ivy lived in London. Her husband Keith was from Yamba in New South Wales and in the Royal Australian Navy. He had a job at Australia House in the Strand. I took the train up to see him a few times. One very good thing about visiting my cousin was that he knew where you could find cold beer!

***

Once you got to London, the wartime feeling intensified.

Approaching London through the vast rail yards at Clapham Junction, I saw streets that had been pulverised by the Luftwaffe bombs. Around Victoria Station, there were lots of blackened ruins, which resembled a burned-out Pompeii.

Bombing patterns were very patchy. Down the Strand and around the West End, there was hardly any bombing at all, but then if you carried on eastwards to Fleet Street and up Ludgate Hill to St Paul's, there was a tremendous amount of devastation. In some cases, there were flattened blocks of land where the rubble had been cleared. In other places, you could see the shells of burned-out buildings, with their walls burst open and the floors inside set at crazy angles, with piles of burned furniture. The bombed-out buildings were very often teetering on the verge of collapse, but were nevertheless very popular with the local children, who saw an adventure playground in every devastated house.

One of the most vivid and moving sights of the war was down into the tube stations at night. People would congregate down there with sleeping bags or blankets and maybe a thermos flask of tea or a packet of sandwiches and sleep on the platforms. I learned that these were some of the thousands that had lost their homes to bombs, who had nowhere else to sleep. The stations were absolutely packed out with mums, dads and kids, all packed together like sardines in a tin. The last trains were at about midnight and the first trains at about 0500, so they cannot have got much sleep. No-one seemed to be downhearted, though, since morale and the determination to win were at very high levels.

Despite the privations of wartime, I was able to do some sightseeing. I started at Victoria Station, which had large, jagged holes in its glass roof from the bombs. I then walked to Buckingham Palace, which was also showing calling cards from the Luftwaffe bombs.

I went down Victoria Street to Westminster Abbey, which was very impressive. You had to marvel at how such a huge structure could be built in the Middle Ages. It was wartime, though, and I can only imagine that people had more pressing things to do, because there were only some half dozen other people in there. It was a pity that the stained-glass windows had been removed, but the powers that be had taken them away somewhere to keep them safe for the duration of the war.

At Hyde Park Corner, I saw the spruikers with all their various philosophies of life and the universe. I could only imagine that in wartime, they had to be very careful what they said. Anything too friendly to the Germans could result in a range of consequences, from a black eye from a member of the audience to a visit from gentlemen in plain clothes who would ask some embarrassing questions.

I took the train out to Windsor as well, to see Windsor Castle and St George's Chapel. I also had a walk in the enormous Windsor Great Park. Another day, I took the train to Richmond, then took the ferry up to Hampton Court. Coming back, I took a different line out of Richmond, which dropped me off at Kew Gardens. If there was one good thing about the war, it certainly gave me the opportunity to travel to some fabulous places!

Regrettably, the realities of World War II were to crash in on my five-star sojourn in Brighton and eager tourism across southern England. The adjutant appeared one day, with the news that I was posted to Operational Training Unit No 29 at Bruntingthorpe, near Leicester. He gave me a rail pass and told me to catch a train from St Pancras station in London. The next day, I was on my way.

5

Operational Training Unit No 29 (Bruntingthorpe)

Now, matters were becoming more serious. We were to train for operations in Wellington Bombers (known affectionately as Wimpeys). These were twin engine bombers, which had been used very extensively on operations early in the war. At the time I joined the air force, they were the frontline bomber and considered to be close to 'state of the art'. Two years later, they were obsolete and rapidly being taken out of the line. The future lay with the four engine bombers – Stirlings, Halifaxes and Lancasters, especially.

We duly arrived at the small village of Bruntingthorpe. I had my sergeant's stripe on my arm, my 'Australia' flash on my shoulder and 11 shillings and sixpence (about one Australian dollar) a day in my pocket. This gave me some four pounds a week. Given that our uniform, board, lodging and food were all covered, that meant that I had effectively four pounds a week pocket money.

I arrived alongside several hundred other 'sprog' airmen. Without ceremony, we were taken to a shed. The Wing Commander told us to form up into crews.

'Form into crews, there's good chaps. I'll be back in half an hour.'

There was no guidance or helpful hints. That was the Royal Air Force way. It was just 'get on with it and muddle through'. Still, we could all recognise each other's crew positions because of the brevets on our tunics.

Almost straight away, a pilot approached me. His name was Flight Lieutenant Thomas Blackham (known as Blackie) and he was from Dunoon in Scotland. Well, that was interesting! I had passed close by Dunoon as the *Queen Elizabeth* had turned hard to starboard before the final run in to Greenock. Apparently, another pilot, with whom I had flown, knew that I had some high scores in target practice, which had led Blackie to make the approach. I accepted immediately. How he chose the other members of his crew was a mystery, though this was quite normal, as most crews seemingly came together by some form of unseen osmosis. I also had an offer from a pilot and wireless operator, both from southern Ireland, who tried to prise me away from Blackie, though I stuck with him. The Irish lads were killed shortly afterwards.

We had to form up into a crew of five:

Pilot	Blackham
Navigator	Jones
Bomb aimer	Godfrey
Wireless operator	Wilkins
Rear gunner	Shuttleworth

The crew came together with a strange but effective wisdom, which Bomber Command displayed in this selection process. The crews had made a choice – albeit for unclear reasons – to live and fight together. This meant that we had all entrusted our lives to the people we had chosen and who had chosen us, which forged a strong psychological bond between us.

The wisdom displayed by the Royal Air Force hierarchy ran out at this point. Its hidebound rules meant that we sergeants were not able to share a hut with the two crew members who were officers. That meant that the pilot, Flight Lieutenant Blackham and the navigator, Pilot Officer Jones lived in one round, corrugated iron Nissen hut. The other three of us were sergeants, so lived in a different Nissen hut with some 17 other airmen. We also used different messes (as we called our social facilities). This was a dreadful way to encourage a crew to form a team. Once you were in an aircraft, it was your job and your expertise that counted. Rank was of no particular use to anyone in a bomber crew when you were at 20,000 feet, with a Messerschmitt on your tail.

***

We were young and optimistic and settled down quickly into a daily routine. During training, we flew out from a nearby aerodrome at Cresswell during the day and sometimes at night. In the evenings, we went to the pub or stayed in the Nissen hut, writing letters and chatting about the events of the day. When we talked, it was about a strangely limited number of topics. We talked about different kinds of aircraft. We talked about girls. We talked about the air force. We talked about girls. We talked about the accommodation. We talked about girls. We never did get around to finding out much about each other's lives before the air force. Being in the Royal Air Force and in the war and in a frontline unit was all-pervading. Any other life outside was, if not forgotten, at least now a million miles away and not particularly interesting. It was definitely not as interesting as girls.

I formed a special bond with Stewart Godfrey, one of the members of my crew and a Scot from Paisley, outside Glasgow. I got on well with all the crew members, but he and I were the same age and had the same outlook on life. With some practice, I could understand what he said.

One wonderful perk of the job was that 'the system' took care of our washing and bedding. Unlike the earlier training facilities, at the Operational Training Unit, we did not have lines of socks or vests festooned around the hut like bizarre Christmas decorations. We did have to look smart though, meaning that our uniforms had to be smartly pressed, trouser creases knife sharp and boots polished like gleaming liquorice. It was odd, looking back, that no-one actually told you that you had to look smart and professional. You just knew.

We formed our own little world. There was our crew and other crews that we knew on the Operational Training Unit. Then, there were the 'erks' – the ground crews who maintained the aircraft and whose skills we depended on if we were to be alive tomorrow. We were really creatures of the system. We had only been in the air force for a short time but were part of the Royal Air Force first and last. We had little to do with the 'civvies' of Bruntingthorpe, although they were friendly enough when we talked to them, which was primarily over the bar at the local pub.

One joke that we did have among us was that if someone was looking for me, they would say 'The first place to look is in the bathroom.' The Australian devotion to personal hygiene was a source of infinite merriment for British servicemen, though I do not recall what Australian servicemen thought of British standards of hygiene.

***

My role was to fire at any aircraft attacking us from the rear. At best, I would bring down any marauding Junkers or Messerschmitt that were after us. However, I was to discover that very few gunners ever brought down a nightfighter, or even fired their guns in anger. Realistically, the best contribution I could hope to make was to tell Blackie to 'corkscrew' as fast as possible out of danger or fire my guns to dissuade a nightfighter from coming close enough to try for a kill.

I had had some experience during training in Australia firing 'go-guns' with a single barrel. We had fired these at drogues towed by other aircraft. However, being thrown in the deep end at the Operational Training Unit, it quickly became clear that in Australia, we honestly had not learned an awful lot. Now, the training was much more intense and my Frazer Nash rear turret was equipped with twin .303 machine guns.

One thing which we learned early on was that any German fighter that wanted to attack us would be equipped with a 20 mm cannon. These had up to four times our range, with shells that exploded on impact. They also fired tracers, which used burning phosphorus.

If a shell were to hit my Perspex turret, I had triple jeopardy from the projectile, the shattering Perspex and splashes of white-hot phosphorus. My twin machine guns offered poor protection by comparison.

If our plane was hit and I received the order to 'bale out', I would have had to have left the turret, got my parachute on, got back in the turret and operated the hand-wheel to reverse its position, upon which I would have fallen out backwards. I would have had some ten seconds available in which to do all this, which was not possible. Really, it would have taken four or five times as long! It is also worth mentioning that we had no training on how to make a parachute jump, meaning my prospects of survival were, in all honesty, not good. However, you had to push this to the back of your mind or you would let the crew down.

Even though we had only been together for a short time, we were bonded, unified and committed to each other. There had already been a sudden shift in our motivation. We had all joined up because Hitler was a nasty piece of work, as well as out of our sense of adventure. However, we were now going to fly for quite a different reason: to pull each other through.

***

As with all crews, our crew became a tightly operating unit.

Our two-month intensive training period on Wellingtons started a couple of days after crew selection. We started with 'circuits and bumps', which were to improve the pilot's ability to take off. Blackie's first attempts to land loosened some of the crew's fillings, but he got gradually better, so that he could land the Wellington very smoothly.

There was one pilot – an old bloke into his thirties – from another crew who just could not get the hang of landing the aircraft. I don't know what happened to him, but he could well have been 'washed out'. If you couldn't do the job to standard, they were very strict. Second chances in training were few. As the trainers never ceased to tell us, second chances on operations were non-existent.

We did cross country flights from Bruntingthorpe. This was highly enjoyable and gave the crew experience in all of the many aspects of working together, including daylight flights, night flights, flights in poor visibility, flights using only instruments, flights not using instruments and so on. Some flights could be quite short, with us travelling just around Bedfordshire. Others might be down to the south coast of England, or up to Yorkshire and over the Pennines to Lancashire. Going over the Pennines was hazardous, as it was notorious for low cloud and bad conditions. A lot of aircraft crashed there in training.

I did learn to like the English countryside, though. I saw a lot of it from the air as we flew around on training flights and also a lot from the ground as I travelled to Lutterworth, Nottingham and Leicester. Nottingham, of course, was very close to Sherwood Forest. I imagined that someone from there had come over and given the name to Sherwood, Queensland, where I grew up. Not only was the green rolling countryside very pleasant to be among, but the country houses were beautiful too. The towns with their incredibly long histories and buildings which went back to times before the settlement of Australia, were interesting and even exotic to my Queenslander eyes.

More importantly, Nottingham was also a good place for an airman at a loose end to meet some girls.

***

Another form of training, which was quite fun, was to be taken to a darkened room. There, profiles of aircraft would be projected onto a wall. We had to identify the aircraft immediately and accurately.

In combat, if we had mistaken a Junkers 88 or a Messerschmitt 110 for a Wellington, we could be dead. The other way round and I could have shot down one of our own aircraft. My score in these tests was around 50:50. It was a dangerous business, war in the air. Still, there was no time to think about it. Over Germany, you would just have to make a decision and hope that you got it right.

***

We progressed to night flying and gradually got to the point where we worked as a unit with minimal orders and maximum harmony. This must have very difficult for Blackie, especially. He had done his initial training in the United States, in sunny conditions and clear nights. Now, in England and Europe, he was faced with heavy cloud and vicious headwinds that you had to fight against. There was a war on, though, and you just got on with it.

The training was so intensive that during my time at Bruntingthorpe, two crews were lost. One crew, under

Sergeant Wilder, was actually sent out on 'on ops'. This was the first time that Bruntingthorpe crews were dispatched on a real operation. According to the official Bomber Command diaries, this was 'to accustom crews to bomb on target-indicator markers'. In fact, the raid, which consisted of 33 Wellingtons, six Mosquitoes and six Halifax heavy bombers, was for a quite different purpose. As per the official diaries, they were told it was an arms dump. Whilst it was of the essence that the exact nature of the target would not be made known to them, the target was, in fact, the Blockhouse at the Foret D'Eperleque in Northern France. This was being prepared as a site to store V2 rockets and to fire some 30 missiles a day at London.

There is an odd twist to this story. The V2 rockets were not destined to hit London until September 1944, meaning this raid was more than one year earlier. Somehow (though this has never been explained), the British government knew the details of the V2 rocket programme more than a year in advance. There were so many odd little things like that in World War II. One thing you did not do was ask questions!

Sergeant Wilder's aircraft lost an engine over the English Channel on the return journey and ditched into the sea near Newhaven. Wilder was the sole survivor; the others were never found. The raids were successful and that V2 rocket site was never used. Later, Sergeant Wilder would pop up again in my life in rather dramatic circumstances.

The other crew, under Flying Officer Clarke, took off for a Bullseye Operation (that is, a simulated bombing attack), with a destination of Fishguard in South Wales and the Irish Sea. An engine failed near Oswestry in Wales, the aircraft crashed and the crew of six were all lost. They did not tell us what happened – merely that the aircraft 'failed to return'. You did not dwell on it. You did not worry about it. You did not ask about it. Most importantly, you did not think about it.

***

During the war, some 5000 were killed in operational training. This was due to a combination of inexperience in the crew and the fact that our training aircraft were clapped out. I don't recall it worrying us unduly. We just thought 'Poor buggers!' and got on with the job. We stuck with the idea that getting killed was always going to happen to someone else. Well, that was almost true.

One afternoon, Blackie was taxiing a Wimpey along the runway. Just on the point of take-off, a tyre burst with a great bang. The aircraft slewed around on the runway. I had no time to collect my thoughts, just to hang on tight. If the aircraft had tipped slightly and a wingtip had touched the tarmac, we would have been 'goners', or worse. Getting incinerated in a crashed aircraft was bad enough but to be semi-incinerated and have to live with the pain and disfigurement for decades was worse. Fortunately, the aircraft gradually stopped its dance of death and came to an undignified halt at a strange angle to the runway. We got out, shaken. Someone would have made a merry quip. We all took off our flying gear, returned our parachutes and went to our separate messes for a nice cup of tea.

***

There was another aspect of life at Bruntingthorpe – one that our ears knew all too well. There was a high-pitched whining sound that went on for weeks and weeks, so loud that it drowned out conversation. It is important to understand that during wartime, if you did not understand something, you did not make enquiries as to what it might be. If you were lucky, any superfluous curiosity could result in a dressing down from the Wing Commander. If you were unlucky, other worse things might befall you. Not until after the war did we find out what it was. It was Sir Frank Whittle and his company, Powerjet, who were developing the jet engine for use in the Gloster Meteor fighter that appeared just before the end of the war.

***

Our time at Bruntingthorpe had its hair-raising, not to say life-threatening, moments. It was not all bad, however, and some luxuries were available through the food parcels that arrived from Australia. We were very pleased with the canned meat, canned fruit and even the odd can of evaporated milk. Some of the local fairs still operated and they were always good fun to go to.

So, one sunny weekend, the crew cycled over to Lutterworth, which was some eight kilometres from Bruntingthorpe. There was a country fair on, which was a traditional sort of thing that they had every summer. There were scary rides, which propelled people through the air strapped into seats. As aircrew, we did have to laugh that people actually spent money to go on these rides, which were considerably less terrifying than what we were experiencing every day in the Operational Training Unit. There were also shooting galleries, candy floss and the like. Everyone was in a good mood. The war was almost forgotten, except that almost all of the men under 40 wore an army, navy, or Royal Air Force uniform. A lot of the younger women were also in Women's Land Army uniforms.

The Land Army was a civilian organisation of young women who were called up for farm work to replace the men who were away at the war. They worked long hard hours for very little pay, though most would later say it was the best time of their lives. The Land Girls had a very distinctive, rather smart, semi-military style uniform, which consisted of a dark green sweater over a cream blouse and brown tie. They also wore buff knee-length jodhpur-style trousers and beige socks. The ensemble was completed by a brown brimmed hat and brown shoes. These had to be kept to the same impossible standards of shininess as ours in the Royal Air Force. During the war, you saw Land Girls everywhere.

'Can you change a "ten bob" note?' someone asked.

'Ten bob' was half of one pound sterling. It would buy several pints of beer or a railway ticket to London.

I looked at the person who had made this unsolicited request. She was a Land Army girl – Joy Barry by name. Although I didn't know it then, the world was about to change. It was interesting when you thought about it. I had chatted with so many girls in training in Australia; so many Women's Army Corps in the United States; so many girls around Brighton; and yet, when I met Joy and her companion, the world and my universe changed in very short order.

There were several Land Army girls in the vicinity. I got talking with one in particular. I can't remember what we talked about, but whatever it was, I do remember that there was a flickering of light. She smoked, but even that didn't deter me. This was serious stuff right from the start! She told me she had never smoked before the war. However, in the Land Army, smokers got a ten-minute smoking break in the morning and afternoon. The other girls encouraged her to join them and 'just hold a cigarette', but she became hooked. The war impacted people's lives in ways that you would never have thought.

She was called Freda. She came from Coalville, a mining town of some 30,000 in Leicestershire, around 30 kilometres away. She lived in a hostel near Lutterworth, with some three dozen other Land Army girls.

***

From then on, instead of hanging around the sergeant's mess or the local pubs, I was now on my cycle to see Freda at every opportunity. Her job was an unusual one, making thatched rooves designed to protect growing crops. Thatching was highly skilled work that a woman would never have done pre-war, but that was the one of the great things for the girls in the Land Army. Pre-war, a woman had one option: grooming to be a housewife and mother. A few women had clerical or nursing jobs, though were expected to give them up when they got married. Thanks to Adolf Hitler, women in the early 1940s actually had the chance to gain other forms of employment.

Remember also that this was a time when women always wore dresses. Many thought that the Land Army jodhpurs were very unbecoming for ladies and tantamount to scandalous cross dressing!

The Land Army hostels were, of course, like moths to a flame for all of us in the forces. However, we Royal Air Force blokes were quite incredibly lucky in one other way.

There were many Italian prisoners of war working in the fields around Lutterworth. They were outrageously good looking, had wonderfully tailored uniforms and would sing as they worked in the fields, or took it easy in the evenings. Their singing was magical, ranging from operatic choruses and Neapolitan folk songs to wonderful harmonies from the Italian Alpine areas. The best aspect, though, was that they were confined to their camps. We were protected from competition for the girls, which worked out well, as otherwise, it would have been a war-time battle, in which we stood no chance whatsoever.

The Land Army girls were, however, critical of the fact that they had to go to their farms on bicycles, whereas the Italian prisoners were taken in the luxury of trucks.

For the rest of my time on the Operational Training Unit, I flew and trained when I had to, but otherwise was back on the bike to Lutterworth and Freda. Life in Hitler's war was really not too bad! Well, not yet.

6

50 Squadron – Skellingthorpe in Lincolnshire

We duly passed out of Bruntingthorpe. There was no final examination, review, or passing out parade. The system passed an order to the adjutant and roughly at Christmas time 1943, we moved on to the Heavy Conversion Unit at Skellingthorpe to learn how to fly Lancaster bombers. This was a large base on the outskirts of Lincoln, with only 50 Squadron and its Heavy Conversion Unit in residence. We were certainly not cramped, so this proved to be quite a good move.

It was also a lucky move. Luck came in various guises. Firstly, the locals told us that winters in Lincolnshire could be bitter with weeks of snow. Freda told me of previous years when buses from Leicester to Coalville would be stuck in the snow and unable to move. This Christmas was relatively mild. That was very much in our favour, as the 'icing up' of Lancasters was a major problem. Ice could form on the wings, which could either make the aircraft unable to take off or unstable in flight and extremely dangerous to fly. We managed to dodge the lot. I did manage to see snow one day that winter, but only a light shower over the 106 Squadron base at Syerston, when I was there one day.

The second slice of luck was that raids were on hold for the first few weeks, when I was on the squadron. This was due not to the cold, but to the thick, impenetrable fog, which make take-off difficult and landing all but impossible.

***

A couple of days after arrival, Blackie went over to the Royal Air Force base at Bitteswell, near Bruntingthorpe. There, he picked up Flight Engineer Walton and Mid-Upper Gunner Ridd, who was from Swansea in South Wales. We were now assembled as a crew of seven to fly Lancasters.

The crew was:

Flight Lieutenant T.H. Blackham	124922	Pilot
Pilot Officer C.R.E. Walton	174051	Flight engineer
Flying Officer D.G. Jones	144926	Navigator
Flight Sergeant S.J. Godfrey	175487	Bomb aimer
Sergeant S.C. Wilkins	1396525	Wireless operator
Sergeant H.G. Ridd	1003849	Mid-upper gunner
Sergeant H.J. Shuttleworth		Rear gunner

At Skellingthorpe, we would carry on our training beyond the world of Wellingtons. We were now to fly Lancasters. The world of wartime was a one of astonishing technological developments and progress. The Wellington bombers that had been at the forefront of technology when I first volunteered for the air force in 1941 had passed through obsolescence and were now obsolete just two years later. They were now only used as trainers. As we had seen at Bruntingthorpe, they were becoming worn out and men died when their engines failed.

The brave new world of the bomber was now the 'heavy stuff': Lancasters and Halifaxes. After the Wellingtons, Lancasters seemed enormous. However, for me, the conversion was relatively simple. The Frazer Nash turret in the Lancaster was very similar to that of the Wellington, except that it had four guns instead of two.

It is also worth noting that no training was provided in the use of parachutes. We knew how to put it on and that we had to jump out of a plummeting aircraft and pull the rip cord to open it. Beyond that though, there was nothing. Once you jumped, you were essentially left to your own devices. You could really imagine our 'betters' in the high command saying, 'Sorry and all that, old chap, but it's really up to you now, so pull yourself together.'

***

At the Heavy Conversion Unit, the rest of the crew went off to do fighter assimilation training, in which fighters would be sent to simulate shooting us down and we would learn how to evade.

Ridd and I were sent to the gunnery school, where we were 'attacked' by Royal Air Force pilots in American Curtiss Tomahawk fighters. Like the Fairey Battles, the Tomahawks had proven useless against Luftwaffe Bf109s and Focke Wulf 190s, though were fine for training. Instead of guns, my aircraft was equipped with cameras, so when I 'fired', it would take a photo of what I would have hit. Our camera guns gave us 30 chances of a hit.

On reporting back to Blackie, he asked, 'How many?'

I replied, '30.'

'No,' he said. 'I didn't mean how many shots you made. I meant how many hits did you make?'

'30,' I replied nonchalantly.

It is fair to say that Blackie was surprised. Actually, so was I, but I didn't want to admit that.

***

We all came back together as a crew for the final round of fighter assimilation training. This was where the mid-upper gunner and I were in centre stage. We would fly on a course given to the navigator. As we flew along, a Tomahawk fighter would suddenly appear below us, getting ready for an attack.

It was my job to shout 'Corkscrew port!' or 'Corkscrew starboard!' to evade the fighter before he came in for the kill. Of course, on operations, 'the kill' meant that the Luftwaffe pilot was literally trying to kill you. It was nothing personal, but life-threatening if he raked your aircraft with exploding 20mm cannon shells.

On my shout of 'Corkscrew starboard!' Blackie would put the huge Lancaster into a corkscrew dive to the right. The Merlin engines would scream, the whole aircraft would shake and the horizon would spin around, as we lost several thousand feet in seconds. Then, Blackie waited for our shout of 'Lost him!' Then, it was up to the navigator, Jones to say, 'Five degrees to port, skipper,' or whatever, to get us back on course.

**

After some weeks of training, we passed from the Heavy Conversion Unit into 50 Squadron proper. This was slightly odd, as the system had allocated me into a British squadron, although there were several predominantly Australian squadrons only some ten to 15 kilometres away. Nevertheless, 50 Squadron was a well-regarded outfit.

One notable figure in 50 Squadron was Flight Officer Leslie Manser, who took part in the thousand bomber raid on Cologne in 1942. Manser had kept his burning aircraft flying straight and level while the other crew members bailed out, thus sacrificing his own life. He was awarded the Victoria Cross.

At the time, if I had ever heard of any of the above, I doubt I would have thought twice about it. Such was the atmosphere of a wartime bomber station. No-one thought of historical details. Instead, all of our efforts, thoughts and focuses were on the job and how well we could fly the aircraft. In my case, the world also focussed on Freda.

There was also something else which we did not think about in 50 Squadron. I wonder what we would have made of it, had we known. It concerned Wing Commander Anthony Heward, our commanding officer. He had a very colourful history. I must say, though, that when I knew him, he was an affable sort of bloke. I remember he picked me up in his car once or twice when I was walking back from dispersals to the sergeants' mess. At that time, none of us knew his amazing story – it would have been all over the base (and Five Group) if we had.

He had been an instructor, apparently, at Royal Air Force Sealand, outside Chester, with the rank of Squadron Leader. His next posting was, incredibly, to the Turkish Air Force. During the war, that would have been strictly 'hush-hush', as Turkey was a neutral country. To even accept training help compromised that neutrality and could have led to Turkey being invaded by German forces.

Had this happened, it would have been remarkably ironic, since Heward was training Turkish pilots how to pilot Heinkel 111 bombers. I could only imagine these had been captured by the Royal Air Force and given to the Turks to bolster up their own air force. This would only further compromise Turkey's neutrality if it leaked out.

At any rate, Heward had found this Anatolian sojourn boring. He was not a man to keep his boredom or his displeasure quiet. A visiting United States Air Force pilot offered Heward a free trip to the USA, which Heward accepted with enthusiasm. Off he flew across the Atlantic, which led to the system declaring him as AWOL ('absent without leave'). Being 'absent without leave' was a very serious business in the wartime armed forces. After some time, Heward decided that a return to the UK was his best plan. He duly organised himself a berth on a ship travelling from the USA. On arrival at Liverpool, he was duly arrested by the Provosts: the stern-faced Royal Air Force Military Police.

Instead of being committed to a court martial, higher authority offered him alternatives. He could either stand trial (which would doubtlessly result in a period of grim imprisonment), or take command of a flight on a bomber station (which was exactly what he wanted). He was posted firstly to 83 Squadron, a Pathfinder squadron, but after a short time, was promoted to Wing Commander. He then became my commanding officer.

None of these details ever leaked out, fortunately for him and the reputation of the Royal Air Force.

He did apparently have the reputation of being a stickler for the niceties of service discipline, though I always found him decent enough. One thing that did impress me about him was that when he gave a briefing before a raid, he would always give his presentation and then select an airman at random to come up onto the podium and repeat all the details. It was a marvellous way to ensure that everyone in the squadron listened very intently!

***

We also attended training sessions on how to get into and out of a dinghy. These sessions were held in the camp swimming pool. We had to jump out of a simulated aircraft and descend in good order into a rubber dinghy.

It was never quite clear whether this prepared us adequately for ditching in the English Channel in the teeth of one of its infamous gales, though we knew that air-sea rescue did a good job in rescuing airmen from both sides. We also knew that if we ditched in the Channel, we would most likely be dead from hypothermia before an air-sea rescue launch got anywhere near us. The fog continued to persist. In those first few weeks on the squadron, it continued to keep us grounded and off operations.

This was wonderful for me, as I could go over to Coalville to see Freda. This sounds idyllic, but with the fog that thick, the roads were completely dangerous to anyone in a vehicle or walking along the road. Driving through the East Midlands with zero visibility was almost as dangerous as flying over the Third Reich. There were no nightfighters after us on the roads of Lincolnshire, but then, over Germany there were no vehicles about to emerge blindly from the fog to cause a fatal collision.

Freda and I had been going out together for some four months when we decided that it was time that I met her parents. The journey was too far to travel by bike and also a very awkward one by rail.

So, I hitch hiked. We did a lot of hitch hiking in the Royal Air Force. You would wait in a good place for a vehicle to stop, often on the road leading out of a village or town. You'd then look pointedly at passing drivers and put your thumb up, pointing in the direction that you wanted to go.

The Royal Australian Air Force uniform led to a lot of drivers picking me up. Normally, the vehicles were trucks of one sort or another, as there were lots of Royal Air Force and army trucks busily going from one place to another. You sometimes got civilian trucks too, but with severe petrol rationing, these were used very sparingly. I was picked up more than once by a 'Queen Mary'. These were enormous articulated trucks that delivered Lancasters in kit form to their operational station. One 'Queen Mary' might have half a fuselage; another, the second half of the fuselage; another a wing; and so on. They were very generous with their lifts, but progress in them was always very, very slow.

If we were really lucky, we might be picked up by a private car, though this was a rarity. Very few people owned cars in 1944 Britain and those that did could rarely run them because of the very tight rules on petrol rationing. I did once get picked up by an Air Vice Marshal and his wife, though. Goodness knows where he got the fuel from!

Whatever the type of vehicle, there was always a pleasant chat (usually on the state of war) with the driver, who inevitably offered cigarettes. At the end, you'd always receive a cheery wave of the hand as the vehicle pulled away. Back then, there was something about hitchhiking that represented the essence of people helping each other out during wartime privations.

Sometimes, the camaraderie cut through the privation, austerity and rationing. Nowhere did we experience this better than down the local pubs, the Red Lion and Black Swan. Both were friendly places with lovely log fires. I was not a heavy drinker by any means, which was just as well, because I had encountered British warm beer in Brighton, and it was just not for me. However, the crew and I would go into the pubs to sink a pint or two 'just to be sociable'. Every night, it seemed there was someone who could play the piano and we would sing songs by Vera Lynn, like 'White Cliffs of Dover' or 'We'll Meet Again'; Flanagan and Allen songs, such as 'Run Rabbit Run' and 'Underneath the Arches'; and favourites of the forces, like 'Bless 'em All' and 'Kiss Me Goodnight, Sergeant Major'. At 10:30pm, the landlord's stentorian voice would bark out, 'Time please, gentlemen!' and ring a bell to say the bar was closed. Under wartime regulations, pubs had to close at that time to make sure that everyone got home and got a good night's sleep to keep them fresh for war work the next day. The bell was also the signal for a slightly unsteady cycle ride home on country roads, with no lighting and vehicles with only the dimmest lights. Some 50,000 people were killed on the dark, unlit roads in World War II Britain, which is rather more than were killed in the Blitz on London.

And so, I met Freda's parents. Her dad was a coal miner. Wartime regulations meant that he was legally barred from joining the armed forces, as Britain was very strict on its 'reserved occupations'. It also meant that, as a miner, his weekly food ration was better than most.

At this stage, Freda and I were just good friends – well, very good friends. Parents know without being told when their daughter brings home someone 'special', so I am sure they understood the situation precisely. They also must have known that as an aircrew volunteer, I was unlikely to survive the war.

They must also have realised that even if I did survive the war, there was a chance that I would take their daughter away to Australia, which meant that they might never see her again. From the start, we always thought of the two of us going to Australia.

Freda's family lived in a 'tied-house', which was a house given to miners for as long as they were working at the mine. This house was one of a terrace (a series of houses all joined together), which was something we had never seen back in Queensland. The house had no bathroom. Instead, baths were taken in a tin bath in front of the fire in the living room. There was also no electricity upstairs. It seemed the mine owners were not given to spending their hard-earned profits to lavish any level of comfort on their employees. However, these conditions led to very tight knit communities, where people bonded together with family, friends and neighbours for help and, in the case of mine accidents, self-survival.

Despite the risks, Freda's parents approved of our relationship and were very much for us getting married, as was Freda's sister, Stella. In the circumstances, their enthusiasm was an act of extreme generosity by all of them. It was a very different era, though. There were many marriages where the husband went back to the army, navy, air force, or marines, then was killed a matter of weeks – or even days – later. It was part of the landscape of wartime life. On the other hand, though, there was always the 'sweetener' of an allowance to a wife married to a man on active service, which was an extravagant one pound per week!

It is also interesting to recall some of the perspectives that were very typical of the time. For example, Freda had a younger sister, Jackie, who played with her food, as children will.

'Stop that!' her mother said, with seriousness in her voice. 'That is costing the lives of the sailors who bring it over the Atlantic!'

Needless to say, there was no wasting food during wartime.

Her father did tell me one very interesting story from her early life. When Freda was a little girl, he would take her for walks and she would say that he was taking her to Australia. Maybe her fate was settled at that early time!

***

After gaining her parents' approval, I would spend more and more time with Freda.

I would call for her at the hostel and we would go for walks or cycles around the lush, green, rolling hills of the Leicestershire countryside.

We'd talk about ... well, everything. We would have those sorts of conversations that just go on for hours and hours and whatever the other said was always fascinating. She wanted to know a lot about Australia and always had questions about it.

Whilst we were in our own private paradise, the war did keep on crashing through. One of the Land Army girls was going out with a member of aircrew. One day, he did not come back. We never heard what happened to him. She was devastated.

∗∗∗

Eventually, in about November, six months after having met her, we reached the crunch point. I have no recollection of what I burbled out, but she said 'Yes!' and we were engaged.

Our wedding day was fixed for the 30 December. I wrote to my parents immediately but knew that by the time the letter reached Australia at about the end of January, I would already have been married for a month.

We were married at a church at Barton Hill, a village in Leicestershire. A lot of the Land Girls attended, all in their uniforms of jodhpurs and pullovers. Such were the times, they did not have any dresses or formal wear to put on. Even nylon stockings were a luxury! The vicar was, however, very put out! Several of the girls were not wearing hats in church and he told them off in no uncertain terms. This was a double sin, because the Land Army uniform included the hat, so they were improperly dressed under the rules of the Land Army as well. However, I do not recall this man's misery causing us too much angst at the time.

On my side of the church, there was just me. The way we fixed the wedding date was one of those supreme wartime opportunities. It is also worth noting that rapid courtships and weddings were very common in wartime England. Wing Commander Heward let us know that in two weeks' time, our crew was granted one week's 'pre-operation' leave. The others were going home to see their families, but we said 'Let's get married!' The decision to take the plunge was very quick and very easy. We would go through with the ceremony, then spend the rest of the time on a brief honeymoon.

There was no wedding reception as such, as there was no money for such a spendthrift event. Back then, even if you had the financial means, you would have had to track down the 'spivs' of the black market for luxuries like tinned peaches or evaporated milk. Nevertheless, someone produced a bottle of Australian wine from somewhere, so they drank to our health – at least, those who got a glass before the bottle ran out did! Then, the girls went back to work.

Freda and I had a very quick but enjoyable honeymoon in London. Returning from our honeymoon, I did fall foul of the hostel manageress for keeping her out too late. *Heck! Freda was a respectable married woman!*

As a married man, I was also now subject to orders about not having aircrew members' wives too close to the station. This was because Air Marshal Harris was very nervous about aircrew members being killed and the bereaved wives organising demonstrations outside the station gates.

7

Winston Churchill, 'Butch' Harris, Lady Luck and Joe Shuttleworth

By some benign twist of fate, I was one of very few people for whom Hitler's war had been a privileged existence. Well, at least that was true until I found myself in the refrigerated weather of Lincolnshire in January 1944.

I had joined the Royal Australian Air Force, a glamorous albeit risky organisation. I wore a spiffy uniform. I had crossed the Pacific Ocean with bright sunshine and no Japanese submarines in sight. I had been royally treated in a train journey across the length of the USA. I had crossed the Atlantic Ocean in my own cabin on the *Queen Elizabeth*. I now enjoyed the status of aircrew in a country that regarded me only one step off being a film star.

The people of Britain had been hammered by Hitler's Blitzkrieg, Luftwaffe and naval blockade through the U-Boat war. Bomber Command air crews were the single and unique body of men who represented the British in the fightback and gave some semblance of belief in ultimate victory. In a more rational world, I might have written to Adolf Hitler and thanked him profusely for two years of truly fabulous life, to have seen things I never expected to see and to have found my life partner.

To mention my life partner brings us to the main participants in my life. If someone had asked me in early 1944, 'Who are the most important people in your life?' I would have answered immediately and without hesitation, 'Freda and the crew.'

As Albert Einstein tells us, 'reality is an illusion, albeit a persistent one.' If only Einstein could have met me, he would have been glad for the proof of his thesis. In these early days of 1944, my entire universe focussed on Freda and, to a lesser extent, the crew. My fate and wellbeing and even my survival, was in the hands of others: Winston Churchill, Air Chief Marshal Sir Arthur Harris and Lady Luck. Two of these I knew about, although how they impacted me was shrouded in mystery. The third I would not know about until a dramatic discovery decades later.

***

Winston Spencer Churchill's contribution to my story was very simple.

The personification of a British bulldog, he had been Prime Minister of the UK since 10 May 1940. The world which Winston Churchill gave to those he led was of pure black and white. The British Empire was good, Nazi Germany was bad. Hitler's Reich was to be put out of business totally and by any means whatsoever. From his time as a war correspondent in South Africa, Churchill had displayed a bias for dramatic action and loved involvement in a really good war.

He also pulled the strings over me.

***

Sir Arthur 'Butch' Harris was another British bulldog. Harris too pulled the tactical strings over me, although the relationship was more complex.

The basis of our relationship lay firstly in our shared history at 50 Squadron. Major Harris had been the officer commanding the unit when 50 Squadron was still part of the Royal Flying Corps in World War I.

Harris had then gone on to distinguish himself dropping bombs on tribesmen in North West India and Arab insurgents on horseback in Iraq in the 1920s. This was where Harris perfected his theory of area bombing, within which I was destined to play a part. Harris had risen through the ranks – firstly as Air Vice Marshal in charge of 5 Group, then as Air Officer commanding Bomber Command, which he was appointed to on 20 February 1942.

Harris had a clear policy on bombing. He gave a clear exposition of this policy in a speech made for newsreels, just after the thousand bomber raid on

Cologne and the entry of the United States Army Air Force into the war.

> *'...Colgnne, Rostock, Lübeck —those are only just the beginning. Let the Nazis take good note of the western horizon, where, at the moment, they will see a cloud no bigger than a man's hand. But behind that cloud lies the whole massive power of the United States of America. When the storm bursts over Germany, they will look back to the days of Rostock, L ü beck and Cologne as a man caught in the blast of a hurricane looks back to the gentle zephyr of last summer. There are a lot of people who say that bombing can never win a war. Well, my answer to that is that it has never been tried yet and we shall see.*
>
> *The Nazis entered this war under the rather childish delusion that they were going to bomb everyone else and nobody was going to bomb them. At Rotterdam, London, Warsaw and half a hundred other places, they put their rather naive theory into operation. They sowed the wind and now they are going to reap the whirlwind.*
>
> *Press on with your attacks! Let him have it on the chin!'*

It is worth mentioning that the Rostock and Lübeck raids of 1942 were conducted as scientific experiments in how to burn wooden-built towns to the ground, rather than for any strategic advantage. Harris was Churchill's boy!

My role was to 'let him have it on the chin', whilst clearly obeying orders and flying where I was told. This has a certain irony to it, as I was to discover years later, Harris was himself blatantly disobeying orders in January when I first arrived at Skellingthorpe.

Harris had developed a list of 50 German cities, most of which, at the time of my going on ops (with the exception of Dresden), had been bombed mercilessly. In November 1943, he had written to Churchill:

> 'We can wreck Berlin from end to end if the USAAF will come in on it. It will cost us 400—500 aircraft. It will cost Germany the war.'

At roughly the same time, Harris also wrote to his superior, Marshal of the Royal Air Force, Sir Charles Portal.

> 'It appears that the Lancaster force should be sufficient to produce in Germany by April 1 1944 a state of devastation in which surrender was inevitable.'

The problem was that the German morale had not broken. The German population shrugged and got on with their job in the same manner as the British population during the Blitz of 1940-41. Worst of all,

German production was not diminishing. Rather, it was still on the increase.

The Battle of Berlin commenced in late 1943, just as I was completing training at Bruntingthorpe. The battle would consist of 19 raids, which were well underway by the time that I arrived at Skellingthorpe. It was Harris' Battle of Berlin that formed the tactical background to my service in the Royal Air Force.

Harris had employed some 76 squadrons over his raids. The vast majority of his aircraft got through. As he had promised, he was, indeed, wrecking Berlin from end to end. Still, German industrial production did not diminish. Harris' gambit was not working.

The War Cabinet, ensconced in the claustrophobic confines of its prison-like, secret bunker below Whitehall, was not impressed with Harris' results. Mutterings in the corridors of power said that he had overpromised and underachieved. Moreover, events had moved on.

By January of 1944, the whole balance of war strategy now shifted to the invasion of Normandy, which was targeted for June. The Cabinet gave Harris orders to cease the saturation bombing of Berlin and to instead concentrate on hitting German aircraft and ball-bearing factories.

Harris paid only lip service to the order. Harris interpreted his orders from the Cabinet Office as meaning that he should continue to bomb Berlin, because that was where many aircraft and ball-bearing factories were situated.

This was the situation in which I found myself when I arrived at Skellingthorpe on a sparkling white, icy cold January day in 1944.

***

The grand sweep of history is one thing, but what happens on the ground is another. Churchill wanted to invade Europe. Harris wanted to knock out Berlin and win the war on his own. I had other agendas – for example, seeing Freda as often as possible; my position on the leave roster; drinking with the crew; and scrounging coke for the stove in the sergeants' Nissen hut.

On bomber stations, many crews also gave some thought as to whether they would be alive this time next week. Some men said that the thought of flying over Berlin broke them out in a cold sweat and refused to fly there. They would prefer to take the unpleasant consequences, including loss of rank, being posted to somewhere awful like the Orkney Islands and, worst of all, having their file stamped 'LMF' ('lacks moral fibre').

However, for Blackham, me and the rest of the crew, this was not the case. Where other crews took on 'the look of death' and died on their next operation, our crew approached this dystopian nightmare with cheery but unrealistic equanimity.

At least it was not that we were stupidly unrealistic. There was a very particular and quite strange reason why this was the case. We have already discussed the first two slices of luck that I had at Skellingthorpe. However, there was a third – and this one was perhaps the best of all.

Of all the 76 squadrons involved in the Battle of Berlin, Lady Luck had put me into that very squadron, which had the lowest casualty rate. Indeed, the squadron's Operations Record Book shows that during my time on the squadron, there was only one aircraft loss out of 150 sorties. That is a loss rate of less than one percent. This is all the more amazing when you realise that 50 squadrons took part in all 19 operations over Berlin.

Some miles to the south, the large Royal Air Force base of Mildenhall was situated. Its early claim to fame was that it had been the starting point for the MacRobertson Air Race to Melbourne, which I had witnessed as a boy. Its sombre claim to fame during Harris' Battle of Berlin was that New Zealand's 75 Squadron, a Stirling Bomber formation, was to lose fully 30% of its strength on every flight that it made over Berlin.

8

Blackham Goes to Brunswick (14/15 January 1944)

In the flight office, the board showed that there 'was a war on' tonight. To our crew's excitement, Blackie was slated to accompany another crew on the raid. In this, he would fly 'second dicky'. He would not actually fly the aircraft but would instead be there as an observer to get a feel of what it felt like to be in proper combat over a real target.

The term 'second dicky' came from the seat on which the supernumerary aircrew member would sit. It was a fold-down seat positioned behind the pilot. The good thing about it was that it provided the trainee pilot with an excellent vantage point to see very well what was going on. The bad thing was that the seat consisted of a single slat of wood, which was intensely uncomfortable for a journey destined to last some six hours.

The raid was made up of 496 Lancasters and two Halifaxes. Of these, 38 Lancasters were lost, which accounted for 7.6 per cent of the force. As ever, lucky 50 Squadron managed not to lose an aircraft, a crew member, or its sense of optimism.

***

The Royal Air Force's wireless surveillance teams could hear the Germans' running commentary, which followed the progress of the bomber force from a position only 40 miles from the English coast.

Many Luftwaffe nightfighters entered the bomber stream soon after the bombers crossed the German frontier, near Bremen. The German fighters scored steadily until the Dutch coast was crossed on the return flight. Eleven of the lost aircraft were Pathfinders.

Brunswick was smaller than the Bomber Command's usual targets. However, the Bomber Command War Diaries say this raid was not a success. The Brunswick city report agrees with this, describing this only as a 'light' raid, with bombs in the south of the city destroying only ten houses and killing 14 people. Most of the attack fell either in the countryside, or in Wolfenbüttel and other small towns and villages well to the south of Brunswick.

There are two sad aspects to the story of this raid, apart from the people who were killed by it. Firstly, Wolfenbüttel is a full 15 kilometres from Braunschweig, which meant that many of the aircraft were not actually bombing the correct town. Secondly, Wolfenbüttel is a place of extraordinary cultural significance through two men who worked there – Gotthold Lessing, who holds a stellar place in German literature and Gottfried Leibniz, who did ground-breaking work in mathematics, including the development of binary notation. This was being used on that very day at Bletchley Park to help break the German Enigma code. Such are the ironies of war.

***

When Blackham returned to Skellingthorpe, the conversation was less on the delights of binary notation and more on what it was like being in a real raid.

'Did you see kites get shot down?'

'What was it like looking down on a burning city?'

'Go on, be honest, Blackie! Were you scared?'

'Who, me? Good Lord! Of course not.'

Gross exaggeration or 'shooting a line' was a popular pastime among the air crews. It was generally regarded with amused and indulgent tolerance.

'At any rate, the crew's "duck" has been broken,' I recall thinking.

One of our crew's number had been 'on ops'. When I look back on it, it was a strange sort of event. Here we all were, pledging our lives to fight Germany, when we didn't have any particular enmity against the German people – only the Nazis. Few on the squadron would ever have met a German. Even fewer would have been there: foreign holidays were not part of life in the 1930s.

Blackie was the only one of the crew who was ever destined to meet a Luftwaffe man. The circumstances of that were so improbable and so unlikely that his story reads like lurid, implausible fiction. However, it is all true.

9

Operation on Berlin (27-28 January 1944)-'Whitebait' and 'Arseweather'

Morale for us at Royal Air Force Skellingthorpe was at a low ebb after the raid on Magdeburg on 21-22 January.

Like the desultory Brunswick raid, this was not a success either. Fifty-seven out of 648 bombers had been shot down, although, as fate normally decreed, none from 50 Squadron. Crews had seen 'a lot of kites going down', although the actual number was not made public.

Most of the fires were outside the city limits of Magdeburg and many crews were lured to bomb on 'decoy' fires outside of the urban area. These were started by the Germans' air raid protection units to protect their cities.

Harris ordered a raid for the night of 25-26 January, which should have been my first raid. However, it was scrubbed due to bad weather and postponed to the next night.

On Thursday 27 January, two code words clattered over the teleprinters to Skellingthorpe and a dozen other Royal Air Force stations. The first codeword was 'Whitebait', which was the code word for the target that night: 'Berlin'. The second codeword was 'Usual'. This meant the bomb loads were to contain one 4000 pound 'cookie' plus twelve canisters of incendiaries.

On the station, there could be no doubt as to our response. *Flipping Berlin yet again!* Harris had been hammering Berlin since the 23 August in 1943. Crews had lost track of how many attacks there had been on Berlin. This was, in fact, the fifteenth.

***

And so, later that night I was to start out in the great adventure for which I had travelled half the world. I felt the Lancaster lurch as Blackie took off the brakes and powered the huge aircraft forwards. It was just gone half past five in the afternoon.

As the aircraft gathered speed, I distinctly remember thinking, 'So, here we are at last. This is what we came for.'

It had been a long, long journey to get here, both in time and distance. I was excited, as I felt that I was finally 'doing my bit', which was extremely important during those war years. I had no thought whatsoever that I could be dead by this time tomorrow if things did not go my way. Still, *here we were* – and it felt right.

All I had to do was 30 of these and I would get through to Pathfinders – an ambition that I shared with the rest of the crew. Nobody told me that the average number of operations before you 'got the chop' was seven. What you needed to get through that tour of duty was a very good crew and a lot – a real lot – of luck.

Even so though, the commanding officer, Wing Commander Heward flew with us on this raid. If the Wing Commander could do it, we could do it too. It couldn't be that dangerous, could it?

***

In Germany, the Luftwaffe waited.

They expected an attack tonight but were not happy. For the German Luftwaffe, the omens were not good. The full moon was past. To make matters worse, the weather forecast was for clear skies over England, which would allow aircraft to take off and land effectively, but cloud over Germany, which made it difficult for the Me110s and Ju88s to find the bomber stream and inflict pain on it. It was what the Luftwaffe called *Arschwetter* [arse weather].

***

Tonight, Harris tried a new ploy. He sent 80 Stirlings and Wellingtons over the German coast to drop mines. This was a spoof raid to draw off the nightfighters, which swarmed around North Holland. In addition, six

Mosquitoes dropped dummy route markers to make it look as though the bombers were going to Hannover, Braunschweig, Magdeburg, or Leipzig.

It worked! The bomber stream in which I was travelling passed over the Dutch coast with the deadly nightfighters in other places, chasing shadows.

In a Junkers 88, *Unteroffizier* [Sergeant] Bruno Rupp caught the bomber stream before it reached Berlin and made a kill. His was the only kill as the bomber force approached Berlin. The only other casualties at this stage were two bombers that collided in mid-air and fell to earth in flames and with full bomb loads.

The sky-marking (parachute flares to give bomb aimers a target) was reported as accurate, but a strong wind blew the burning target indicators off course. Seventeen different districts within the target area of Berlin were hit but a further 61 non-combatant communities outside and to the east of Berlin were bombed also.

The flak barrage was noted as feeble on this night. However, once the attack started, large numbers of nightfighters arrived and the number of Royal Air Force casualties began to mount rapidly.

***

One man from 50 Squadron, James Brown, who was a mid-upper gunner of Flight Lieutenant Keith's crew, had a hair-raising tale to tell.

'The attack badly damaged our Lanc, starting a fire in the No.1 starboard petrol tank. I opened fire on the Ju88 and actually saw him nosedive into the blazing target area, badly hit. But as we were more concerned with our blazing petrol tank, nobody witnessed my claim for a kill. My view of the tank on fire from the mid-upper position was of a colossal flame that stretched from the wing trailing edge, right past the fin and rudder, with a furnace of sparks coming from a great hole in the petrol tank.

'I reported this to the skipper and I remember him saying that Lancs had flown back with only one wing, which I thought was a bloody stupid remark, considering the shit that was flying about.

'From his position, the pilot could see very little. Nevertheless, he did ask me what he should do. This was after we had got rid of the bombs. I said that all he could do was a vertical dive to see if the wind force could abate the fire.

'In a split second, the nose went down and we screamed from 22,000 feet to 15,000 feet and pulled out. This had a great effect on the fire, but it didn't go out completely. I told him to do it again, quickly.

'The nose went down again. The wind noise was deafening. I never thought the Lanc would stand so much air pressure in a dive.

'The skipper said that the altimeter showed 11,000 feet. By a sheer miracle, the flames and sparks subsided and he pulled out straight and level at 10,000 feet, with not a spark to be seen.'

The skipper and engineer nursed the Lanc back to Skellingthorpe, where it was placed in the graveyard as a complete write-off. The four officers in the crew got the Distinguished Flying Cross, but the three non-commissioned officers got nothing.

Regrettably, in the Royal Air Force, the discrimination between the officer class and 'other ranks' was by no means unknown.

***

On the way home, one Lancaster from 61 Squadron ditched in the sea. Three members of the crew drowned, but four were rescued.

Flight Sergeant Arthur Morris of 115 Squadron was heard making distress calls over the North Sea. He was not seen again.

***

Blackie's report of that night, which was made to the intelligence officer and recorded in the Operations Record Book, reads as follows:

BOMBING ATTACK ON BERLIN

Up at 1732. Down at 0221

Primary target attacked at 20.34 hrs from 21,000 feet. 10/10ths cloud cover, tops above 8–10,000 feet. Target identified by Wanganui flares green with red stars and red TIs (target indicators). Bombed centre of three Wanganui flares, glow of fires could be observed through the clouds. Monica and Window carried. Sortie completed.

'Window' was the code word for aluminium strips. Some aircraft carried large amounts of these, which they threw out of the aircraft to confuse the Germans' radar-guided searchlights.

'Monica' has a more sinister explanation. The 'Monica' box was situated at the rear of Lancaster bombers. It was an electronic device to detect the radar beam from a pursuing fighter, at which point it would give an audible beep. It was my role as tail gunner to report this to the pilot. Unfortunately for the Royal Air Force, the Germans had deconstructed a 'Monica' box from a shot down Lancaster. Their boffins had devised a means whereby the on-board 'Lichtenstein' radar on a nightfighter could use the signal from the 'Monica' box as a beacon to hone in on the aircraft.

Essentially, the Germans were using the signals from 'Monica' to locate and shoot down British bombers. This was not discovered until several months after the raid.

'Wanganui' flares were 'Christmas Tree' flares, which Pathfinders dropped onto their targets. They received their name from New Zealand air crews, because the town of Wanganui had been the first to adopt electric Christmas tree lights.

The Bomber Command Diaries for the raid read as follows:

515 Lancasters and 15 Mosquitoes despatched to Berlin. The German fighters were committed to action earlier than normal, some being sent out 75 miles over the North Sea from the Dutch coast. A number of elaborate feints and diversions had some effect; Half of the German fighters were lured north by the Heligoland mining diversion and action in the main bomber stream was less intense than on recent nights. 33 Lancasters lost, 6.4 per cent of the heavy force. The target was cloud-covered again and skymarking had to be used. Bomber Command was not able to make any assessment of the raid, except to state that the bombing appeared to have been spread well up and down wind.

Total effort for the night: 697 sorties, 34 aircraft (4.9 per cent) lost.

10

Operation on Berlin (28-29 January 1944)

'Oh God! Not bloody Berlin again!'

In reality, the language employed at Skellingthorpe and dozens of other Royal Air Force bases was somewhat stronger than that.

The crews were still tired from the long trip to Berlin the previous night. However, it was not only the crews who were tired of the trips to Berlin. So was higher authority.

Harris had had his orders as early as 10 June 1943 to attack aircraft and ball-bearing factories. Harris had pointedly ignored this and wilfully kept on bombing Berlin on the expectation that he could win the war with his bomber force. In his view, the invasion of Europe would not be necessary.

General Eisenhower was not impressed and said so in his charming diplomatic yet firm manner. It had not worked. Harris' headquarters were only a short distance from Churchill's weekend home, Chequers. This led to frequent informal dinners between Harris and Churchill and in turn, to Churchill's support for

Harris. Others were not only less supportive of Harris, but livid at his insubordination.

Air Marshal Bottomley had written to Harris on 14 January and again on this day, 28 January. The letters were becoming terser:

> *'I am accordingly to request that you adhere to the spirit of the directive forwarded in the Air Ministry letter dated 10 June 1943 and that you attack as far as practicable those industrial centres associated with the German fighter air-frame and ball-bearing industry.'*

Once again, Harris ignored it. The temperature in the Allied High Command was assuming the proportion of a large steam engine, which rocked on its bearings and gave off angry sounds just before it exploded.

For this raid, Harris ordered his right-hand man, Deputy Chief of Staff Sir Robert Saundby, to change the tactics. Three Mosquitoes dropped a small load of 500-pound bombs on Berlin in the early evening. The hope was that the Germans would decide that, since the Mosquitoes had paid them a visit, the 'heavies' would not mount a main force raid that night.

Saundby also sent mine-laying operations to the great German naval base at Kiel and directed the bombing of individual Luftwaffe airfields in Holland to further the subterfuge. Meanwhile, the code word 'Whitebait' had gone out to airfields across eastern England. *Bloody Berlin, again!*

Then it looked as though the raid would be scrubbed due to bad weather. This was not entirely problematic, as it meant the Germans would find even more convincing arguments to believe a raid was not on. This might just make them complacent.

A spoof raid went over Hannover to complete the web of deception. The crews duly took off, cursing and swearing, for the 'Big City' yet again.

***

Little action took place on the way to Berlin. The subterfuge seemed to have worked and we all gave a sigh of relief at the relatively easy ride.

However, this feeling of wellbeing ended in short order, as the bomber stream overflew the outskirts of Berlin. There were nightfighters in the hundreds, like angry, malevolent monsters, awaiting their imminent arrival. That night, this defence of the German capital also introduced a new tactic: high-flying Luftwaffe aircraft dropping flares to illuminate the bomber force and make it easier for nightfighters to find kills. Most notable among the flare-dropping aircraft were the massive Focke Wulf Condor maritime-reconnaissance aircraft.

During my trip across the Atlantic, these were the feared aircraft that I had spent hours looking out for during my stints on watch. In the few months since that time, the aviation world had moved swiftly on. The Condors had been pensioned off from the North

Atlantic after ship-borne Hurricane fighters started shooting them down in large numbers. They found their final role as transport aircraft. Their use as flare-dropping aircraft on this occasion may have been the only time they were ever used for this purpose.

I do recall this raid for a very particular and strange reason. On the truck out to the dispersal was a padre and he was in flying gear. This raised eyebrows. No-one had ever heard of a padre on 'ops' before. He raised even more eyebrows when we discovered that he was to fly with our crew as 'second dicky'. Our feelings were a mixture of wonderment and amusement, but we did think he had guts. This was particularly so because the flares set off by the Luftwaffe made the sky as bright as day. Through the gaps in the clouds, we could see the red glow of the fires across Berlin. Normally, the cloud over Berlin was so thick that you could not see anything through it.

The raid was notable, also, for the large number of aircraft that returned due to badly iced wings. Also, executive pressure 'from above' led to many of the Halifaxes being 'bombed up' beyond their normal level and were quite overloaded. This meant they flew slowly, were easy prey for nightfighters and consumed petrol more quickly, meaning that many could barely make it back to the English coast. Two Halifaxes were abandoned by their crews, who bailed out over south England. At least two others came down in the sea, with no survivors.

Another notable point was that as the raid was so late and the aircraft returned in daylight, we were amazed to see hundreds of American B17 aircraft on their way out to bomb Frankfurt in a daylight raid.

Blackie's report, as enshrined in the Operations Record Book, reads:

BOMBING ATTACK ON BERLIN

Up at 0037. Down at 0904.

Primary target attacked at 03.28 from 22,000 feet. 9/10ths cloud – tops above 10/12,000 feet. Target identified by red and green target markers, fighter flares and searchlights. Bombed on green target indicator. Fires illuminating cloud. Explosion seen at 03.15 hrs. Monica carried, sortie completed.

The record shows all details of the crew and that we flew in a Lancaster VN-S LM 435. There is no mention of the padre. Presumably, Blackham was doing something slightly dodgy and without the sanction of Wing Commander Heward. I recall that he had what Australians call a 'larrikin' streak. He probably reasoned that if he failed to return, then he would, at least, avoid an embarrassing court martial. However, it does raise the question as to what would have happened if the aircraft had been shot down?

The Bomber Command Diaries for the raid read as follows:

28/29 January 1944

Berlin: 677 aircraft – 432 Lancasters, 241 Halifaxes, 4 Mosquitoes. Part of the German fighter force was drawn up by the early diversions and the bomber approach route over Northern Denmark proved too distant for some of the other German fighters. The German controller was, however, able to concentrate his fighters over the target and many aircraft were shot down there. 46 aircraft – 26 Halifaxes, 20 Lancasters – lost, 6.8 per cent of the force. The cloud over Berlin was broken and some ground-marking was possible but the Bomber Command claim that this was the most concentrated attack of this period is not quite fully confirmed by German records. The western and southern districts were hit but so too were 77 places outside the city.

63 Stirlings and 4 Pathfinder Halifaxes carried out mine laying in Kiel Bay 5 hours before the main Berlin operation; this was the first time that Pathfinder aircraft helped a mine laying operation. 6 Mosquitoes bombed Berlin 4 hours before the main attack and 18 Mosquitoes bombed nightfighter airfields at Deelen, Leeuwarden and Venlo. 4 Mosquitoes carried out a diversionary raid to Hannover and 6 more Mosquitoes flew

Serrate patrols at the same time as the main raid. 2 Stirling minelayers and 1 Serrate Mosquito were lost from these operations. 16 OTU Wellingtons carried out leaflet flights to France without loss.

Total effort for the night: 794 sorties, 49 aircraft (6.2 per cent) lost.

Serrate was an on-board radar system designed to warn of the presence of Luftwaffe nightfighters by picking up on emissions from their radar.

Flight Lieutenant Burtt did not return. 'Aircraft missing', said the Operations Record Book. This was highly significant, as the loss of this aircraft was the only failure to return during my time at Skellingthorpe. This is also prima facie proof of the supernaturally good fortune 50 Squadron enjoyed during this period.

11

Operation on Berlin (30-31 January 1944)

'What? Bloody Berlin yet again? When is this ever going to stop?'

The words were echoed from Skellingthorpe to Whitehall, to General Eisenhower's headquarters up the Thames in Teddington. Soon, they would too be echoed in Berlin.

Air Marshal Harris now had three written, formal and point-blank directives on file, telling him to hit the German aircraft and ball-bearings industries and 'For God's sake, leave Berlin bloody well alone!' By this time, the Air Ministry, General Eisenhower, the Royal Navy, the British Army and everyone involved in organising the forthcoming 'D-Day' landings was on the phone to Churchill.

'Pull Harris into line, or he will wreck the invasion!'

Three operations in four nights on the worst possible target was taking a toll on the aircrews. Sergeant Chalklin of 207 Squadron asked a friend to send a cardboard box home to his mother if he did not come back.

'Mail it yourself,' said the friend. 'You'll be back tomorrow.'

Sergeant Chalklin lies in the war cemetery in Berlin. Harris was pushing not only his luck, but also his men into fatalism.

***

I recall very well the bomb load employed by 50 Squadron at this time. It was the typical combination of a 'cookie', plus 200 small incendiaries, which resembled the batons used in a relay race.

A 'cookie' was a massive 2000 kilogram bomb that looked like a large water tank. The intention was that the cookie would cause a huge blast and punch a hole in a factory or demolish several houses. The incendiaries, which were made of phosphorus, would rapidly set fire to the rubble.

***

Tonight, Harris had decreed a simpler raid with no feints, deceptions, or subterfuges.

The Air Marshal had a reason for this. The older mark II and V Halifaxes were being shot down at a rate much higher than the Lancasters or later Halifaxes. Harris ordered Saundby to organise the raid on a shorter route, directly across northern Germany. This would allow selected squadrons to carry heavier bomb loads.

There would be a quarter to half-moon on the outward flight. This latest attack was going to be more dangerous.

Take-off was late in the afternoon. The weather fine and clear. I had a wonderful view of the bomber fleet as it assembled, formed up over Norfolk and headed over the North Sea. Although the bomber force was huge, from my position in the rear gun turret, I could see dozens, rather than hundreds.

The early part of the journey was very straightforward as the daylight disappeared and the bombers flew on in pale moonlight.

For whatever reason, the German nightfighter response was slow. One theory for this is that the Luftwaffe controllers held off, as this might be yet another mine-laying diversion. Another theory is that they thought Harris would be mad to attack Berlin with the moon rising and thereby bring his force into danger. The German nightfighters took off late and mainly headed for the wrong areas.

***

One such was *Oberfeldwebel* [Flight Sergeant] Hallenbruch, who took off from Venlo with his radar operator, *Unteroffizier* [Sergeant] Vollert.

Vollert described his view of the raid.

> *'We thought that we were off too late to catch the bombers, but we picked up a contact on*

radar – it was 10 to 13 kilometres away. I guided the pilot, Hallenbruch, onto it.

'We thought it was a bomber, but we were surprised to find it had only two engines. We had strict orders not to attack any twin-engined aircraft unless we were absolutely sure that it was an enemy. We argued about it. I thought it was a British Beaufighter (nightfighter), because it had a thicker fuselage than a Junkers 88. The pilot said, No, it's a Ju88 – another poor sod like us.'

'We decided to turn away and leave it alone. We did so and were turning back for Venlo, when this aircraft suddenly attacked. He hit us in the right wing between the engine and the fuselage and the whole wing broke off.

'I tried to pull the cockpit cover open and, with some effort, did so. The aircraft was by now spinning and the air pressure pushed me back into the cabin, but I knew that I mustn't give up. I tried again and again and got out in the end. I opened the parachute at once, because we were over the sea and that the strong west wind would carry me to the coast. I came down in the water, but it was so shallow that I could stand up.

'The aircraft crashed some ten kilometres out to sea. I never found out what happened to

Hallenbruch. They only found a hand, which may have been his.'

***

The nightfighters caught up with the bomber stream about 100 kilometres before Berlin. Some 20 bombers were caught on the way and shot down. There were more kills on the way home and several crippled Lancasters crash-landed when they got back over the English coast. A Halifax from 640 Squadron crashed on landing at RAF Leconfield and killed all the crew.

Skipper Harry Widdup, a pilot of 100 Squadron, said that crews were now beginning to display signs of hopelessness. *'No-one talked any more about when they would finish their tour. That would have been tempting fate. Our rear gunner had gone "LMF" on being posted to the squadron and our mid-upper gunner did the same after this raid.'*

For Royal Air Force crews, to have that stamped on your personal file was more horrible than a trip down 'Happy Valley'. Some Wing Commanders would quietly transfer an 'LMF' man to a far-off post in the North of Scotland, where they might be put on menial duties and reduced to the rank of Aircraftman. Other Wing Commanders would parade a man before the entire squadron and give him maximum public humiliation 'to encourage the others'.

Widdup met the disgraced mid-upper later in the war and the mid-upper said, 'I never expected to see you again.' He meant it in more ways than one.

***

During the raid, Werner Schlecking of the important Hollerith Werke, which made electrical equipment in Berlin, took shelter in the underground railway station at Nolledorfer Platz.

> 'It was very deep and secure, but the ground began to shake and heave from all the explosions around us. Then, there was a tremendous concussion. A heavy bomb must have gone deep into the ground nearby.

> 'The lights flickered and went out. People began to scream. The emergency lights came on. The panic broke out. We heard a rushing and a gurgling sound coming nearer and the terror was complete when someone shrieked, 'My God – water!' This cry of horror swept over the whole platform, which was packed tight with people.

> 'We realised that the big water main, which lay underground, had been broken. The panic-stricken mass raced like mad to the stairways leading to the upper platform. The stairs to the upper platform became clogged with desperate people trying to escape. Parents tried to hold their children above their heads, so that they would

not be trampled on. The panic was made worse through people having brought a lot of pets into the shelter, strictly against orders. People behaved in panic and irresponsibly. Utter chaos reigned and it was impossible to get to the upper platform and away from the onrushing water.

'Fortunately, I was able to use my knowledge of the area to escape. I pulled my wife back and guided her into the water, which was becoming deeper by the minute. The water was numbingly cold, but I knew that this was our one chance to escape. I pulled her into the railway tunnel, which was pitch black, with the water already at waist height. We forced our way against the swirling water and then I felt my plan beginning to work: the tunnel was gradually ascending and the water was becoming less deep.

'We slowly came out of the swirling flood. The water only came to our knees, then our ankles and we found an air shaft. There was an iron ladder inside it, which we climbed and came out onto the street. Fortunately for us, there were fires raging all around us, so we dried out and warmed up very quickly.

'There were many people killed in the panic, but this was not reported in the papers. To talk of such things could bring you into a concentration camp, so I never found out how many.'

***

On the ground, Berlin was a burning, shattered mess. They had suffered 17 heavy raids since the start of the Battle of Berlin and now three massive raids in four nights. In the last three raids alone, the number of people rendered homeless was 171,000. The city authorities would not be able to give a report on casualties until March. Some 30 square kilometres of the city lay in ruins.

However, due to the 100% cloud cover, the bombing was dispersed. While it had done massive damage, the bombing did not result in the huge fires achieved in November. Moreover, the large areas of cleared debris inadvertently created firebreaks, across which the flames could not spread. Harris needed those fires, if his thesis of breaking Berliners' morale was to work.

Public utilities such as railways, trams, gas and electricity production were severely hit, but not fatally. They kept working.

There was a worse fact which would have chilled Harris had he known it. Despite the heavy raids and vast devastation across the city, the lack of precision bombing left the main war industry factories barely damaged. Most factories were still operational. Certainly, all of the big firms like Siemens would have experienced some damage, but there were few crippling hits on the industrial works.

War production in Germany in general and Berlin in particular, was still on the increase.

**

If Harris's air crews were tired and losing heart, the people of Berlin were at screaming pitch.

It was midwinter and snow lay on the ground. Berlin was freezing cold and gloomy. There were massive heaps of rubble all over the city. Many streets were too dangerous to walk down, for fear of collapsing debris, bare electrical wires, or gas leaks.

People looked on in silence as teams of concentration-camp inmates in black-and-white striped pyjamas were forced to remove unexploded bombs, which could – and did – detonate without warning.

**

Blackham's report reads:

BOMBING ATTACK ON BERLIN

Up at 1721 Down at 0013

Primary target attacked at 2031 hrs from 19,000 feet. 10/10ths cloud tops 10,000 feet. Target identified by flares red with green stars. Bombed leading Wanganui of a line of three. Rather wide formation of Wanganui. Bombing results not observed owing to cloud. Fire glow just discernible. Monica carried. Sortie completed.

The Bomber Command Diaries read:

30/31 January 1944

534 aircraft – 440 Lancasters, 82 Halifaxes, 12 Mosquitoes – to Berlin. There were no preliminary diversions on this night and the attempt by the German controllers to intercept the bomber stream over the sea failed. The bombers were, therefore, well on the way to Berlin before meeting any fighters but the Germans were then able to follow the bomber stream until well into the return flight. 33 aircraft – 32 Lancasters and 1 Halifax – lost, 6.2 per cent of the force.

22 Mosquitoes to Elberfeld and 5 to Brunswick, 8 RCM sorties, 7 Serrate patrols, 12 Stirlings mine laying in the River Gironde, 22 OTU sorties. No losses.

Total effort for the night: 610 sorties, 33 aircraft (5.4 per cent) lost.

After this raid the new moon period was coming on and squadrons were stood down for 13 days.

***

On Sunday 13 February, Harris began operations again. It was to be Berlin again.

Crews would have looked at each other in despair. Eyes would have rolled to heaven. Shoulders would have gone down.

'Oh Christ! Not bloody Berlin again? When, if ever, is this going to bloody end?'

However, the weather was very bad and the operation was scrubbed.

Across bomber stations from Yorkshire to Lincolnshire, to the fens of rural Norfolk, the victorious cry went up. 'Brilliant! Let's go down the pub!'

***

In the midst of all this wartime activity, thought must be given to Freda. She would not know when I was on ops. As soon as an operation was called, the station was sealed off. There was no communication outside.

For the last month, in her Land Army hostel, she would have heard the deep roar as the bombers took off. When she heard hundreds of them, she would have known there 'was a war on'. Each time, she was bound to have had three thoughts: 'Is Joe up there in the middle of all of that activity? Will he come back? Will he come back in one piece?'

She had certainly known many, many Land Army girls whose husbands and boyfriends had failed to return. Sometimes, it wasn't until weeks later that they heard their loved one was dead. Or sometimes, they learned after some months that he was in a prison camp. Worst of all, sometimes they heard nothing and never would.

I may have been optimistic that 'it would always happen to the other bloke', but it is unlikely that Freda shared that feeling. That all-pervading roar of Merlin engines across the green and pleasant lands of rural Leicestershire would have triggered a feeling of black inescapable dread in the pit of her stomach.

Did she ever talk about that? Of course not. There was a war on.

12

A Breakfast in Leafy Buckinghamshire

Springfield Lodge, Great Kingshill, Buckinghamshire – 0700 hrs.

It was a cold, unpleasant morning in the depth of an overcast, cloudy, gloomy English midwinter.

Two men met over breakfast. Their deliberations set the course for my subsequent life and some tens of thousands of other men. It is strange to think, but the deliberations that morning also saved my life.

The first man was the tenant of that palatial residence, Air Marshal Sir Arthur Harris – known as 'Bomber Harris' to the general public, 'Butch' to his men and 'Bert' to his friends.

The second person was Harris' house guest, Air Vice Marshal R.H.M.S. Saundby. He was known as 'Bob' to Harris and 'sir' to everyone else. He lived with Sir Arthur and Lady Harris for an entire six years, during which he did not take a single day's leave. He remained unmarried for the whole of his life and represented the epitome of the British eccentric.

He was an interesting man, with three great passions in life. The first was fishing, hence why the code for Berlin as 'target for tonight' was 'Whitebait' in secret communications. Similarly, Hamburg was referred to as 'Weaverfish', Munich as 'Catfish' and so on. Whether it took a German equivalent of Bletchley Park to break this code is one of the untold stories of World War II.

Saundby's second great enthusiasm was the massive model railway that he had constructed in a room above the mess at headquarters in High Wycombe.

His third was collecting butterflies. This had led to his arrest by an assiduous policeman, who had seen Saundby chasing a rare specimen up a tree. The earnest limb of the law promptly took the hapless but innocent Air Vice Marshal in charge, under suspicion that he was spying for Hitler's Reich. Rumours persist that the constable was then assigned to directing traffic for the rest of his life, though no official record confirms this.

As Senior Air Staff Officer, it was Saundby's job to plan the tactics, operations and minute details of every major raid by Bomber Command in World War II.

In the main though, it was Harris himself who had chosen the Royal Air Force's bombing targets for the two years since his appointment in February 1942. Harris' belief that the bomber war would inevitably lead to victory was echoed by his men, who were fiercely loyal to him.

By now, quite honestly, I was of a different mind. My loyalty was to the crew; to their survival and our shared aspiration to complete the tour of 30 operations, before a well-deserved move into the prestigious Pathfinder Force. My intent was to keep on bombing Hitler's Germany, in between hitch hiking to Nottingham and Leicester to steal some time with Freda.

***

For Sir Arthur and therefore me, there existed a large problem. The Royal Air Force had expended an extraordinary level of bombs, aircraft, men and money in attacking Germany. An even more extraordinary effort by the German Minister for Armaments, Albert Speer, had resulted in an increase in the German production of aircraft, tanks and all the other material of war. Not one to be embarrassed easily, Harris had a clear view of his next moves. The increase in German productivity merely meant that the amount of 'biffo' that he was giving to 'the Hun' was not enough. More 'biffo' was in order!

His superiors were losing patience. They did not want 'biffo'; they wanted tangible progress in the war! But it was not happening.

By the time of this breakfast on a freezing Buckinghamshire morning, Harris had now received three extremely pointed and increasingly directive letters from Sir Archibald Sinclair, Churchill's Secretary of State for Air. These told Harris that his bombing was now required to fit in with the planned invasion of Europe. Each successive letter had demonstrated a greater level of that polite but firm snottiness at which the Brits excel.

Winston Churchill had backed him as far as possible. Now, even Churchill was telling Harris that he had to change tack. Even worse, bloody Eisenhower was starting to run the show. Eisenhower! This was the general who had only ever aspired to one battlefield command: the disaster on the beaches of Italy at Anzio. This yank amateur was telling Harris how to run his show!

It was a matter of distaste, irritation and outrage to Harris that Eisenhower had set a date of 5 June for Operation Overlord – the invasion of Europe.

***

That breakfast, Harris said, 'It's no good, Bob. Winston's not backing me anymore. I told him I could wreck Berlin and bring Germany to its knees by April of this year. He's stopping me and its only February. I could have done it, I really could. As from tomorrow, I am to talk to Eisenhower's people and find out what targets they want me to hit.'

Harris' oft-quoted line from the time of the thousand bomber raid on Cologne in 1942 was that the Germans had 'sown the wind and would reap the whirlwind'. Maybe he could get them to reap just a little more whirlwind before he was, in effect, demoted from strategist to service-provider to bloody Eisenhower. A ripping big show on Berlin would be just the thing! I was destined to be involved.

'Tell you what, Bob. Let's have one last really good show on Berlin. What was the name of that big opera that Wagner wrote?'

'Götterdämmerung, Bert. *The Twilight of the Gods,*' Saundby replied.

'Yes, let's give them one of those tonight. That's the ticket! Remember, Bob, they've sown the wind and they'll reap the bloody whirlwind.'

'Yes, Bert.'

∗∗∗

High Wycombe, Buckinghamshire – 0830 hrs

After breakfast, Sir Arthur Harris followed his invariable routine.

He proceeded at breakneck speed to Bomber Command Headquarters. Sir Arthur's chauffeur, Maddocks, was under orders to drive as quickly as possible through the leafy back lanes of Buckinghamshire in the black, two-seater Bentley.

On one occasion, a passing police car had stopped them and admonished him, 'If you are not careful, you will kill someone!'

Harris replied to the constable, 'And that, young man, is what I am paid to do!'

Saundby was left to drive his own Rolls Royce to Bomber Command HQ outside of High Wycombe. Saundby did, however, never take that noble conveyance shopping, because he felt it encouraged shopkeepers to overcharge him.

***

On arrival, Sir Arthur's secretary, Peggy Wherry, brought to his office the most urgent signals and the files of potential targets, which he had requested the day before.

At 0900 precisely, Maddocks drove Sir Arthur, together with the large pile of files from his office, across to the Operations Room. This was in a dingy, claustrophobic underground bombproof shelter, known and loved as 'The Hole'.

It was in this subterranean warren that Harris conducted a daily meeting commonly referred to as 'morning prayers'. On the wall were large maps of Europe and charts showing the 50 or so top priority targets laid down by the War Cabinet for Bomber Command's treatment. It was the 'hit-list' par excellence! Sir Arthur took pride that 49 of the targets had been reduced to ashes and piles of debris. Dresden was the sole survivor to remain irritatingly intact.

Everyone would have stood up and scraped their chairs backward as Harris entered the room. Typical attendants at these meetings were:

Air Officer Commanding Bomber Command and Air Marshal	Sir Arthur Harris
Air Vice Marshal and Senior Air Staff Officer	Sir Robert Saundby
Meteorological Office (a major player in the meetings)	Magnus Spence
Royal Navy Intelligence	Captain de Mowbray
Army Intelligence	Colonel Carrington
Group Captain – Royal Air Force Operations	
Group Captain – Royal Air Force Intelligence	
Chief Radar Officer	Dudley Saward
Royal Air Force Navigation Officer	
A representative of the Special Operations Executive	
Ad hoc Wing Commanders and Squadron Leaders from Intelligence and Operations	

The first agenda item was invariably a review of the previous operations. This was irritatingly thin due to poor weather and the full moon being too dangerous for bombing operations. If Harris could have arranged better weather by having someone more effective from the Meteorological Office, he would probably have done so. He did not like outrageous factors, such as the caprice of the Northern European weather, getting in the way of delivering a bit of well-deserved 'biffo' to the enemy.

On this day, his review consisted of a low-level precision raid on 8-9 February on the Gnome and Rhone aircraft factory in Limoges. Eisenhower wanted to interrupt the delivery of aircraft to the Luftwaffe to make the Overlord landings easier. On 10 February, Harris had dispatched 21 Mosquitoes on a daylight flight to assess the damage. On that same night, he had sent 26 aircraft to France at the behest of the 'cloak-and-dagger wallah' from the Special Operations Executive. The following night, he had sent ten Lancasters to bomb the Antheor viaduct to slow down troop movements from Italy to the upcoming battlegrounds in Normandy. He also had 25 aircraft out on mine laying operations to hinder German sea patrols in the run-up to Overlord.

The second agenda item was Magnus Spence's weather report. Harris was sharply aware that his predecessor, Sir Richard Peirse, had ignored a weather forecast regarding a raid on Berlin in 1941, which had led to a massive loss of aircraft and Peirse's demotion to India. Spence was the only man apart from Churchill, who was allowed to dictate to Harris. In essence, Spence told Harris which targets were not available to him because of weather limitations. Thus, by elimination, it told him which *were* available. Harris was delighted to find that the weather report for the night of the 15-16 February was very promising for a change. It was going to be a clear night at high level, but with low level cloud. Best of all, the moon was waning. This meant Spence had effectively given

Harris virtual carte blanche over the whole of Europe within operational striking distance. In general, he could send his armadas – and me, in particular – anywhere he wanted. And he wanted Berlin again.

The third agenda item was the formal decision on 'target for tonight'. Only a few short months ago, there was no discussion as such. Harris had decided on behalf of everyone else. Now, he was receiving directives from his immediate superior, Marshal of the Royal Air Force Sir Charles Portal, which told him where Eisenhower wanted bombs to drop. There was pressure for raids on Leipzig to hit factories that manufactured Messerschmitt 109 fighter aircraft; to damage ball-bearing factories in Schweinfurt; and to destroy the Augsburg factories that made diesel engines for U-boats. The list was endless.

It was a great relief to Harris that the pressure on that particular morning was of a generalised nature and not too specific. Maybe Harris could just pull off one more outing over Berlin. Not only that, but it should be a big one. In fact, it should be bloody huge because it was the last chance he might get.

'We'll show 'the Hun' what a spot of 'biffo' means!'

***

'Well, for tonight we have no specific requirements from the Admiralty or Army and no specific requests from the War Cabinet. We have now had some two dozen raids on Berlin. I sent some Mosquitoes over there for photo reconnaissance a couple of nights ago.

'Berlin is a mess, but I would like to make it a bit more of a mess before we turn our hands to some of the other targets, which orders will later tell us we are to hit. Saundby, what are our chances of a thousand bomber raid on Berlin, just to bring a climax to the whole series?' Harris asked.

'The returns, which I have from the squadrons, are some way short of a thousand, Sir Arthur. If we can include a couple of Operational Training Units and Heavy Conversion flights, we should be able to muster 900 though.'

This raid was, indeed, destined to involve the largest number of bombers of any Royal Air Force raid of World War II, apart from the thousand bomber raids over Cologne, Bremen and Essen. As Saundby had calculated over breakfast, because the Royal Air Force now used much bigger bombers than previously, the bomb load would, in fact, be the greatest of any air raid in aviation history up to that point.

'Good show. Well, that should bring tears to Adolf's eyes. Over to you, Saundby. I'm sure you can sort out the detail. Just one thing, though.'

'Yes, Sir Arthur?'

'The German nightfighters have been getting a little too frisky lately and we have lost quite a lot of kites.

Would it be possible to send the bomber stream a bit further north – say, over Denmark?'

'With a bomber stream this big, I don't think we can send all of them on a route as far northerly as that. It would cut down the total bomb load as well, but I'll see what can be achieved.'

'And another thing, Saundby. Could you send one squadron on a diversion flight? I would like to try and draw off some of the nightfighters if we could. We haven't had a go at Frankfurt an der Oder for a while, have we?'

'No, indeed, Sir Arthur. One squadron it shall be.'

'Wizard! And another thing, Saundby.'

'Yes, Sir Arthur?'

'Look, we've got to sort out some of those bloody German nightfighter squadrons. Find out from Intelligence which are the five worst of them and find 20 or so Mosquitoes to bomb the living hell out of them.'

'Certainly, Sir Arthur.'

'Oh and another thing, Saundby. We have a war going on between Cochrane at Five Group and that Australian chap Bennett in Pathfinder Force. Whatever you do, make it completely clear that Pathfinders will be marking the targets tonight and not Five Group. But try and be diplomatic about it, if that's at all possible.'

'Will do, Sir Arthur.'

'Good man. Right, gentlemen. Any questions?' He paused and looked around the table. 'If not, the meeting is closed.'

Harris would then have breezed out of the room, as the chairs scraped back once more and everyone stood.

***

From 0930–1000, teleprinter messages would clatter out to the Bomber Groups. It was 'Whitebait' and 'Usual' again. The messages conveyed Saundby's calculations to tell them approximately how many squadrons and what classes of aircraft should be on standby. In the case of 50 Squadron and me, the teleprinter would be to Five Group Headquarters at Morton Hall at Royal Air Force Swinderby, under the leadership of Air Vice Marshal Ralph Cochrane.

Saundby would then return to his office for some two hours of furious activity. It was his personal task to organise a team to calculate routes, aiming points, bomb loads, take-off times and rendezvous points. At 1130, he would present a handwritten draft to Harris, who would approve the draft, perhaps with changes in detail. Saundby would finalise the orders and have them typed and forwarded to Group commanders. Orders would then pass to individual squadrons and thence to individual crews. At the end of the chain, Blackham, myself and the rest of the crew would visit the flight office at Skellingthorpe to discover there 'was a war on' that night and their participation was required.

Of all the previous procedure, machination, drafting of orders and transmission, myself and the rest of Bomber Command were totally oblivious.

During World War II, we operational airmen never knew of the existence of 'the hole' beneath the affluent fields of Buckinghamshire. We did not even know that Five Group Headquarters was at Royal Air Force Swinderby.

More to the point, neither did the Luftwaffe.

13

The Day Before the Raid

Royal Air Force Skellingthorpe – 15 February 1944

A sprained ankle was hardly the stuff of Victoria Crosses or Distinguished Flying Medals, but the previous couple of weeks had been painful for me.

It was looked at carefully by the Medical Officer. *Was it genuine?* Yes, it certainly was. *Was it self-inflicted, as a means to get out of flying more bloody trips to Berlin?* No, there was no sign of this.

The Medical Officer packed me off to Moreton Hall Commando Training Centre to improve my physical fitness and briefed me to look out for any developing 'LMF' cases trying to dodge the column. It was good to be back with the crew.

'Come on Joe, let's get char and a wad (tea and a sandwich). The girls in the NAAFI are waiting for your Australian charm!'

***

It was early morning and not long light. The Spartan accommodation in the rounded Nissen hut was warm, thanks to a coke fire. The locals had said it wasn't a bad winter, but when you came from Queensland, the weather in the East Midlands was perpetually cold and bleak, though quite honestly, I can't ever remember worrying about it. Our heavy blue serge uniforms kept that cold at bay and the heater in the hut kept it perfectly warm.

There were not many perks to the job, since the accommodation was not exactly luxurious and the good people of Lincoln, Nottingham and Leicester were getting a bit fed up with the many airmen around town and their perpetual high jinks. However, breakfast was one of the highlights of the day and offered great compensation. Just outside of the Royal Air Force station's perimeter, such luxuries as bacon were in short supply due to wartime rationing. Civvies might be restricted to eight ounces (227 grams) of bacon a week, to go with their eight ounces of cheese and one pound (450 grams) of jam per month. On the base though, it was different. We had as much sausage, fried eggs, beans and tea as we wanted, along with anything else a man could need, though the sausages were fairly awful and seemed to be primarily composed of bread.

Cigarettes in the navy, army and air force institutes were not only cheap, but we had a free allocation of cigarettes and cigars each. This was a cynical ploy by Wills and Players, the major tobacco companies, to get as many people as possible addicted to their product – well, those that survived. In our crew, there were only two who smoked and I was not one of them. Oddly enough, that was typical in Bomber

Command and I do not know why, as this was a time when 90% of the general public smoked.

On an operational station, the conversation over sausage and eggs was usually about the last night's raids – making sure that everyone had returned, nightfighter activity and any other point of interest. When Flight Lieutenant Burtt failed to return from an operation over Berlin, we might have said, 'Poor buggers!' but we all knew that you could not dwell on missing comrades in arms. That way lay defeatism.

Today was different. In fact, the whole of February 1944 had been different. There had been no bombing raids from Skellingthorpe during my two-week sojourn with a sprained ankle.

Europe was in the throes of winter. Cloud cover was thick. Even with the new navigational aids of Gee, H2S and Oboe, flying bombing raids over Germany was just too hard. With brilliant moonlight too, the nightfighters would have committed ritual murder on the Royal Air Force crews. Perhaps the worst aspect of winter flying though was the icing of aircraft wings. That could make an aircraft difficult, or even impossible to fly.

Down in Italy, the yanks were having a hard time on the beachheads south of Naples. The landing on the Anzio beachhead, which was supposed to open the road to Rome, had stalled. The British Army was held up against ferocious opposition at the Benedictine monastery at Cassino. On the Eastern front, the

Russians were just advancing on Kiev in the south and Estonia in the north. We could only assume that the casualties were appalling.

For us at Skellingthorpe, it was a different sort of war. Most of the crew hitch hiked into Nottingham, which had the attraction of lots and lots of girls who worked in the factories. Outside Nottingham Town Hall, there were two large bronze lions said to roar if a virgin walked past. As a married man, I cannot comment on this.

Myself, I would hitch hike down to Lutterworth or Coalville in Leicestershire to see Freda. Our war was not one of frostbite, muck, bullets and bayonet charges. Nevertheless, we could be dead by this time tomorrow.

Sometimes, Blackie would take us for a ride around the midlands for an aerial tour. There was one fabulous trip when he took us all the way up the east coast of Scotland to John o'Groats and brought us back down the west coast. That was an unusually brilliant clear day, with blue skies more suited to Queensland than the bleak northern end of the British Isles.

On another occasion, we actually got up to 25,000 feet in an empty Lancaster with no bombload. As a trained pilot, Blackie must have known that this was 500 feet higher than the specified 'ceiling' (maximum allowable altitude) for a Lancaster, which means that I may hold the record for having flown in the highest-flying Lancaster bomber of all time. We did not talk about it too much, or Blackie would have been court martialled.

***

'There's a war on,' said one of the crew later that morning.

We knew that one or two friends were already down to go, so thought we'd better see if we were 'on' as well.

Walking into the Flight Office, we headed for the Wing Commander's office.

There we were on the board: Blackham's crew allocated to Lancaster No DV368, 'S – Sugar'. At this stage, we had no idea where the target might be.

'Morning, chaps!' said Wing Commander Heward, in his clipped military manner.

'Morning, sir.' We snapped to attention and saluted in the prescribed manner.

'Briefing is at 1500. See you there.'

'Very good, sir.'

We had noticed that the one telephone available to us in the sergeant's mess was tied up, so that no-one could make calls out. The station was now in 'blackout', which was a state of virtual quarantine. This meant that no-one could enter the station from the outside and we could not go out. Strictly speaking, you could get out if you made a determined effort, since the wire around the perimeter was less than formidable. However, such a move would not be a good idea and would lead at least to a court martial. If the authorities thought a man was communicating the 'target for tonight' to anyone outside, then the consequences would be severe, or worse.

The next part of the procedure was to walk over to the petrol pumps.

'How many today, Chiefie?' I asked.

The question to the Flight Sergeant in charge of petrol was for how many gallons to be put into the aircraft. That would give us an idea of how far away the target might be.

'1,950 gallons, Joe.'

Darn it! That was the same petrol load as for the previous raids. Surely we could not be going to bloody Berlin again?

'Couldn't we be having a go at somewhere different, like Leipzig or Frankfurt?'

'It's about time we had an easy one. How about over the alps and down into Italy?'

There were not too many raids down there at this stage, but you never knew. Blokes who had been on raids to Milan and Turin said they were much easier targets that Germany, with the added benefit that you got fabulous sights of the Alps in the moonlight.

Berlin still felt like the 'front-runner' though. Surely to God though, not again?

We then went over to dispersal to check out the aircraft's serviceability. Already, the aircraft had tradesmen swarming all over her. Specialist ground crew would be checking her engines, instruments and moving parts like wing flaps, as well as checking her over for any flak or unexploded cannon shells from nightfighters. I was interested to see that the 'erks' (the aircraftmen technicians) had polished the Perspex on the rear turret to make sure that I had a clear view during the flight. This was important, because what looked like a smudge on the Perspex could turn out to be a Junkers 88 lining up for a kill.

The armourers were driving the bomb trains to the aircraft. Our load that night was the normal load for this sort of raid: a 4000 pound (1814 kilograms) high explosive 'cookie' and some 200 small incendiary bombs.

***

After the morning pre-ops ritual, we then had some six hours to kill before the briefing.

Some crew members had standard pre-flight tasks. For example, the radio operator had to change accumulators for the intercom and navigators had to check their direction-finding equipment.

The technical work for my guns was all done by the armourers, so I had some free time. The normal way to pass time before a raid was to read the papers or have a quick game of cards or football.

I do remember, though, that I still did not feel frightened. Before an 'op', you could often see that crew members would be tense, especially those who had had close shaves with the Luftwaffe. So far though, we had not had a nightfighter on our tail, or even seen one. During my month on the squadron, there had been raids on Berlin, Magdeburg and Brunswick, but the squadron had still only lost Burtt's crew.

I don't think we ruminated over whether we were lucky, well managed, or invincible. We still had that confidence of the young. In our own minds we were obviously invincible.

***

At 1500, there was a buzz as the whole squadron gathered outside of the large main briefing room.

There was tension in the air. You could feel it.

A Royal Air Force policeman ushered us in. We took our places on long wooden benches. Many lit cigarettes, causing the air in the briefing room to turn into a blue fog within seconds.

In front of us was a heavy curtain, which masked a large map of Europe. On the stage waiting for us was the Station Intelligence Officer, Meteorological Officer, Engineering Officer and Flying Control Officer.

First, there was roll call.

Then, the platform party – the Group Captain, Wing Commander Heward and the Squadron Leaders – entered. There was a sudden scraping of furniture legs, as everyone stood smartly to attention. The Royal Air Force police closed the door behind them and stood guard outside to maintain security. Any non-authorised person approaching an operational briefing without just cause faced immediate arrest and a lengthy interrogation as to what they were doing there. They would need to have a very convincing story for the stern-faced provosts.

The Station Intelligence Officer opened proceedings by drawing back the curtain. This was the moment that everyone had been waiting for.

Red tapes on the map showed a route from Skellingthorpe to a common rendezvous point over Norfolk, then over southern Denmark and down over Schleswig Holstein to ... where the heck is that? Oh NO! It's bloody Berlin again.

'Tonight's raid, gentlemen, is on Berlin. Can we have the blinds drawn and lights out, please?'

A ripple of excitement, surprise and tension passed through the room. Sprog crews were excited. Those of us who had been there before accepted it with an air of resignation. Some of the more experienced crews became very quiet, probably thinking, *Why, oh, why did we not get easy jobs such as 'nickelling' (dropping leaflets) or 'gardening' (dropping mines)?*

Wing Commander Heward took over.

'Thank you, gentlemen. As you will all know, we have carried out some 18 main force attacks in this series on Berlin. The red spot on the photograph shows the aiming point. This is

Siemensstadt on the west side of the big city. It is a major centre of important German war factories.'

Well, that was just 'delusions of accuracy'. Berlin was nearly always covered in ten tenths cloud. All the bomb-aimer could do was to aim at the bright lights of the target indicator flares and put their trust to luck. The chance of hitting a specific target in Berlin was akin to winning a lottery and as for aiming at something as small as Siemensstadt? If we actually hit the Berlin metropolitan area, we thought we were doing well. Our large 'cookie' bombs did not have any fins, meaning that once dropped from the aircraft, they would land where they wanted. If that was where the bomb aimer also wanted them to, then that was just luck.

'The weather conditions tonight are easing. The bad weather of the last couple of weeks is abating and the moon is less full. The PM wants Mr Hitler to know that his capital city is going to be razed to the ground if he persists in his ludicrous war. This raid on Berlin is all in line with Air Marshal Harris's policy of de-housing the German work force, destroying vital services and industries and breaking their morale.'

'De-housing', in theory, meant destroying the houses where workers lived with the purpose of destroying their morale. In practice, it meant killing as many of the civilian population as possible to terrorise them into surrender. Well, Adolf had started it.

A diversionary raid of 24 Lancasters was to go to Frankfurt an der Oder to confuse the German defences. Tonight there was to be a huge main force on Berlin: 561 Lancasters and 314 Halifaxes. The bomb load on this raid would be greater than the much publicised 'thousand bomber raid' that had devastated Cologne.

Sixteen Mosquitoes from the Pathfinder Force were to drop target indicators. That was the job that I wanted. You had to increase your tour of operations from 30 to 45 if you transferred across, but to have that winged golden eagle on your tunic was good for prestige. Actually, it was *very* good for prestige!

There was a big Australian contingent on the raid. The Australian bomber squadrons 460, 463, 466 and 467 were to provide no less than 74 aircraft between them.

Heward continued, 'We are to form a force with aircraft from other bomber groups. On a huge raid like this, they are too numerous to mention. We form up as usual over Norfolk and follow this path here. However, tonight, we are routed north to pass over Denmark and come down through Schleswig Holstein, passing Bremen and Hannover and so on to Berlin.

'Does the diversion over Denmark mean we carry a lesser bomb load, sir?'

'Good question that, man. I would certainly expect that the mark II and V Halifaxes would carry a slightly lower bomb load, but that is not the case in Lancasters. Flight Engineers, you might want to keep an eye on fuel expended, but I don't expect any great problem.'

The briefing proceeded with known intelligence on the German defence line over Holland and Belgium, which was the area of greatest danger. This route, however, would take us around the top end of these defences and possibly miss out on nightfighter activity altogether.

'Searchlight positions on the map are shown with a green overlay and flak with a red overlay. Your headings are as on the map, with several diversions to keep the opposition on their toes. Let us be quite clear, gentlemen. The Germans will be expecting us. They know the meteorological conditions and the phase of the moon as well as we do.'

He then proceeded to give the estimated times of arrival at each control point on the route out, as well as the height for bombing.

The Flying Control Officer was the next to speak.

'Tonight's duty runway is runway A. Start-up times are at 1645 and we want you marshalled and ready for take-off at 1700. Synchronise your watches. The time is now 1527.'

The Meteorological Officer then gave a briefing on weather conditions. It was going to be clear at higher altitudes, but lower down, it would be cloudy and visibility was going to be bad. The navigators would need to be on their toes, as would the Pathfinders, who would drop yellow markers to show us where to change course.

Then came Heward's speciality. He would randomly select a crewman – any crewman – to stand in front of the assembled squadron and repeat what he had said in the briefing. It made us all extremely keen to be totally on top of the details!

A group of Women's Auxiliary Air Force members then entered the room with bags for personal items. Every item in the aircrew's pocket had to be put into one of these bags. Even a ticket for the Lincoln City football ground would tell a Luftwaffe intelligence man '5 Group.'

Blackie went off to the map store for the night's map, so that he could mark out the route. Flying Officer

Jones, the navigator, went off to another room to draw the tracks to Berlin on a map with Mercator projection, which gave accurate bearings. He would then check and double check his calculations with slide rules and protractors.

***

Later, the crews returned to the mess for the pre-operation meal, which was known as the 'last supper'. At Skellingthorpe, there was always a fried egg, which was considered a luxury in wartime Britain.

Some would be quiet. Some would eat heartily. Some would not eat at all, although it was better to eat to summon up energy for the ordeal ahead.

Once again, it was easy to pick out the raw crews on their first trip. They were eager and asked questions, whereas the old hands were mainly quiet.

There was an unwritten rule that if there was any conversation, then it had to be cheerful. But each was locked up with his own thoughts, which must have wandered to who was really having their 'last supper' that night.

On the previous raid, we knew that many heavy bombers had not returned. In fact, the number was 33. That meant that some 231 airmen had not returned. With average survival rates, some 100 were in prisoner of war camps. The rest were dead. Did we think about that? Not one bit. At least, not that we would admit to.

At this point, it is highly likely that there was near silence. Perhaps there were some weak jokes that everyone laughed at in too hearty a fashion. Or perhaps not at all.

***

When we were done, we made our way to the stores to pick up fresh parachutes and Mae Wests. We then proceeded to the locker rooms to put on the flying gear.

First, we drew on the silk socks and heavy woollen stockings. Underneath the battledress, we typically wore a heavy, white sweater. Lancaster bombers only had heating in the cockpit for the pilot and flight engineer, so the other crew members had to wear substantial Sidcot flying suits over the fleece-lined Irvine flying jackets to keep the fearsome cold at bay.

The two most unfortunate crew members were we two gunners. We had to wear a massive Taylor suit, which required help from other crew members to put on. These were so huge that they made us look like the India-rubber man that advertised Dunlop tyres. They gave us protection against the cold, but also contained heating elements to protect us further. The temperature at the back of a Lancaster at 18,000 feet could be minus 20 degrees.

Around our neck was a silver whistle, which was to attract attention if we bailed out into the sea. If we bailed into the North Sea in February, death would come in five minutes if we were lucky and six if we were not. In my heavy Taylor suit, I might have lasted six – that was, if it didn't become waterlogged and pull me downwards into the deep.

Finally, we pulled on the heavy flying boots lined with lambswool.

Women's Auxiliary Air Force members handed out flasks of tea or coffee, together with chocolate and barley sugar. Perhaps the most harrowing part of the process was the point where each crew member gave over his locker key. This was a precaution just in case you didn't make it back.

Outside of the locker rooms, crews waited for the Women's Auxiliary Air Force members that drove the trucks – joyfully known as 'blood wagons' – to take us to our dispersal.

We piled in without ceremony. We were quiet. No-one spoke.

We still felt confident, but you never knew. *You never knew.*

It was Blackie's job to do a check of the wing flaps, tyres and undercarriage gear and confirm that all the other crew members were happy with their equipment.

My job was to check out my turret. Did it move correctly? Was the Perspex clean enough? Were the gun mechanisms operating correctly? I had also had to do an additional check of the wings.

'OK, skip!'

Blackie then signed the Form 700, which he gave to the ground crew Flight Sergeant to formalise his acceptance of the aircraft.

***

We then sat on the grass and talked to pass the time. Wilkins and Ridd were the only two smokers, who would practise their risky habit unenvied by the rest of us. Mind you, when it came to risky habits, flying over Berlin was up with the best.

Eventually, we saw the bright green flare from the Verey pistol fired from the control tower. This told all crews to climb into their aircraft.

The final burst of conversation could be about football, a beery night in a pub, or anything. Well, anything except the upcoming operation.

We all took up our well-rehearsed positions in the aircraft. The odd exception was that of Stewart Godfrey, the bomb aimer, who sat in the forward turret of the aircraft until the bombing run was about to begin. At this point, Blackie would order him to his bomb aimer's position.

'Intercom working?' said Wilkins, the wireless operator.

'Intercom working,' we all replied.

One after another, the 'erks' climbed under the wings and pump-primed the powerful Merlin engines until they roared to life. The whole aircraft shuddered with the vibrations. I waited to feel that jolt of movement, which meant we were on our way.

Berlin, here we come. Again.

14

Operation on Berlin (15-16 February 1944)

This was my final raid. As Harris had decreed, it was a raid that was attended by several records up to that date.

These included:

- The greatest number of aircraft sent to Berlin.

- The greatest number of Avro Lancasters on a single raid.

- The greatest number of Handley Page Halifaxes on a single raid.

- The greatest bomb tonnage of any raid in history, being more than the thousand bomber raids of 1942.

***

Against the bold statistics, there was a human side to these vast bombing raids.

Leading Aircraftman E. Howell was a Flight Mechanic (Engines) at 44 Squadron. He was based at the large

Waddington base, close to my home base of Skellingthorpe.

He wrote as follows:

'Just before take-off was a very uneasy time for us ground crew, as we were viewing men who were risking their lives in a most unpleasant manner several times a week and the ground crews were helping to send them on their way in this endeavour. Some were tense and uncommunicative, others seemed to be at fever pitch and very hyper, but all appeared to be in full control of themselves. There was an air of unbelievability to the whole situation, as if this could not possibly be happening to them.

After a certain time, they would board the aircraft and start the engines, which had to be accompanied by one of the ground crew climbing up under the undercarriage and pumping a Kygass priming pump for each engine, until each engine was running. At their signal, we would pull the chocks away, give them the thumbs up and away they would taxi to the top end of the take-off runway. At this time, the whole station would be at high pitch and if prayers really counted, every one of those gallant aircrew would have returned to Waddington. But that was not to be.'

***

I saw the 'erks' run backwards, carrying the chocks that held the wheels steady. They gave a 'thumbs up' to the pilot and flight engineer. We were ready for 'the off'.

This was it then – a fifth bloody trip in a row to bloody Berlin.

I felt a jolt, as the huge bomber with its 14,000 pounds (6400 kilograms) of bombs and 1950 gallons of fuel lurched forward. I could hear the Merlin engines screaming as Blackie held the brakes against them. We moved forward at walking place off the dispersal and along the pathway, towards the runway. As it was February, it was really important that the aircraft stayed on the tarmac. If it went off to the side, it would be stuck in the winter mud. Trying to get it out would have held up all the following aircraft and the wrath of the 'Wingco' would have been terrible.

In their forward seats, the skipper and flight engineer watched the first aircraft take off down the runway. Over the intercom, I could hear the navigator, Jones, give Blackie the initial flight plan and instructions for climbing. The aircraft before us, Thornton's crew, moved onto the runway, then after a quick flash of the bright green Aldiss lamp at the end of the runway, disappeared rapidly into the twilight.

It was 1735 and our turn. Blackie moved 'S-Sugar' onto the runway. He peered through the gathering gloom of a bleak Lincolnshire twilight for the green light. There it was! The green lamp flickered at the end of the runway to tell the skipper it was our turn.

It was the Flight Engineer's job to sight this and report it to the pilot. 'OK, skipper. You've got green. Take her away.'

Blackie jammed on the aircraft's brakes and ran up the engines until they screamed like a bull in pain. He held the nose down as the aircraft eased down the runway. Over the intercom, I could hear Walton, the flight engineer, going through the orders and confirmations with Blackie concerning the pressures, electric charges and propeller settings.

The rest of us tuned in more when Walton began to count our speed as we hurtled down the runway. That meant we were about to take off.

'95 knots, skipper. 100 ... 105 ... 110 ... 120 ... 130.' Blackham pulled the control column back, the aircraft nose went upwards and the runway was left behind. After a slight thrill of weightlessness, the runway slid away as the aircraft shuddered, the engines screamed and we took off.

Behind us, I could see Robinson edge his aircraft onto the runway, lining up for the take-off.

Jones reported, 'Airborne 1737, skipper.'

'Thank you, navigator.'

There was always a feeling of relief after a take-off. It was one of the most dangerous parts of the journey. The aircraft was heavy and the bomb load and petrol were a deadly combination if they came to grief on the wet, slippery and oily runway.

As tail gunner, I had a good view of the 30 or so well-wishers seeing us off. They were a motley gathering of Station Commanders, senior officers, drivers, Royal Air Force police, ground crew and Women's Auxiliary Air Force members.

I still did not feel frightened. Anything that was going to happen would happen to someone else. Our squadron had still only lost Burtt, who I didn't know, during my time there. Nevertheless, it was good to know that there was plenty of moral support.

'Retract undercarriage, engineer.'

'Retract undercarriage,' repeated Walton, like a man reciting a litany in church. He pulled the lever that retracted the wheels until we heard and felt the familiar 'clunk'.

We waited for the next part of the litany.

'Turn the oxygen on, engineer.'

'Wilco, skipper. Going to turn on the oxygen.'

'Wilco' meant 'will comply'.

Walton descended into the bomb-bay of the aircraft, where the oxygen bottles hung in racks.

'Oxygen on, skipper.'

'Skipper to crew. Turn your oxygen masks on, everyone.'

'Wilco, skipper.'

***

As we rose above the flat lands of Lincolnshire, there was not a light to be seen. The blackout was complete. Nevertheless, I could see the metallic shine of the railway lines which led from Grantham, Doncaster and Nottingham, as they converged on the main railway station in Lincoln. I could also see the huge, impressive outline of St Mark's cathedral, as we edged further and further away from it.

Blackie followed the navigation lights of Thornton's aircraft upwards, just as Robinson, who had now taken off, followed ours. The airborne procession continued at some 200 miles per hour (320 kilometres per hour), to somewhere over rural Norfolk. Jones would know the precise point, which was where the individual squadrons would form up into a bomber stream.

'Navigation lights off,' Blackham ordered.

'Navigation lights off, skipper,' Walton repeated.

From my position at the rear of the aircraft, I could get some idea of the size of the operation. The darkness was almost complete, especially as there was little moonlight. Even so, I could see that there were dozens and dozens of four engine bombers.

From below, the sky would be covered with uncountable numbers of Lancaster bombers, who would soon be joined by more uncountable numbers of Halifaxes. We were an armada. We were invincible. *This is what I joined up for!*

At a precisely choreographed time, which was confirmed by the navigator, the huge armada formed into a single stream of ten miles (16 kilometres) long and departed for the target area. We were to fly to the Island of Texel, off North Holland, then proceed to the Danish border. We were on a more northerly route than usual for the three-and-a-half-hour journey to Berlin.

The sea now glinted in the dim light. The British mainland was just a matte black mass beyond where the glint of the sea ended.

'Mid-upper to skipper.'

'Receiving, mid-upper.'

'OK for a test fire?'

'Yep. Try not to hit anything!'

'Very funny.'

I could not hear it because of the roar of the engines, but the aircraft shook briefly as the twin Browning .303 guns fired tracers towards the sea.

'Mid-upper to skipper. They're working.'

'Sounds like it to me. Skipper to rear gunner. Give them a test shot, Joe.'

'Wilco, skipper.'

I slid home the bolts, cocked the guns and pressed the firing trigger. The aircraft reverberated for a couple of moments as I fired the quadruple .303 Brownings.

'OK, skipper.'

'Thank you, rear gunner. Navigator, how long to enemy coast?'

'Thirty minutes, skipper, on this bearing.'

Jones passed on orders to the skipper to fly low, to keep the aircraft hidden from the German radar. This was the point where we gunners – Ridd and myself – came into the picture. Our job was to scan left and right, up and down, for any sign of nightfighters. We also had to report if any other aircraft was coming too close to us.

The wireless operator, Wilkins, tuned his radio to pick up broadcasts on winds, which were given out from time to time. Jones followed the information from the Gee navigational aid (known as the 'goon box') to ensure we were following the correct course.

'Navigator to skipper.'

'Yes, navigator?'

'The goon box is dying, skip. Jerry's up to his old tricks again. We must be getting near the coast.'

In the 'cat and mouse' game of the bomber war, each side made rapid technological advances, only for the other side to capture the technology, reverse engineer it, then devise a counter measure.

A few minutes later, Godfrey, the bomb aimer made the time-honoured announcement.

'Enemy coast ahead.'

'OK, bomb aimer.'

We slid over the dark coastline of Denmark, somewhere over Schleswig Holstein and to the south of Esbjerg.

'Navigator to skipper. Climb to angels' nine.' This meant 9000 feet.

'Thanks, navigator. Could you just have a look through the astrodome and see if you can spot anything out there?'

The astrodome was a Perspex bubble on the top of the fuselage, which enabled crew members to look around the aircraft.

'Wilco, skipper. Nothing out there but absolute hundreds of Lancasters and Halifaxes. Going back to my table.'

The aircraft weaved and dipped to port and starboard and port again. This was to make it easier to spot any nightfighters.

'Anything out there, gunners?'

'Mid-upper to skipper. Not a thing.'

'Rear gunner to skipper. Nothing either.'

We were being lucky again.

At this stage, the crew was high on adrenaline, but everyone was involved in his allotted tasks, which had been ingrained in us to work like clockwork. The Royal Air Force had trained all of us so well, so hard and for so long that we could probably have done an entire flight without using a single word. We knew our duties for every second of the whole trip.

For us gunners, it meant that we had to keep a perpetual watch and be very clear as to what was a smudge on the Perspex and what might be a nightfighter. If you stared into the blackness too long, you could start to see things, which you might decide to ignore. This was dangerous, as it meant vulnerability to nightfighters.

This night, over the south of Denmark, there was no flak activity. We were all quite clear on what the lack of visible activity meant – that nightfighters were on the prowl somewhere. The ploy on this raid was that we were too far north and off the nightfighters' beat. If we were not lucky and they were out there, then we could only hope that we would see them before they saw us.

Each individual pilot had his preferred way of flying once over enemy territory. Some flew straight and level, whereas others weaved left and right as far as the bomber stream would allow. Others changed throttle settings, or desynchronised engines to confuse the enemy radar.

One canard, which many crews believed, was that if the pilot left on the Identification Friend or Foe (IFF) transmitter, then it confused the German radar in some way. This was later proved to be untrue. Another such fallacy was that the Germans used 'scarecrows' to frighten us. These were believed to be large explosive shells, designed to look like exploding aircraft, which were sent up with the intention of demoralising aircrew. After the war though, it was discovered that the Germans did not use any such techniques. Rather, the aircrews were seeing Lancasters and their bombloads explode in mid-air.

We slid over south Denmark and Jones gave a new course.

'First of all, go up to angels' fifteen, skipper.'

'Up to angels' fifteen, navigator. Wilco.'

Without being told, we knew that Walton would be watching the altimeter.

'Angels' fifteen, skipper.' Walton's voice crackled through the intercom.

Jones now gave us a bearing to take us mid-way between the blackened ruins of Lübeck and Rostock. That meant we would dodge the flak from those two well-guarded industrial centres. It also meant that we were within range of nightfighters from both.

We approached the Baltic shoreline over Germany. We looked down into the black heart of Hitler's Third Reich. From the air, it looked remarkably like England – a large black mass, with a few shining railway lines and rivers. You had to wonder what the people down there felt when they heard these enormous bomber streams passing overhead. Well, it was them that started it and interrupted all of our lives.

Jones confirmed our position.

'Navigator to skipper. Just passing Fehmarn to the north.' 'Skipper to gunners. Are you keeping your eyes open?' Well, so far, we were in luck. There was no sign of any flak, nor any nightfighters – at least, none so far.

'Rear gunner to skipper. There's nothing out there. No flak.

No activity at all.'

'Mid-upper to skipper. It's all calm, skip. There's nothing out there. The Herrenvolk must be a bit snoozy tonight.'

Some time later, we heard Jones say, 'Now over Germany and shortly to pass to the east of Rostock. Berlin ETA (estimated time of arrival) 43 minutes at this speed. We are right on schedule.'

BANG! There was a tremendous crash at eleven o'clock high. There was a flash of lightning across my face and a hot, searing pain. I passed out.

15

What Happened When Joe was Unconscious

From his pilot's seat, above the drone of the engines, Blackham heard a sound like the rattle of hailstones hitting a tin shed. With each individual impact, he felt small shockwaves pass through the airframe, the fuselage and his seat.

What the heck?

Whatever was hitting the aircraft was hitting it with some force. It had to be cannon shells.

That was the point where his oxygen failed. What on earth had happened? They clearly had been hit. But there was no flak. No nightfighter activity. How could the aircraft have been hit?

His heart must have raced. Well, he had known the risks. Was this it? Was the kite going down? Was he going to live or die within the next minute?

The aircraft was not handling properly. That was ominous.

He was the skipper. He had to keep calm.

The oxygen was clearly off. He was starting to fight for breath. His absolute first priority was to get that back on. If the oxygen would not come back on, he would have to descend to a lower altitude and head back for home. The nightfighters would be waiting and Blackham knew – as they all knew – they would be very unlikely to make it back.

'Engineer, my oxygen has gone off. How about yours?' Blackham's voice was tense but controlled. The endless training over two long years was kicking in.

'Mine's off, skipper.'

They were at 20,000 feet. Without oxygen, they would soon all pass out.

'Shall I check the oxygen, skipper?'

'Just have a quick look and report back immediately. I need you here for a minute, just to tell me if the kite is going to keep flying.'

'Wilco, skipper.'

Walton clambered down from his flight engineer's seat, then down into the bomb bay to the vital rack of oxygen bottles. Their serviceability would decide whether the crew lived or died.

The thinness of the oxygen made every breath a desperate gasp. Walton's body felt two or three times its normal weight. If he could not restart the oxygen supply at that high altitude, they were all going to pass out and ultimately die. It was time to suppress the terror and remain icy calm.

'Skipper, bomb aimer here. Sorry, skip. I'm passing out. It's the oxygen.'

'OK, bomb aimer, we'll do what we can. Try and stay awake if you can.'

'Wilco, skip, but it's all going bloody hazy'.

'Wireless operator, check the gunners, would you?'

Wilkins unhooked his oxygen mask and intercom connection. He made his way towards the back of the aircraft.

***

Wilkins' legs still dangled down from his position in the mid-upper turret. He was at least still in one piece.

He pulled on the leg of Ridd's flight suit.

'Ridd, are you OK?'

Ridd bent down. There was a hole in the Perspex cover of his turret and the 200 mile an hour wind howled through it. Ridd's flying helmet was torn where Perspex shards had lacerated it. Wilkins thought it was probably pretty bloody inside.

'Feeling pretty groggy. Something hit the turret and it smashed me in the head. God! It hurts like the devil. Why does this aircraft feel so lumpy? It just doesn't feel right.'

'Can you carry on? Come on, quickly. I have to report back to the skipper'.

'Yes, I can carry on. Wouldn't mind a drink of tea if you can manage it.'

'Good man. I'll see what I can do.'

Wilkins worked his way backwards and negotiated the main spar halfway back on the fuselage. The main spar halfway along the inside of the fuselage in a Lancaster bomber was a nuisance. It was a huge girder that held the aircraft together but was awkward to negotiate when a man went aft to the rear turret.

***

Wilkins clambered to the far back of the aircraft, to Joe's position in the rear turret. He opened the two sliding doors into the back of the turret. As the doors opened, Wilkins was filled with a cold, creeping horror.

The Perspex of the turret was smashed. Joe was slumped, lifeless, away from him and over the breeches of the four guns. Beyond the turret was an inky blackness – an endless black void, leading down 20,000 feet to the territory of our blood enemy. With the turret gone, there was a terrible cold of perhaps minus 30 degrees.

Wilkins had to get Joe out of there. If the turret disintegrated any more, it was going to fall out into the night and take Joe with it to certain death.

Wilkins put his arms around Joe's massive Taylor suit. He gasped with the effort. Joe was not the tallest man, but inside this huge protective suit, his weight was like that of a dinosaur. He was either completely unconscious or dead. Wilkins had to prepare himself for that. Joe might be dead, but at all costs, he had to get Joe – or Joe's body – out.

Wilkins carefully undid the safety harness, the intercom, the leads which powered the heating elements inside the Taylor suit and the oxygen mask. He had to be as careful as possible, so as to not to disturb the fittings that held the turret to the aircraft. If they gave way, it meant certain death for both of them.

So far, so good. The various impediments were unfastened. Now, how the heck could he get him out? He could not pull him out backwards; the seat would not allow it. There was only one way.

At the bottom of the rear-gunner's seat was a handle. Wilkins grasped it and, with some difficulty, turned it. Ah! It worked! He cranked the lever some more. God! It was hard to move the darned thing. By putting all of his effort into it, the seat began, at last, to swivel around towards him. Wilkins had to position and reposition Joe's lifeless arms and legs to enable the turret to turn.

Joe was a dead weight. Wilkins could still not see if he was alive or dead. He could only hope and strain and ... The turret and lifeless form moved a bit more. Just a bit more and ... That was it! The turret was completely turned around.

He gasped with relief. He pulled Joe out of the turret and into the back of the fuselage. Wilkins was nearly passing out. His lungs were receiving hardly any oxygen at all.

***

In the cockpit, matters were becoming worse.

'Where the hell is Walton?'

Blackham was becoming desperate. Time was running out.

Without notice, the hiss of the oxygen supply restarted. Blackham let out a sigh of relief. Almost immediately, the flight engineer returned from the bomb bay. He gave a thumbs up sign. There was no time, or even enough breath, for an answer.

Blackham now had to look for that decision point, which would tell him to give the order, 'Everyone out!' That time was close but not yet.

Firstly, he needed to know if everyone was all right.

'Skipper to crew. Is everyone OK?'

'Engineer, skipper, OK'.

'Navigator, skipper, OK'.

There was nothing from Godfrey, Ridd, Wilkins, or Shuttleworth.

At least the aircraft was still flying, the oxygen was on and the intercom was still working.

Without gunners though, he was flying blind. If another nightfighter was on their tail, they would not see it coming. Having said that, they never saw the first one coming, either.

'Navigator, will you step up into the astrodome please and see what damage there might be.'

'Wilco, skipper'.

'Flight engineer, how are we looking? Is the kite still OK?'

Walton replied with tension in his voice, 'This aircraft is not handling right, skipper. It just doesn't feel right.'

Blackham nodded. 'Yes, I can feel it in the joystick.'

'Engineer, tell me quickly your assessment on the aircraft's state.'

Wilkins was, by now, beginning to find signs of life. Slight movements from the depths of the Taylor suit showed that Joe was still breathing. *He was still alive!* But oh hell, what a mess! His flying helmet was cut to ribbons from shards of flying Perspex and his face was covered in blood, which was still clearly flowing.

Wilkins dragged Joe, in his huge protective suit, one foot and then one yard at a time. He had to haul Joe's lifeless form over that bloody nuisance of a main spar, onto the floor of the fuselage and then onto the rest bed, which Lancaster bombers had as standard equipment for just such emergencies as this. Wilkins lay him on his side, so that the blood would flow away from his body. He placed a dressing over the wound to try to stop the flow of blood. He tried to make him as comfortable as possible.

At least Joe was alive. At least he was out of that shambles of a turret.

Wilkins made his way back to his position and reconnected his intercom cable.

'Wireless op to skipper...'

'Wilkins, where the hell have you been? How are the gunners?'

'Ridd is injured, skip, but he can carry on. Shuttleworth's in a bad way. He is completely out cold. I thought he was dead. His turret is smashed up and he is bleeding from a nasty head wound. I had to get him out or he was done for.'

This was not an exaggeration. With open head wounds exposed to temperatures severely below freezing, if Joe was not moved quickly, frostbite would have soon taken over and a long, losing battle with that particular form of torture would have ensued.

'Wireless op, will you go back and put a bandage on that wound? Just do whatever you can.'

'Wireless op to skipper. Wilco.'

'Engineer to skipper. Electrics OK. Hydraulics OK. We are losing petrol. The rate is not bad yet, but it could get serious.'

'Thank you, engineer.'

The situation was beginning to look extremely threatening. If they lost petrol, the aircraft was gone. Five would be able to bail out, but Shuttleworth and Godfrey would have to be left to die in the aircraft.

'Skipper to crew. Be prepared to bail out, but do not do so without my order, is that clear? Once again, do not bailout without my express order.'

'OK, skipper,' came from several different voices.

Blackham still did not hear the voice of the bomb aimer. He had presumably passed out through lack of oxygen.

'Engineer to skipper, wilco.'

'Bomb aimer, are you hearing me? Bomb aimer, come in please.'

There was silence.

At least the crew were not panicking. Had they panicked, the aircraft was doomed. Their survival depended on Blackham remaining calm and issuing clear, concise orders, which would maintain discipline and give them some chance. To Blackham's relief, the crew all sounded calm, although each man was in terror for his life.

'Navigator to skipper. I've had a look through the astrodome. The tail aircraft is shot up, the elevators have taken a savaging and there is a hole in the tail aircraft that you could crawl through. There is no fire though. Repeat. No fire.'

'Thank you, navigator'.

The kite was responding to the controls, but still felt very lumpy and uncertain in flight. He may still have to give the 'bail out' order, but he did not have to do it yet. That was a relief.

'Skipper to crew, I am not giving the bail out order yet. Please confirm that you have heard this order.'

Those who could responded.

'Engineer to pilot. There's a load of damage down in the bomb bay and the pipes from the oxygen bottles have become dislodged. Is yours coming through, skipper?'

Blackham turned to his right and nodded.

'Engineer, do the bomb release mechanisms look as if they are in working order?'

'Hard to tell, skipper, because it is bloody dark down there. I checked as well as I could though and as far as I can see, they are OK.'

The aircraft droned on. Blackham felt that the controls for the tail aircraft remained wonky, though were holding. The question was, how long would they hold for? In the far distance, an aircraft plummeted to ground in flames.

'Skipper to crew, there's a kite going down at two o'clock. There are no searchlights, so there must be nightfighters. Keep your eyes peeled.'

It occurred to him that Joe could not hear him and he was not sure if Ridd or Wilkins had either. The thought chilled him. He now had no rear gunner and an injured mid-upper. They were his eyes looking for nightfighters, meaning that now, he was effectively blind to any more attacks. There was nothing for it but to press on.

'Bomb aimer, skipper here. Can you hear me?'

The Scottish lilt was drowsy. 'Bomb aimer here, skipper. Feeling a bit seedy, to be honest'.

'But you're still with us?'

'Still with you, skipper. The oxygen is back on.'

'Engineer to skipper. The loss of petrol has stopped.'

'What? Really?'

'Yes, as far as I can see. The self-sealing feature in the petrol tanks must have worked.'

'Skipper to crew, stand down from orders to bail out. Repeat. Stand down from orders to bail out. Confirm that you have heard this order.'

'Wilco, skipper,' came from five voices.

The aircraft was maintaining air speed and height. It was responding to the controls. It did not feel right because of the damage to the tail aircraft, but at least it was doing everything that it should do.

Walton spoke next. 'Is it worth turning back, skipper?'

'Skipper to engineer. We wouldn't stand a chance. The nightfighters would have us for supper if we were on our own. Skipper to crew. We are not turning back. We are pressing on with the attack. Is everyone clear?'

From the intercom came a chorus of 'OK', 'Wilco' and 'Very good.'

'Navigator to skipper. Just approaching Güstrow. Time to target is 25 minutes.'

That is when they began to see more aircraft shot down.

From the height of 20,000 feet, well above the clouds, any burning aircraft were clearly visible. The first was at 2111, dead ahead. At 2113, a second went down to their left. At 2115, a third went down behind them.

At 2120, a fourth was shot down in flames ahead of them and at 2129, a fifth behind them.

Nightfighter activity suddenly stopped. They knew what that meant. The sky was alive with flak from thousands upon thousands of anti-aircraft guns. The tracers from the shells were so thick that afterwards, crews said you could have walked on it.

Training kicked in. Blackham did not have to think. He issued the order. 'Bomb aimer to position.'

'Bomb aimer, wilco!' Godfrey moved from the forward turret, where bomb aimers customarily spent the outward journey. He took his place in the Perspex nose of the aircraft, where the bomb aiming equipment was situated.

In the distance, they could see the red glow through the clouds, where the first bombers had arrived and had dropped their bombloads.

'Bomb aimer to skipper. Just keep heading for that red glow. Waiting for the target indicators, skipper.'

'Thanks, bomb aimer. Mid-upper, look to the rear. Can you see any of our little friends out there?'

'There's a couple of kites going down in the distance, skipper.

Can't see any fighters around here.'

'Thank you, mid-upper.' Ridd was starting to sound alive again. That was a big advantage.

As ever, Berlin was covered with a heavy layer of cloud. From somewhere underneath the clouds, the spread of the dull, menacing, red glow from hundreds of fires was giving the cloud blanket a quality of a scarlet nightmarish inferno.

Up ahead, the Mosquitoes of the Pathfinder crews were dropping their markers.

'There we are, skipper! Right on cue! Can you see those green flares with the red stars coming out of them? Just head for there. Here we go, everyone! Hold on tight!'

The aircraft surged forward for a minute or so. All fear was now forgotten. Training kicked in. There was a job to do and each man knew his part perfectly.

'What do you want me to do, bomb aimer?'

'Left a bit, skipper. Left a bit. That's it! Left a little and...'

The huge aircraft suddenly felt weightless as it leapt in the air, with 6000 kilograms of bombs suddenly let loose.

'Bombs gone, skipper!'

This was now the worst part of the raid. Blackham had to fly the aircraft straight and level for a minute until he saw the brilliant burst of the photoflash, whose photograph would prove that the aircraft had indeed bombed the target. Without the photoflash image, the Wing Commander would not credit the crew with a completed sortie and that final target of 30 completed raids would be no nearer.

As the aircraft droned on for that interminable minute, the spreading red inferno was visible through the thick cloud. They braced for another nightfighter attack, but none came.

Blackham had one gunner out cold and another still groggy. If a nightfighter was to come onto their tail, there was little chance of a warning. Not only that, but if he did corkscrew the aircraft to escape an attack, it could rip the tail aircraft off. Still though, no attack came.

The photoflash went off. 'Navigator, give me a course for home.'

***

They passed over Hannover, Osnabrückand the Dutch borders on the fraught way back to Skellingthorpe. There were still no nightfighters.

Then, over the Ijssel Meer in central Holland, they were to have the most incredible luck.

Oberleutnant [First Lieutenant] Hans-Wolfgang Schnaufer was waiting for them. Schnaufer was the top scoring nightfighter ace of the entire World War II. He was ultimately to be credited with 121 kills. That night, he was to get a Lancaster off Den Helder at 2258, another over Hoorn at 2319 and a final one over Waddenzee at 2333.

Blackham's crew with the unconscious Joe were just approaching the area where Schnaufer plied his trade of death. Schnaufer was just approaching another Lancaster – possibly even Blackham's – when he was racked with abdominal pain. The pain became insistent, agonising, all-consuming.

He could hardly fly his Messerschmitt 110. He could only make it back to his base at Leeuwarden, where he immediately received a diagnosis of appendicitis. That was a lucky let off for some Lancasters that night, especially considering Blackham's aircraft was exactly where Schnaufer had been looking for more victims.

***

'North Sea ahead, skipper.'

It was Godfrey. Blackham could already see the shining expanse through the broken cloud.

'Skipper to mid-upper. can you hear me?'

'Mid-upper, skipper. Loud and clear.' He sounded better.

'Watch out for intruders. If you see a twin engine kite, fire at will, but be bloody sure it's one of theirs and not a Bristol Beaufighter escorting us in.'

'Wilco, skipper.'

***

Back at Skellingthorpe, the priority was to have Joe, who was still unconscious, taken by ambulance to hospital. He really did look in a bad way.

Walking around the aircraft on terra firma, the crew were shocked at what they found. The tail of the plane was badly shot up with a hole that – as someone had already said – 'a man could crawl through'. The elevators and rudders showed evidence of cannon shell explosions. There were cannon shell marks on the underside of the fuselage. There was clearly one cannon shell that had breached a wing and entered a petrol tank. If that cannon shell had still been live and exploded in the petrol, then the aircraft would have exploded without warning in a fireball. The crew would have been incinerated.

On average, only three men would successfully bail out of a stricken Lancaster. Four would go down with the aircraft and die. The self-sealing feature in the tank had clearly worked very well, as it had allowed them to press on with the attack and brought them safely down the runway and back to Skellingthorpe. It was against all possible odds, but no-one was dead.

The debrief with the intelligence officers would be controversial that night.

***

When they returned to the Operations Room, a Women's Auxiliary Air Force member was waiting by an urn to give each crew member a cup of strong hot cocoa.

They would look at the operations board to see who was back. Litherland's crew had not returned. This was not a crew that they knew, but within that band of brothers, they all hoped that everyone would return from every trip. A non-return at this stage was not a matter of immediate concern, as there was always a chance an aircraft had 'boomeranged' with engine trouble and put down at another station. Alternatively, they might have ditched into the sea to be picked up by a rescue launch from one side or the other – well, if they didn't die of hypothermia first.

'Oh, he's probably had to touch down at Manston (the emergency airfield near the English Channel) or something,' someone is bound to have said. This was not unusual.

Blackham's crew would be called in for the well-worn routine of debriefing. They would sit in front of two intelligence officers and a Women's Auxiliary Air Force member would take minutes as they spoke. The station top brass hovered in the background, overhearing intently but without comment. It was good to see, out of the corner of their eyes, that another Women's Auxiliary Air Force member chalked their time of landing – 0039 – on the control board – only ten minutes late, with a shot up aircraft. That was really not a bad effort. *They had survived another one!*

The debrief on immediate arrival was important. Memories would be fresh.

The Intelligence Officer beckoned them forward. 'Do be seated, Flight Lieutenant Blackham. How come there are only six of you?'

'The tail gunner was shot up, sir. He's in a bad way and on his way to hospital.'

'Sorry to hear that. We want to hear all the details, of course. Perhaps we can just start from the top of the questionnaire and work our way down to it?'

'Engineer, how much fuel did you use?'

Walton replied from his notes.

'Did you see any nightfighters or flak?'

Ridd, the mid-upper gunner, was in the best position to reply. 'We saw absolutely no flak, sir, over Texel or Holland, or anywhere en route, up to the point where we were attacked. We saw no activity from nightfighters, either, until we were hit. Then, there was heavy nightfighter activity over the coast around Rostock and over the target. Over the target, the flak was ferocious, but it always is over Berlin.'

'Did you see any aircraft go down?'

Blackham answered, 'We saw several go down over the target, but I agree with Sergeant Ridd – none before we were attacked.'

'So, how do you account for the attack, Flight Lieutenant Blackham? There are only two possibilities and yet you say you saw neither.'

'We had a look at the aircraft, sir, after we landed. There is evidence of cannon shells on the lower fuselage towards the aft end. There is no sign of flak damage. It had to be a nightfighter.'

'Ah, but Flight Lieutenant Blackham, nightfighters typically approach from behind and fire deflection shots ahead of your aircraft with tracer shells. When a nightfighter attacks, he normally fires a stream of shells for the target to fly into. Did you not see anything like that?'

'There were no trails of tracer bullets, sir.'

'That is correct, sir,' Ridd added.

'Well, in that case, he would have had to come up behind you and execute a climb at around 80 degrees to hit you as you flew past at 200 miles an hour. Is that what you are saying?'

'I cannot imagine a German nightfighter attacking at an angle as steep as that. It would probably stall. Even if it did not, such a manoeuvre would have been clearly visible to the mid-upper gunner. As would the tracers, which overshot us. We saw no such thing.'

'Well, then, it's a mystery, isn't it?'

'Sir, I can only say that we saw no flak and no sign of nightfighter activity. We were hit very suddenly and without any warning or sign of an enemy aircraft whatsoever.'

'Let's move on, Flight Lieutenant Blackham. Did you drop bombs exactly as briefed?'

'Yes, sir.' He gave details.

Further questions included:

'Navigator, did you receive all the messages on wind speed and cloud cover?'

'Did you see any shipping movement of interest, especially German battleships?'

'Was there any other aircraft activity which you observed?'

'Was there anything of interest when you flew over Holland?'

Then, 'Right, thank you all. You may go.'

'Sir,' butted in the Women's Auxiliary Air Force secretary, uncertainly. 'What do I write for the reason the aircraft was damaged?'

The report recorded in the Operations Record Book reads as follows:

BOMBING ATTACK ON BERLIN

Primary target attacked at 21.24 hours from 21,500 feet. 10/10ths cloud, tops 9–10,000 feet. Target identified by Wanganui flares, red with green stars. Bombed centre of two Wanganui flares. Several small red glows were seen through the cloud and Wanganui flares appeared concentrated. At 20.50 from 20,000 feet aircraft hit by heavy flak. Damage to rear turret, part tail plane, elevator and rudder. Rear gunner injured. The attack was a successful and concentrated one. Sortie completed.

The entry in the Operations Record Book was wrong. The Royal Air Force had not yet realised that Luftwaffe nightfighters were firing upward-pointing cannons, with no tracer.

'Right, chaps. Dismissed.'

***

The crew would then strip off the paraphernalia of flying – the Sidcot suits, the Irvine jackets, the helmets and the Mae Wests. They ripped off the facemasks and threw them into wooden lockers. They returned parachutes to the drying room.

They would then go on to the store. First, they would return their unopened escape packs and retrieve their valuables and documents.

They would have turned in at about 0300.

There had been no further word of Litherland and his crew. The Station Commander had ordered that the flare path be turned off.

Then came the post-operations nervous response. The crew had spent so much time and effort in fighting off sleep that when they finally got to bed, many found sleep difficult. The eight hour burst of adrenaline was hard to hose down. It is likely that some of Blackham's crew were still awake two hours later to hear a van quietly draw up and crunch the gravel outside. There would be a short interlude of clattering boots and banging of empty cupboard doors as the Committee of Adjustments men came in and removed the personal effects of Litherland and his crew.

The boots came to the door of Blackham's crew. A torch flashed.

'Wake up. Which is Shuttleworth's locker?'

'That one there.'

For a few seconds, there was the sound of personal effects being stuffed unceremoniously into bags.

'Got it all?'

'Got it, corp.'

The hob-nailed boots tiptoed out.

The van quietly drew away.

***

When the new day dawned three hours later, there was no trace left of Joe Shuttleworth.

He was off to hospital, though the crew had no idea where he might be.

Blackham just hoped that Joe would be all right. He had looked bad when they loaded him out of the aircraft in the blackness of that freezing February morning. Blackham hoped also that his new rear gunner would not be some green sprog.

The official Royal Air Force Campaign Diary was to describe the night's work as follows:

15/16 February 1944

After a rest of more than 2 weeks for the regular bomber squadrons, 891 aircraft – 561 Lancasters, 314 Halifaxes, 16 Mosquitoes – were dispatched to Berlin. This was the largest force sent to Berlin and the largest non-1,000 bomber force sent to any target, exceeding the previous record of 826 aircraft (which included Stirlings and Wellingtons) sent to Dortmund on the night of 23/24 May 1943. It was also the first time that more than 500 Lancasters and more than 300 Halifaxes were dispatched.

The German controllers were able to plot the bomber stream soon after it left the English coast but the swing north over Denmark for the approach flight proved too far distant for many of the German fighters. The German controller ordered the fighters not to fly over Berlin, leaving the target area free for the flak, but many fighters ignored him and attacked bombers over the city. The diversion to Frankfurt-on-Oder failed to draw any fighters. 43 aircraft – 26 Lancasters, 17 Halifaxes – were lost, 4.8 per cent of the force.

Berlin was covered by cloud for most of the raid. Heavy bombing fell on the centre and south-western districts and some of Berlin's most important war industries were hit, including the large Siemensstadt area.

This was really the end of the true Battle of Berlin. Only one more raid took place on the city in this period and that was not for more than a month.

The *Melbourne Argus* of 17 February wrote the following report:

Greatest Raid of War on Berlin

Well over 2,500 tons of bombs – a heavier load than in any previous attack on any objective in air warfare – was dropped by the RAF on Berlin last night.

The same edition reports that the monastery at Monte Cassino has been destroyed.

That night marked the end of Joe Shuttleworth's operational career. It also marked the end of Sir Arthur Harris's battle of Berlin. He was interviewed in 1961 by controversial historian David Irving and still maintained he could have won the war with Bomber Command if only Churchill had let him keep on bombing and not got involved with a costly invasion of Normandy. A work colleague of the author in 1977 was a personal friend of Sir Arthur Harris. The man was a Battle of Britain pilot and had risen to the rank of Air Commodore. He said these words. 'Harris was mad'. The person cannot be identified.

16

In the Hospital

Back in Skellingthorpe, I had my own war to fight. I was groggy and confused. What on earth had happened to me? I came to. Looking back, I do not remember it clearly.

***

It dawned on me that I was in the station hospital. How on earth had that happened? Where was Blackie and the rest of the crew? Did Freda know?

Everything was so vague and murky and the world around me was out of focus. Whether the next events took minutes or hours or days, I did not know and did not much care.

It was all so hard to take in. We had seen no nightfighter activity. There was no flak. There was no equipment at the back of the aircraft that might explode. How on earth did this drama happen?

The well organised world of the Royal Air Force had no time for conjecture or ceremony. Someone organised me briskly into an ambulance and took me to the No 4 Royal Air Force Hospital Raunceby, a half hour drive from Skellingthorpe to the outskirts of

Grantham in Lincolnshire. The hospital had been built as a lunatic asylum in the nineteenth century, which invited a whole barrage of completely predictable jokes. Anything to keep morale up!

***

The doctor sat beside the bed. He got straight to the point.

'We can't save your eye, old man. It will have to be taken out. Would you sign this consent form, please?'

What the heck did he mean that he couldn't save my eye? And why were there all these bandages around my head? Why was my eye bandaged up so that I could not see?

I do recall that there was no pain whatsoever. How could it be that I was so badly wounded? I supposed afterwards that they must have given me a large dose of morphine.

I learned that there had been an explosion at the back of the aircraft. It didn't make sense. I couldn't understand why or how there could have been an explosion.

There was, however, one way in which I had been extremely lucky. Initially, I thought I had been hit by flak. I found out later that I had been hit by a German fighter with an upward firing cannon. In order to maintain their clandestine method of operation, these aircraft, unlike conventional fighters, were not equipped with tracer shells. Had tracer shells exploded into my turret and spattered me with the white-hot phosphorus of the tracer, the 'erks' back at Skellingthorpe would have had to hose me out of the aircraft.

The operation took place and the Royal Air Force surgeons did an excellent job. I was still alive and otherwise very much in the land of the living. I was, however, very unhappy. This inconvenient wound meant that I now would not meet my ambition of joining the Pathfinder Force and getting that highly desirable golden eagle on my tunic.

My being in aircrew had been exceptionally worrying for Freda. She knew that I had undertaken some operations over Germany. On any one night, however, she would never know if I was on an operation or not. So every night, she must have thought 'Is he over Germany tonight? Will he come back?' Lincolnshire was 'bomber country', with some 50 plus bomber stations. Every night, apart from times of full moon, the local population heard them going in their hundreds. Each time, they knew that some would not come back.

Freda came to visit me at the hospital as soon as she heard I was injured. She had had a telegram from Wing Commander Heward and also a telegram from my parents via the Red Cross. It had told her that that I was doing fine, but she knew that if an aircrew member was in hospital, it was serious. She was worried that I had been wounded. At least I was still alive and not horribly burned like some of the other poor blokes at Raunceby.

She found her way from Lutterworth to Raunceby several times to see me. There was nothing in the world that was so good for my morale! The first time was the worst, when she found out what condition I was in. We had spoken on the phone beforehand, however, so she was forewarned what to expect. On those train journeys to Grantham, she must have thought so many times, 'If one of those shells had been just a few inches left or right...'

I didn't see the crew. The Royal Air Force did not welcome crews keeping in touch with former members: they saw it as a threat to morale. It is most likely that the Adjutant told the crew that I had been given to the medical people; that I was in their charge now and the administrative machine at Skellingthorpe didn't know where I was. In essence, this was correct. I was sorry that it had to be like that. We had lived together, trained together, fought together and we were really fighting the war to keep us alive – not to beat Hitler, or anything political. Now, literally in a flash, I was gone out of their lives. My war up until that morning had certainly had a 'best of times' flavour to it. That was clearly at an end.

***

The facts and figures about Raunceby tell a truly wonderful, but unsung, war story.

In 1943 alone, there were:

1398 major operations

2926 minor operations (mine was one of eight performed that day)

1452 orthopaedic patients

1233 medical patients

163 burns patients

48 orthodontic patients

1791 psychiatric outpatients

141 psychiatric inpatients (including 47 aircrew)

Admissions totalled 5337, with 18,650 outpatients.

The hospital had 1000 beds, plus another thousand in store in case of an invasion.

Squadron Leader Dr Fenton Braithwaite was to achieve fame for his skills as a plastic surgeon and Archibald McIndoe for his remedial work among the terribly burned aircrew.

***

I spent some six or seven weeks there, then was transported to the Royal Air Force's rehabilitation centre at Hoylake, on the Wirral Peninsula 'over the water' from Liverpool.

Due to the large number of rapidly developing liaisons between recuperating Royal Air Force crew members and nurses, this was unofficially known as the 'Royal Air Force Conception Centre'.

Unlike the gloomy history of the lunatic asylum at Raunceby, this was a commandeered private school and rather comfortable. I had a single room all to myself. Apart from the loss of an eye and the loss of the crew, this was not too bad!

Freda could not get the time off from the Land Army to make the long trip to Hoylake but, as I was in convalescence, I managed to get a few rail-passes to go and see her. This, however, involved taking four trains there and four trains back. I don't know if Freda ever realised the devotion I was showing on those journeys: the journey from Hoylake to Coalville was harder than getting to Berlin! Admittedly though, there were no nightfighters waiting for us!

I was amazed to find one resident who I had known at Bruntingthorpe at Hoylake – Sergeant Wilder. He had been the sole survivor of a raid in Northern France. Now, both of his arms were in plaster. He had been posted to a squadron flying Stirling bombers, which had a cockpit that was extremely high off the ground. Wilder had fallen out of a Stirling onto the tarmac below and broken both arms.

At Hoylake, I was pleased one day when Stewart Godfrey walked in through the door, grinning and with his familiar Scottish amiability. I suppose he must have found out about my whereabouts from Freda. I was glad to hear that the crew were all still alive and assigned to some targets other than flipping Berlin. His visit was good for my morale and he left me in no doubt that when he reported back, it would be good for the crew's morale.

The big event when I was at Hoylake, though, was some weeks later: the D-Day landings. The precise, clipped tones of the wonderful broadcaster, John Snagge, came on the BBC's one o'clock news.

> *'This is London. London calling in the home, overseas and European services of the BBC and through united nations radio, Mediterranean. This is John Snagge speaking. Supreme Headquarters, Allied Expeditionary Force have just issued communiqué number one and in a few seconds, I will read it to you.*
>
> *Under the command of General Eisenhower, allied naval forces supported by strong air forces began landing allied armies this morning on the northern coast of France. I will repeat that communiqué. Under the command of General Eisenhower, allied naval forces supported by strong air forces began landing allied armies this morning on the northern coast of France.'*

Everyone from Wing Commanders with Distinguished Flying Crosses and sergeants like myself to the ward orderlies, nursing staff and men who did the garden jumped into the air. They were shaking hands and embracing each other and waving their arms in the air (though Sergeant Wilder, with his two broken arms, was probably spared this). Others were kissing nurses: any excuse was better than none!

It was the Melbourne Cup, Grand Final and Ashes series all in one. At last, the end was in sight!

Well, so we thought. Then it didn't happen. The American, British and Canadian forces were bogged down in Northern France for months.

***

A few weeks later, I was also able to make a trip back to Skellingthorpe. I thought I would walk in on the crew in the same way that Stewart Godfrey had walked in on me. A wonderful reunion would then occur.

The crew were gone. They had been shot down in early May. No-one knew if they were alive or dead. 'Aircraft failed to return. Terribly sorry, old man,' said the adjutant, quoting from the Operations Record Book. That is all that anyone knew. I could only hope that they were still in one piece. I also knew it was unlikely. They must have been shot down just a few days after Stewart had visited me.

It was good to see the 'erks' again though – they were still there and confirmed the adjutant's sad news. 'Poor buggers.'

Still, the war had to go on. It was now surprising how many new faces there were on the squadron. During my time on the squadron, only Burtt's crew had not returned. It was now clear that over the last couple of months, an awful lot more had not come back.

I made the short trip into Lincoln, which we had all rather ignored when we were a crew together. I walked around the outside of St Mark's Cathedral which was extremely impressive. This had been a major navigation point when we were flying. It was locked and I could not go inside – probably due to some wartime regulation, of which there were thousands. I don't think I was too bothered though. My thoughts had more to do with grieving for the crew. It was a chilling thought, but as far as anyone knew, I was the only surviving member of the crew.

After some weeks, my posting came through to work at the headquarters of the Royal Australian Air Force at Kodak House, 63 Kingsway, London. I found myself living in Finsbury Park, which was famous for the fighting of duels in the good old days.

I had an easy journey of some five underground stops down the Piccadilly Line to Kingsway station. At last, the railway system worked in my favour for once! Commuting on the London 'tube' was a different experience to that which I had known in Queensland. The trains were packed like sardines. You rubbed shoulders in a very literal sense with people from every country of the world and of every possible colour. Brisbane was more like a large country town, but London was probably the greatest city on earth. Just outside the office was the Kingsway tram tunnel, where trams would disappear at one end of Kingsway and pop out at the other end. There was nothing like that in Australia. One thing I would have to credit Adolf Hitler was that he certainly broadened my horizons!

My job was to file and organise occurrence reports, which gave details of all the raids and the crews who were on them. They included details of many crews who were missing on operations, many of whom were friends. When the reports came in, you only knew that a crew was missing: nothing more. It would be some time before the Red Cross would confirm if they were alive and captured, or if they were dead. Sometimes, they disappeared without trace. The reports were fascinating stuff to read, although often not in a good way. I got 'a rocket' a few times for being unproductive, due to reading too many of the reports and not getting on with my clerical job.

***

This was the time of flying bombs and rockets. Firstly, these were the V1 attacks. These had started on 13 June. Pilotless aircraft by the dozen would appear over the horizon, coming towards us. They gave off a strange whining noise, which led to them being called 'buzz bombs' or 'doodlebugs'. When you saw one, everyone in the street would stop to watch it as it passed over. Then, the engine would cut out. Everyone would hold their breath as the thing silently came to earth, then went out of sight. You then heard the enormous explosion as it hit the ground and detonated.

There was little we could do about them, except pray, if you thought that would do any good. Anti-aircraft fire shot down a few. Some intrepid pilots were able to run Spitfires or Typhoon fighters up against them, bat them wing on wing and turn them sideways. Some buzz bombs had wings ripped off by the heavy wire cables that tethered the barrage balloons.

Whilst the V1s were quite scary, they were not in sufficient numbers to worry a city that had endured the Blitz, even though some two thousand were fired at London. The explosive payload was less than half that of the 'cookies' that we dropped on Berlin. This was just not going to win the war for Adolf!

***

Then, something else happened. We heard bigger explosions, but no buzz bombs. Officialdom explained these initially as gas explosions, though the sceptical public was not convinced. After half a dozen, it was beginning to seem odd that every gasworks in London was spontaneously exploding.

The powers-that-be were forced to come clean. They were rockets called V2s, which were being sent over from Germany. They were so fast that you heard the huge explosion first, then the 'whoosh' of them coming afterwards. Bad though the V2s were, again, it was too little and too late for Germany's war effort. People in London just got on with their lives.

***

I was at Kodak House from July to December of 1944. I then got the orders to return to Australia, once again via America.

By this time, the war was in anti-climax mode. The Germans were being squeezed from the east, west and south and were known to be taking terrible casualties.

I was back up to Greenock and discovered that my return journey was, once again, on the *Queen Elizabeth.* Not only that, but they gave me, for some unfathomable reason, a cabin to myself. Unlike the first journey, this was not because I was on watch for U-boats. Now, there were no U-boats to watch for. Perhaps I got special treatment, being wounded. If so, then it was a very double-edged sword. I did not want special treatment – I just wanted to get on with my life with Freda, as soon as we were able.

***

Our arrival in New York was an utterly spectacular event.

The *Queen Elizabeth* berthed beside the *Queen Mary*. What a wonderful sight that was! Two of the largest and most beautiful ships in the world right beside each other, albeit painted in war-time grey. As if this was not enough, the two of them were berthed next to the French super passenger liner, the *Normandie.* Whilst the two British ships were a spectacular sight, the Normandie was an arresting but ugly sight: it was a blackened hulk. A huge fire had gutted the ship some months previously and left this wonderful, majestic ship a dejected, pathetic wreck. There were rumours that the Mafia had burned the ship to demonstrate their power to the American government, but I do not believe this was ever proven.

The Americans continued to treat us Australian servicemen extremely well. A family called Clark had a huge and very impressive townhouse at 55th Street and Fifth Avenue. They made it available for British and Commonwealth servicemen to stay without charge. There were perhaps 30 of us staying there. Oddly enough, I never got to meet the Clarks. Two housekeepers ran the property and made sure that we were looked after. From this house, we could walk to Central Park. Someone invited us out to Great Neck to visit the place where millionaires live. The Great Gatsby, in Scott Fitzgerald's novel, lived there.

It was rather wonderful that during my months in hospital, I had spent hardly any money at all. This meant I had lots of spending money for my month in New York, so I went to Macy's and Bloomingdale's to buy some clothes for Freda. This was incredible! After a couple of years in Britain where everything was 'on the ration' and clothes were in short supply and rather dowdily designed, here was a land flowing with milk, honey, fabulous dresses, sensational blouses and endless people who had the money to buy them. The impression was that America had done rather well out of the war.

Buying clothes without ration-coupons was a very liberating experience. I bought so much of various things that I had to buy an extra kitbag to carry them all in.

Almost next door to Macy's, I found the Empire State Building. The view from the top has stuck with me for the rest of my life.

***

America really struck me as a land of tremendous contrast. On someone's recommendation, I walked along 50th Street and took a bus northwards up Fifth Avenue. I was glad that I did. In Midtown, there were the expensive shops, the hotels and, after a few blocks, Central Park on my left. It was all so lovely. The bus went for block after block, past the classy Frick Mansion and the imposing Metropolitan Museum.

Then, a few blocks onwards, it all changed. I was coming into Harlem, which was where the black people lived. This was very dramatically different. It was the same Fifth Avenue, but the mansions had given way to mean, smoke-blackened tenements, four stories high. Ugly fire escapes led from the roofs to street level. The standard of living of the black people was awful. I was now the only white man on the bus and the only white man in the street. There was no way I was getting off that bus! I took it to the terminus in Upper Manhattan and came straight back. Nightfighters over Berlin were one thing but being a white man in Harlem did not feel that much better.

I got off the bus about halfway down Central Park and took a stroll. That was so lovely. The park itself was wonderfully green and well-kept and surrounded on all sides by exotic skyscrapers. Well, they looked exotic to me and so many of them were well-designed. There was nothing like this in Brisbane, or probably the whole of the world.

***

On another day, I joined a guided tour around China Town. It hummed and seethed with life.

It was more like being in the Orient than being in America. I really did have to think that 'the best of times' had come back into my life.

Also, I do not know why, but I decided to take a bus up to Rhode Island, several hours out of New York.

It was one of those things that seemed like a good idea at the time. In one sense, it was an anti-climax after the hustle and bustle of New York, but in another sense, it gave me a view of the affluent, well-heeled and well-functioning United States of America. No wonder they could just spend their way to win the war.

***

My biggest trip, though, was down to Washington.

My departure point was the cathedral-like Penn Central station. It was cavernous, so beautifully designed and so utterly impressive.

The rail journey to Washington takes some three hours and goes through Philadelphia and a lot of wonderful countryside. One detail that I remember very well was that you had to put your rail ticket on the back of the seat in front of you, so that the conductor could check your ticket was correct.

We were diesel-hauled as well! In Australia and England, I had always been pulled by steam engines. It just seemed that America was so advanced in many aspects of the world.

In Washington, I did a tour, starting with the Jefferson Memorial, which was so classical and exquisite in its design.

Next, we went to the Smithsonian Institute, the Lincoln Memorial and the Capitol. I was very impressed with Washington. It was so beautiful and well laid out!

I went past the White House as well, but in those days, you were not allowed to go into it – probably because hostilities were still going on.

From the peace and tranquillity of the Mall in Washington, it was hard to think there was still a war going on. As a serviceman in a blue uniform with the Australia shoulder flash, I fell into talking to a delightful young woman and spent some time with her. I wish I could remember her name. One odd spot, though, was that a man came up to the two of us out of the blue and said in a worried voice, 'I wouldn't stay around these parts after dark'.

Just two blocks from the White House were areas that were not pleasant or wise to visit. There was nothing like that in Brisbane, I thought. Beautiful place America was, it did have its seedy side.

***

I travelled by train back over the United States to San Francisco, where some kind locals gave me a ride over the Golden Gate bridge.

I travelled on the *Monterey* as far as New Guinea, where we trans-shipped to the *Hollandia.* We all complained that the food on the *Hollandia* was not that brilliant, but someone discovered that the ship was carrying a cargo of thousands of cartons of tinned salmon.

After that, we dined on tinned salmon.

The final leg from Brisbane to Sydney was on the *Swansea.*

***

From February of 1945, I was back in Brisbane. As with my departure, no-one had told my parents. I phoned home and my mother answered.

'It's Joe,' I said.

The reply was not quite what I expected from a mother with no sight of her son for a couple of years. Then, the penny dropped: she thought it was my cousin.

The penny must have dropped with her as well. 'Joe!'

The important thing for my parents was that I was back and more or less in one piece. By this stage of the war, an awful lot of boys, many of whom I knew, had not come back. There was so much to tell. I had gone away a Queensland boy and come back a well-travelled, decorated war veteran (having earned my Air Crew Europe Star). I was also a family man with a wife.

***

On 23 March, we heard that allied forces had crossed the River Rhein and were on German soil.

Still, the buggers would not give up. It had been clear for two years they were finished. Adolf Hitler clearly intended to fight to the last drop of someone else's blood!

It was now three years almost to the day since I had joined up. The local Royal Australian Air Force found a job for me, reporting on aircraft in the sky. I am quite unsure how this helped the war effort or any other effort. Nevertheless, I had come full circle and survived.

I still knew nothing of the rest of the crew and could only hope that as many as possible had survived. I knew it was unlikely.

I now waited for Freda to come and join me.

***

She arrived in September 1945 on the *Empire Grace.* Fortunately, as a war bride, the Royal Air Force paid for her passage and the Ministry of War Transport organised the journey.

I was back in 'Civvy Street' now.

I avidly read the war books – *The Dam Busters, Carve Her Name with Pride, Reach for the Sky* and so on – and saw the various films.

Still, being a Lancaster gunner had been the most vivid adventure. Over the years, it always surprised me that very few people ever asked about it.

Would I do it all again?

Yes.

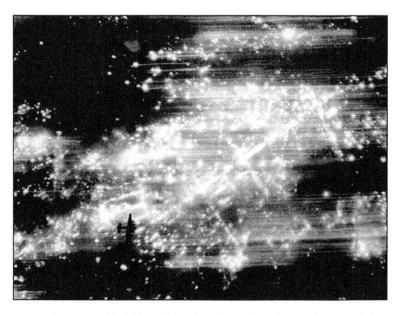

Berlin burns under an RAF attack: Joe's view from his rear turret.

NAME _____

DATE _____

Cunard White Star Liner 'QUEEN ELIZABETH'

As Joe had said, the Queen Elizabeth was full to overflowing!

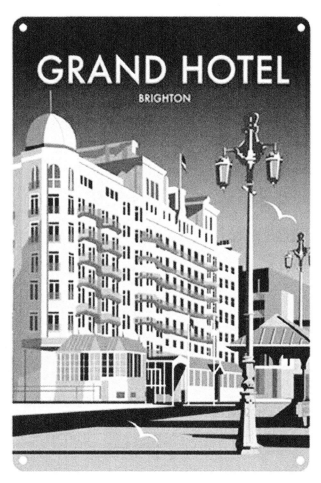

An advertisement for the Grand Hotel in Brighton where Joe cooled his heels for some weeks.

Joe and Freda: he with his 'air gunner' brevet and she in her Land Army uniform of jodhpurs, blouse and long socks.

Tom Blackham and crew undertake a ritual involving a teddy bear before leaving on a raid. Joe may have taken this photo as he is not in it.

'Bombing up' a Lancaster before a raid.

Joe and Freda on their wedding day.

'Blood wagons': the trucks taking the men out to their aircraft before a raid over Nazi Germany.

A Lancaster rear gunner.

Aircrews listen to the Wing Commander's briefing before a raid.

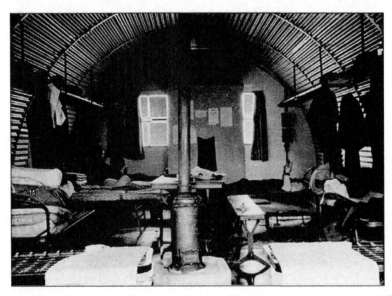

The interior of a Nissen hut: cosy if not luxurious. Officers and other ranks were, of course, not allowed to cohabit!

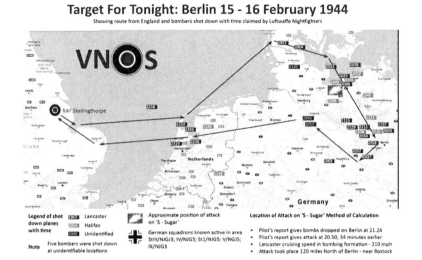

Target for tonight': the flightpath of Joe's aircraft on his final operation showing where the plane was attacked.

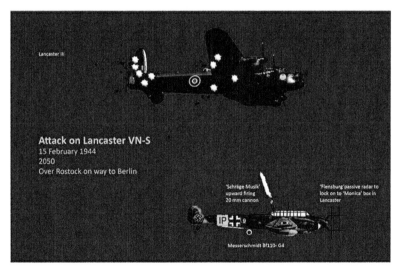

How the attack on Joe's plane was carried out. The RAF hierarchy did not accept for some weeks that the Luftwaffe used upward-firing cannons.

Young Joe' as sketched by a cartoonist at Skellingthorpe.

Drury Lane, London as a V1 rocket explodes not to far away.
From Joe's nearby office he would have heard the bang.

Joe, homeward bound, at dinner in an upmarket club in New York. Officers and 'other ranks' at the same tables? What would the RAF hierarchy have said?

Tom Blackham after his return to the UK.

Tom's story as it appeared in the RAF Flying Review in 1954.

Jacques Desoubrie, who betrayed Tom and hundreds of others to the Nazis.

Squadron Leader Phil Lamason RNZAF, the Senior British Officer among the men sent to Buchenwald to be murdered.

Maquisards: one of the Resistance groups who fought against the German occupation. It was a group similar to his with whom Tom fought.

'Jedem das Seine' [You get what you deserve]. The sinister message on the entry gate to Buchenwald.

Oberführer [Colonel] Hermann Pister: the man responsible for the criminality, inhumanity and suffering in Buchenwald concentration camp.

Buchenwald: how it was for the inmates.

British Airmen at Stalag Luft III: a heavily posed photograph but shows that life there was at least several rungs above that at Buchenwald.

'Dodkin' or whoever he was. This image was taken some days before his last flight into Nazi-occupied France.

The sinister German scientist Sturmbannführer (Major) Doctor Erwin Ding-Schuler, who conducted bogus medical experiments in Buchenwald concentration camp.

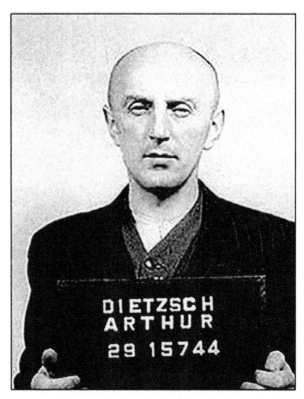

Artur Dietsch: Ding Schuler's right-handman who took part in the subterfuge to let 'Dodkin' escape.

Sturmbannführer Max Schobert, Pister's Adjutant, said to have attended 300 executions.

PART 2

TOM'S STORY

Whilst Joe's story was of happiness, seeing the world, swashbuckling adventure and gaining a wife, Tom's story was radically different.

The two men travelled together from training to operations, until Joe's severe wound caused them to part ways. Although they only spent a few months together, the bond and 'band of brothers' comradeship aircrews felt for each other is not to be underestimated.

We are able to track Tom's dramatic and challenging story through a piece which he published in an RAF journal in 1954. We are able to build on this memoir through a book written about his best friend during the worst of his challenges. Other sources then allow us to piece together what happened during Tom Blackham's 'worst of times'.

17

Tom is Shot Down

Back at Skellingthorpe in February of 1944, life moved quickly for Tom Blackham and the crew.

Joe had been invalided out. The last Tom had seen of Joe was when they stretchered him to the base hospital, still unconscious. An ambulance had whisked him away somewhere. There was no chance to say goodbye. There was no forwarding address. That is how it worked when a man returned injured.

To Tom's relief, the Medical Officer had reported that whilst the wound to Joe's eye was onerous, he was going to pull through. According to the sergeants in Joe's Nissen hut, the Committee of Adjustments Men had been in before dawn to remove Joe's effects.

Then, Joe disappeared quickly and irrevocably into 'the system', wherever that might be. Flight Sergeant Dixon appeared a day or so later to take his position as rear gunner.

It was the norm that when a man or a crew disappeared, those left behind in the Nissen hut and the mess would mourn his loss with the time-honoured words, 'Poor bugger.' There was a war on and there was no looking back: they had to think about the next raid.

Whilst crews did not usually contemplate their own demise, death, or disfigurement, it lurked like a malicious goblin in the back of their minds: 'Maybe me, next'.

It was dangerous to think about those who had gone. For Blackham, as skipper, it was his job to keep the crew, with their new rear gunner, concentrated on the next raid. He hoped the new rear gunner would fit in and be accepted as Joe's replacement. Still, crews could be clannish when one of their own was lost, so Tom kept his fingers crossed.

Some weeks later, Stewart Godfrey returned from Hoylake to tell the crew that Joe had lost an eye, but was otherwise was living it up just outside of Liverpool.

***

The men at Skellingthorpe did not know it, but the ructions at the top level of the Allied High Command had progressed from disagreements to bitter quarrels, to white hot enmity. The schism between their strategy in the hands of General Eisenhower as Supreme Commander of allied forces and Royal Air Force operations in the hands of Air Marshal Harris had progressed to an acrimonious crisis. Eisenhower was taking the Allies to a landing in Normandy, now only some dozen weeks away. Harris found all of this irrelevant at best and at worst, inconvenient. His preferred option was to win the war on his own initiative via Bomber Command.

Harris' 19 raids on Berlin had not impressed Churchill or Eisenhower, who saw them as pointless and wasteful of resources. Up until now, Harris had been protected by his superior, Marshal of the Royal Air Force Sir Charles Portal. This protection had been wearing thinner and thinner since the turn of 1944.

Eventually, push came to shove.

'I cannot support you anymore,' Winston Churchill had said to Harris. That meant neither could Portal.

Harris was now directed very firmly what his bomber crews should hit and what they should not hit.

***

A couple of days later, Tom Blackham and crew filed into the briefing room at Skellingthorpe to discover 'the target for tonight is Leipzig'. You could only imagine the burst of applause that Wing Command Heward received from his airman, for this simple bland announcement.

The purpose was to hit marshalling yards and disrupt the enemy's ability to switch forces from the Eastern Front to the Western.

The theory was that Berlin was the toughest target. Nevertheless, the Leipzig raid proved to be no easier.

Nightfighter activity started in Holland, which pursued them all the way to the target and all the way back again. Tom and crew were relieved to touch down in safety.

The Leipzig raid was the first of Blackham's raids after Joe Shuttleworth had been wounded.

Date	City	Target	Size of raid
19 February	Leipzig	Hit residential and industrial areas and railway installations. This was the first raid to be followed up by a daylight raid by the USAAF on the next day. 970 people killed.	823 aircraft; 79 lost

There was an extremely high rate of loss on this raid. Nearly 20% of these losses would later be put down to the unrealised use of upward firing 'Schräge Musik' [jazz music] cannons.

Fortunately for Tom Blackham, 50 Squadron was not rostered for the disastrous raid on Nuremberg on 30 March. There, 95 out of 795 heavy bombers were shot down, again largely through 'Schräge Musik' activity.

The penny had still not dropped for many senior officers that the Germans were indeed using upward-firing cannons. This was an extraordinary failure by Royal Air Force intelligence.

The Blackham crew's raids then progressed as follows:

Date	City	Target	Size of raid
20 February	Stuttgart	Daimler and Porsche automotive factories, which produced tanks and military vehicles. In total, 4560 people were killed in all raids on Stuttgart.	598 aircraft; 9 lost
24 February	Schweinfurt	Ball-bearing factories	734 aircraft; 33 lost
25 February	Augsburg	M.A.N. diesel works, which produced submarine engines.	594 aircraft; 25 lost
9 March	Marignane near Marseilles	Aircraft factory	44 aircraft; no losses
15 March	Stuttgart	As above	863 aircraft, approximately 25 lost
18 March	Frankfurt	Industrial areas	846 aircraft; approximately 18 lost
22 March	Frankfurt	Industrial areas. 1000 civilians dead.	816 aircraft; approximately 20 lost
24 March	Berlin	Berlin railway yards. This was the last main force raid on Berlin.	811 aircraft, 72 lost (unusually, 50 of these were by flak – a very high percentage)
26 March	Essen	Krupp armament works	705 aircraft, 9 lost

Since Joe Shuttleworth had been injured, Blackham's crew had now completed ten more raids. Joe had been the second member of 50 Squadron to be wounded or killed during his time on the station.

A month later, the situation had changed radically. Many airmen had now failed to return. On the morning after a raid, there were now increasing numbers of empty places at those lavish breakfasts at Skellingthorpe. The clattering boots of the Committee of Adjustments men were heard more and more frequently at 0500, as they removed personal effects.

More new crews, clean and keen appeared. You could spot them in the 'last supper' before a raid. They were the ones who talked.

Blackham had seen German cities burned to the ground. Goodness knows what it would have been like down there under the raid. Still, he was already halfway through his tour of 30 operations and still alive.

The mood of the crew now was different to that which Joe had known. During his time on the squadron, optimism had been in the air. Now though, that optimism was evaporating day by day, as the casualty list climbed ever higher. Still, 50 Squadron continued to have fewer casualties than other squadrons. This was down to luck more than any other cause. Across 5 Group, they knew that in 44 Squadron at Waddington, only 5% of crews finished their tour of 30 operations. Other squadrons based around Lincoln had similar loss rates. These were not published and the figures were top secret. However, crews met other crews in the pubs of rural Lincolnshire and word got around. Even though the news of the lost airmen was not based on reliable statistics, but on anecdotal evidence, it was nonetheless worrying.

***

Unexpectedly, a couple of weeks after the Essen raid, Wing Commander Seward summoned Blackham to his office.

'Thought you might like to see this, Tom.'

Blackham took the magazine from his Commanding Officer's hands. It was the 7 April edition of *The London Gazette*.

'Group Captain Jefferson said to keep mum about it until you were 'gazetted'. Didn't want to raise false hopes and all that.'

Citation for the award of the Distinguished Flying Cross.

'Flying Officer Thomas Henry BLACKHAM (124922), Royal Air Force Volunteer Reserve, No.50 Squadron.

As pilot, this officer has participated in a number of sorties and has displayed outstanding determination, fearlessness and devotion to duty. This was well illustrated on a recent occasion when detailed to attack Berlin.

On the outward flight the aircraft was hit by anti-aircraft fire and the elevators were damaged. Soon afterwards the bomber was struck by bullets from a fighter. The rear turret was rendered unserviceable and the oxygen installation was damaged.

The target was still 100 miles distant but Flight Lieutenant Blackham continued his mission. On the bombing run, 3 members of his crew became unconscious through lack of oxygen.

The flight engineer successfully repaired the oxygen system and the effected members were revived. Flying Officer Blackham then pressed home a determined attack and afterwards flew the damaged aircraft to base.

A few nights later, this officer again displayed praiseworthy skill and resolution in a successful attack on Augsburg.'

'Good God! I don't believe it! I'm to get a DFC. That's absolutely wizard! Sir, that was the raid where Joe Shuttleworth was hit. It's terribly decent of Group Captain Jefferson to nominate me, but the crew will say I am shooting the most terrible line. This detail is all pure nonsense. There was no anti-aircraft fire whatsoever and we didn't see any enemy aircraft – at least, not until later. When the old man's secretary drafted this, she might have mentioned that Joe got hit. And what is that about Augsburg? That was about four raids later.'

'Well, if you don't tell Air Marshal Harris those details, I won't either. I saw the kite after your return. It was bloody peppered with cannon shells and if there were any shards from exploding flak, I'm darned if I saw them. Tom, there are rumours that Jerry has fighters with upward firing cannons. Do you think you might have been hit by one of those?'

'Hard to say, sir, but it would certainly fit in with our observations.'

They shook hands.

'Do I have to keep mum about this until the award, sir?' Tom asked.

'Not at all. It'll be all around the station by now. Drinks in the mess at seven tonight. First one's on me!'

He got on with the business of waging war.

***

Tom's attacks followed to:

Date	City	Target	Size of raid
10 April	Tours	Marshalling yards	180 aircraft; 1 lost
11 April	Aachen	Railway installations	341 aircraft; 9 lost
18 April	Juvisy	Railway installations	202 aircraft; 1 lost
20 April	Paris	Marshalling Yards at La Chappelle	269 aircraft; 6 lost
22 April	Brunswick	Industrial sites. Used new technique of low-level marking.	255 aircraft; 4 lost
24 April	Munich	Town centre	250 aircraft; 9 lost
26 April	Schweinfurt	Ball-bearing factories. Used low-level marking again. Sgt Norman Jackson of 106 Squadron awarded a Victoria Cross for climbing out on a wing in full flight to extinguish a fire in an engine.	217 aircraft; 21 losses
28 April	St Medard	Explosives factory. Not successful; hidden by smoke screen. Master bomber ordered crews to retain bombs and return back to base.	92 aircraft, no losses
29 April	St Medard	Explosives factory: successful this time.	73 aircraft, no losses
1 May	Toulouse	Explosives factory and aircraft assembly plant at St Martin du Touch	139 aircraft; no losses

By now, it was clear that many of the targets were to soften up the Germans for the inevitable invasion. There were rumours of invasion every day. It seemed that everyone in the entire country had secret inside knowledge as to when and where it would take place. Some thought it stood to reason that the invasion would be across the Pas de Calais, as that was the shortest route. Others thought it would be further east – possibly as far as Normandy, even. Pilots who had flown over the south coast reported seeing a build-up of landing craft, tanks, warships of all types, trucks and all the other paraphernalia of war. They all reported that it was on an unimaginable scale.

Every day, they got up and turned on the radio, only to be disappointed. It hadn't happened yet.

***

On 3 May, Blackham took a stroll down to the flight office.

There it was on the wall! The crew were allocated to Lancaster LM480 (VN-U).

He was interested to see that he was to take a pilot officer, an Australian chap by the name of C.E. Stephenson, as 'second dicky'. This was his first Australian since Joe Shuttleworth, although Stephenson was from Tasmania, an awfully long way from Queensland. Blackham hoped Stephenson would have better luck than Joe. He knew from the bomb aimer, Stewart Godfrey that Joe was in convalescence, having lost an eye, but at least he was alive. Plenty of others who had survived that terrible raid on Berlin had ended their life in burning wrecked aircraft in Germany.

'There's a war on,' Blackham announced to the crew.

Checking with the fuellers, the tanks were only half full. Checking with the armourers, he found that the bomb load was of a hitherto unknown mix. Instead of the 'Usual' load of one 4000 pound 'cookie' and a large number of incendiaries, the bombload tonight carried the code-name 'No-ball'. This load was of a 4000 pound 'cookie', plus 18 x 500-pound high explosive bombs.

'What, no incendiaries?' Blackham is bound to have asked of the armourers.

'Nope, just lots of high explosives. Please let us get on – we have a load of work to do. There's good blokes.'

'France again?' mused Ridd. 'Strange bomb load, though. We haven't had all high explosive and no incendiaries before, have we?'

'Probably not,' they all agreed.

The half full tanks suggested a raid on France. That was good and at least it wasn't flippin' Berlin or Leipzig or 'Happy Valley'. This was the 26th raid now for Thomas Blackham – only four more to go and he had finished his tour. Then, the prestigious world of Pathfinders beckoned. He was so close to that golden badge he could almost feel it in his fingers. He must already have been thinking about the end of the tour and leave, including how to traverse the lengthy and complex rail connections from Lincoln Central railway station to his home station at Dunoon.

***

In the time-honoured manner, the crew filed into the briefing room and took their seats. The mood among crews was positive. It had to be France, or possibly Belgium, but at least it was not going to be one of the horror trips.

The entry of the platform party disturbed his daydream.

Wing Commander Heward opened the curtains, which hid the map from view.

'*Now,*' thought Blackham and every other airman on the squadron. '*Where are those red ribbons taking us tonight?*'

'The target for tonight is Mailly le Camp in central France. We have to hit a large German army camp and stores depot.'

Previously, the bomber group targets were whole cities or, if possible, specific targets like the MAN works in Augsburg. With the upcoming invasion, the targets were now much smaller and much more specific in nature. This was an important camp east of Paris.

The depot at Mailly le Camp housed a lot of tanks. These were not ordinary tanks. Rather, intelligence had, through its secret mysteries, reported it as a base for Panzer VI 'Tiger' Tanks. The standard allied tanks – the Shermans or Cromwells – stood little chance in a straight fight against one of those enormous beasts. To make matters worse, there were reports that Mailly le Camp also had an allocation of Panzer VIb 'King Tiger' Tanks, which were 75-ton monsters that had not been deployed yet. It was clear to all who knew about them that these threatened devastation at a level that allied tanks could not compete with, let alone halt. Only a few knew about these new tanks; most Germans did not know about them. They were in that mysterious wartime category of 'hush-hush'. Even more 'hush-hush' was how British Intelligence knew about them.

Mailly was bound to be a difficult target because accuracy was paramount. The bombing runs were to be at 7000 feet, as opposed to the more normal 17,000–20,000 feet. There were also known to be several nightfighter units in the area.

The raid was planned as a 'smash and grab'. There was to be a diversionary raid on a German airfield to draw the Messerschmitts and Focke-Wulfs away, but that advantage would not last long. It was necessary to get in quick, drop the bombs and leave the area as fast as possible. To make matters worse, the variations in bombing heights from one aircraft to the next was only 100 feet. That meant that Blackham and all other pilots would need to be very vigilant if they were to avoid collisions.

***

The Pathfinder force of 14 Mosquitoes was led by a famous name that night: Wing Commander Leonard Cheshire.

Passing over the English Channel, the medium-sized attack force of 346 Lancasters met little resistance. The Luftwaffe, by this stage of the war, was running out of steam. Over French territory, there was little to trouble them. This was beginning to look like a very straightforward, easy raid.

An hour after passing over the French coast, Blackham ordered Godfrey, the bomb aimer. to take up his position. Right on cue, the target markers were falling to earth up ahead of them. The initial target marking was very accurate. The Master Bomber then called in the main force.

Then, it went wrong.

On arrival over Mailly, the Master Bomber instructed crews to proceed to a point some 15 miles (25 kilometres) away and circle a yellow marker until called forward to bomb.

Blackham and the crew would have been unhappy. They had been told to get in and get out as fast as possible. Hanging around over a target was a very risky business when nightfighters were not far away. It was a bright night with little cloud, which meant they were visible not only to the radar, but also to the naked eye of a Luftwaffe pilot looking for his next kills. Such a night favoured the defenders, not the attackers. Fortunately, they had not seen any enemy aircraft yet, but that was unlikely to last.

Matters went rapidly from bad to worse. In the aircraft, Blackham's wireless operator, Wilkins, waited to hear the voice of the Master Bomber telling him to proceed to target. Instead, 'Deep in the Heart of

Texas' blared out in full exuberant volume, with handclapping and the noises of a boozy party.

Somewhere in the background was a voice, but it was garbled and unintelligible.

'Wireless operator, what the hell is going on?' asked Blackham.

'This frequency is playing the American Forces Network, skipper.'

'What? Are you bloody serious?' Blackham attempted to maintain that note of sangfroid, which Royal Air Force pilots were trained to use even under the most challenging circumstances. This idiocy made the maintenance of that tone very difficult indeed.

'Afraid so, skipper. I'll try a different frequency.'

'Skipper to crew. We're going to circle again until our American cousins have sorted out tonight's musical offerings.'

Still, no order came to attack.

'Skipper, I've tried a whole range of frequencies. There is no order coming through.'

And so it was that the bomber fleet of 346 Lancaster bombers circled around and around the target area of Mailly le Camp for a full 30 minutes. This was a raid which they were told must be 'quick in and quick out' and yet they were forced to keep circling and circling and circling on a bright moonlight night, in complete view of the enemy who didn't need radar to find them – just a pair of standard-issue eyes.

As they circled and circled, 346 Lancaster pilots were incandescent with rage and perfectly prepared for a declaration of war against the United States, so that they could joyfully bomb the blithering idiots who had messed up their radio frequency and put a complete operation and 300 odd crews at risk.

***

After half an hour, Wilkins made his announcement.

'The Deputy Master Bomber has come through on another frequency, skipper. We are to commence the bombing run immediately.'

The raid was to commence but all advantage of surprise had been frittered away by some idiot American.

The attack order was at last given when the Messerschmitts and Junkers returned from the spoof diversion raid. Lancasters instantly started crashing down in flames all around them. The night was so clear, it was possible to see the aircraft plummet towards the ground with one, two or, at most, four parachutes emerging. They could see the dull red glows as the aircraft exploded on hitting the ground.

At last, it was Blackham's turn for the bombing run.

'Pilot to bomb aimer. Take over please.'

After the half hour delay, the swiftness of the run-in to bomb was all the more galling.

'Wilco, skipper. Stay on this bearing. A little right and ... just a bit more to the right. That's it. Steady, steady, steady, steady. Now!

The crew felt the now-familiar thrill of weightlessness as the aircraft lurched upwards. For a moment, Blackham hoped he would not collide with another kite that might be flying just above him.

'Bombs gone, chaps. Hang on if you would.'

Blackham flew the aircraft straight and level for one minute. Then, after the brilliant burst of the photoflash, which would confirm to authority that they had dropped their bombs, Blackham spoke into the intercom again.

'Navigator, course for home please.'

They had escaped the mess over Mailly. Behind them, the jollities of the American Forces Network had resulted in 42 Lancasters being shot down, with 258 airmen lost.

***

The aircraft headed due south towards Troyes before a scheduled turn westwards to take it home.

Despite the aircraft losses, 1500 tons of high explosive bombs had hit the training camp and destroyed 150 barrack buildings and transport sheds, together with over 100 vehicles, including many of the feared 'King Tiger' tanks.

The official record was to state 'no civilian fatalities.' Regrettably though, this was yet another instance of an official mouthpieces telling lies. More accurate information was to confirm that over 100 French civilians had been killed, together with prisoners of war and forced labourers.

'Any sign of the Herrenvolk, gunners? Keep your eyes peeled.'

'Wilco, skip.'

They were some five minutes away from the Witches' Sabbath over the target zone now and approaching Troyes. Blackham took the aircraft into clear, quiet air space.

'Skipper!' shouted Dixon in the rear turret. 'Corkscrew right, skipper! We've got a fighter on our tail. Corkscrew right!'

Blackham took the aircraft into a dive and turn manoeuvre immediately. The engines screamed and the airframe shook. The crew members felt themselves becoming heavy with G-force.

'Is he still there, rear gunner?'

'He's still there, skipper. Corkscrew left! He's gaining on us and he's following us.'

The engines screamed again as the aircraft shifted to the opposite tack.

'Quick, skipper! He's drawing a bead on us.'

With a deafening roar, a livid red flash engulfed the aircraft.

'Christ! Put on chutes, chaps.'

Months of training meant that his voice still retained that calm, authoritative tone. Inside, Blackham felt utter panic, but he was captain of the aircraft. He knew that he had to hang on.

Ridd, the mid-upper gunner, jumped down from his seat. Dixon, the rear gunner, frantically rotated the wheel of his turret to reverse it. Godfrey, the bomb aimer, headed for the escape hatch, opened it and felt the suction and the cold draught of air; he was ready to jump out. He would be the only one to do so.

The intercom sizzled, crackled and died. The pink, livid red glow on the port side persisted. The petrol in one of the wings was on fire and the burning fuel was finding its way through the wing roots and into the fuselage.

Blackham knew they had only seconds. He had to keep the aircraft flying straight and level to give the crew a chance to escape.

'Everybody out!' he ordered, though it is doubtful if anyone heard it.

A second explosion rocked the huge aircraft. What happened next was a matter of panic, confusion and that terror of staring death squarely in the eyes.

***

Three other Lancasters from 50 Squadron were lost that night.

Pilot Officer Ronald Hanson was shot down on leaving the target area. Only the wireless operator, 'Dickie' Richardson survived. He was badly burned on his face, body and hands. A few days later, advancing allied troops found him in a cellar, blind and with a gangrenous right hand. He was air lifted to England and given a new nose, ears, chin, eyelids and upper lip. Still, his hand was amputated and he was blind. He received treatment at the 'guinea pig' hospital in East Grinstead for five years.

Pilot Officer Handley was shot down too. All eight of his crew members were killed.

Pilot Officer Dobson was also shot down. Four were killed, one was taken prisoner, but two, providentially, were to make it back to the UK.

18

Es Kommen Die Englischer Gentlemen

The order had come in from the Luftwaffe headquarters in Berlin.

'All personnel to return to base. Attack expected tonight.'

The moonlight was right. The cloud cover was right. This was not a surprise.

'Now, where would they hit tonight?' asked the Luftwaffe men on their air base in Central France. It was largely a rhetorical question.

Krause looked pensively at the map of northern France.

'Of course, the trouble is that we don't know where their idiotic invasion is going to land.'

German personnel were divided about how successful any landing might be. Some thought it would be disaster for the Allies, but some thought it would be curtains for Germany. They did not know that General Rommel had advised Hitler 'if they establish a beachhead for 24 hours, we can't hold them.'

As with Royal Air Force stations, Luftwaffe stations – and indeed the whole of Europe – were beguiled as to where the inevitable landings would take place. The Pas de Calais was the betting man's favourite, with a clear majority predicting a landing around Dunkirk. Others thought Normandy and still, others thought Norway.

'Oh well. All we can do it wait for orders from Control.' Krause's radio operator and gunner shrugged their shoulders and lit another cigarette.

As a *Hauptmann* [Flight Lieutenant] in Night Fighter Wing 4, it was Krause's job to make sure his BF110 nightfighter was serviceable and loaded up with petrol, cannon shells and bullets. He also had to make sure that his two-man crew were present, sober and prepared.

Tonight, there was going to be another inevitable attempt at holding back the tide of bombers, which came now without ceasing, without flinching and without pity from the north. Since the battle of Stalingrad two years ago, there was no question of winning the war. It was just a question of putting off the inevitable defeat for as long as possible. Obviously, you could not say that, or you would be sent to one of 'those places' that no-one knew much about, except that you didn't want to end up in one.

***

Two hours later, another message came over the loudspeaker.

'*Es kommen die englischer Gentlemen!*' [The English gentlemen are coming!]

Now was the time of tension. Luftwaffe Control could always tell when a raid was imminent. Radios in northern France could always pick up an increase in the volume of radio traffic from over the channel, even if they could not always interpret what it said.

Now was the time for silence and introspection, smoking more cigarettes and thinking about that possible Knight's Cross you'd get if you shot down enough enemy aircraft.

'*Startalarm! Startalarm!*' [Scramble! Scramble!]

This was it, then. The order over the loudspeaker was the message to assemble in the briefing room as quickly as possible.

The *Major* [Wing Commander] briefed Krause and the other pilots quickly. The raid comprised some 80 heavy bombers, which appeared to be heading to the large Luftwaffe base at Montdidier. This was some 100 kilometres to the east. It would take them 15 minutes to arrive there.

To Hans Krause, the attack was, in one way, an extremely pleasant prospect. If he could be first there, he would have the pick of the targets and boost his tally. In the world of the Luftwaffe, the number of confirmed kills was the most important number to be attached to his name.

On this day, Krause had already had a dozen kills to his credit. This had led to the award of the Iron Cross (First Class), which established him as an 'expert'.

With another dozen, he could expect an upgrade to the Knight's Cross. That would establish him as pride of his squadron, his parents and everyone with whom he was in contact

With a couple dozen of kills beyond that, he could expect his Knight's Cross with the Oak Wreath, which would establish him as a national hero. Over at Nightfighter Group 1, the *Kommandeur* [Wing Commander] Major Prince Egmont zur Lippe-Weissenfels had received the Oak Wreath from the Führer himself!

***

Krause got the wave from the ground crew.

'Everybody ready?'

'*Ja, Herr Hauptmann.*' ['Yes, sir.']

They were off.

In less than 20 minutes, he could see it. The Montdidier base was lit up in the distance by the eerie sweep of searchlights and the flak ascending to the heavens like deadly fireworks.

'Erich, put out a message to Control that we are arriving and for God's sake tell them to turn that verdammte flak off or they'll shoot our entire squadron down.'

'Jawohl, Herr Hauptmann.' ['Yes, sir.']

Krause drew his Messerschmitt 110 closer. After a minute or so, the flak stopped. He could see the base more clearly. He could see the flashes from the explosions as the bombs hit the ground. There were quite a lot of enemy Lancasters to be seen. There were already some nightfighters active, presumably from Montdidier itself. Now, where could he find a nice juicy victim?

Suddenly, the wireless operator spoke urgently into the intercom.

'Herr Hauptmann, Control have ordered us to leave the area immediately. This raid is a trick. There are several hundred heavy bombers hitting the army base at Mailly le Camp. We are ordered to proceed there immediately.'

'Order understood. Tell Control we are on our way.'

He winged the aircraft over urgently, making himself and the two crew members temporarily weightless and slightly nauseous.

'What is the bearing for Mailly and what is our estimated time of arrival?'

There was a moment's hesitation.

'Herr Hauptmann, fly on a bearing of 130 degrees. Estimated time of arrival, 23 minutes.'

'The clever bloody sods. They've put up a spoof raid again! In 23 minutes, they will have finished and be on their way home again.'

He willed the aircraft to fly faster.

'Radio operator to skipper.'

'*Ja?*'

It was the radio operator again. 'Control, advise they are approaching Mailly from Chalons in the north and are then flying to Troyes before turning westwards. I recommend you head south east of Troyes and see if you can catch them there.'

'Recommendation accepted. Same bearing?'

'Bearing 147, sir.'

'Bearing 147. *Schon gut!*' ['OK, then!']

As Krause approached Mailly and flew south of the town, he could see that this was a vastly bigger raid than the one on Montdidier. They were attacking at 2500 metres. That was unusual – they normally attacked at three times that height. The reason was clear. They were going for accuracy. They were out to really clobber the army base. The other unusual thing was that the raid had only just started. What the heck had these idiots been doing for the last half hour? There was no time for questions.

'Approaching Troyes,' announced the radio operator over the intercom.

'God! There's an awful lot of them, I'm swinging south of Mailly to see if we can pick them up as they turn right for home.'

In a minute, he asked, 'Radio operator, position please?'

'Just passing St Mesmin, Herr Hauptmann. Troyes is dead ahead.'

'There's one! I'm going after him. Hang on, boys!'

The aircraft was leaving the target area and banking to the west. It was Blackham's aircraft.

'He's seen us!' Krause muttered through his teeth.

The Lancaster began to circle in a corkscrew dive. Krause followed him. The Lancaster pulled into a tighter turn. Krause cut his air speed as fast as possible and went into a sharp dive to fly beneath the Lancaster. Their ears popped as the aircraft lost altitude rapidly.

He looked up. There were the luminous, red hot exhausts of the Lancaster some hundreds of metres ahead of him. He increased air speed.

'He thinks he's lost us.'

Krause manoeuvred the aircraft beneath the Lancaster.

'Hold on, boys. Hold on!'

Now, he was 200 metres underneath the Lancaster and flying on a parallel course. He was in the aircraft's blind spot. He guided the aircraft higher – 150 metres below that unsuspecting fuselage, 100 metres below.

'Wait for my order, gunner. Wait for it!'

He eased the nightfighter to 50 metres below the Lancaster.

'Fire!'

The nightfighter rattled with the vibration from the twin cannons. As was the custom with upward firing cannons, the ammunition did not carry tracer. The gunner could see the flashes as the shells peppered the petrol tanks in the wings.

Debris from the Lancaster spattered through the night sky. Some were chunks as big as a man's hand. If one of those shards, no matter how small, hit one of his own plane's propellers, Krause's Me110 aircraft was doomed. Other chunks as big as a man's head flew around them. If one of those hit the wing or Perspex of the cockpit canopy, they were finished.

'Get out of it!' shouted the gunner.

Krause pulled the nightfighter into a tight turn as fast as the air frame would allow him. One second later, the sky was lit up with a livid yellow flame as the petrol tanks blew up.

A few seconds later, the gunner said, 'Looks like two of them got out! Christ though – what an explosion!'

***

Krause did, indeed, go on to earn his Knight's Cross. He was to shoot down 28 Royal Air Force aircraft and survive the war.

19

Tom Blackham's Memoir – Escape to Hell

Tom's own memoir, takes up the story of his being shot down. Despite the trauma and shock which would have caused a lesser man to despair, his command of the details of the story is excellent and depicts something about his character.

***

On the night of May 3–4, 1944, our target was the German Panzer Barracks at Mailly-le-Camp, in the French wine country near Epernay. Although the barrage was fierce and fighters numerous, we went through the target safely. But after half an hour on the homeward journey, we were attacked by a nightfighter. He knocked out my starboard engine, fired the main tanks and damaged the tailplane.

I could only hold the Lancaster in a rapidly steepening spiral long enough to let the crew bale out. Then the starboard wing folded up and the plane spun. I remember seeing the brilliant full moon in a lovely clear sky as the aircraft hurtled towards the ground. Then the tanks exploded and I was blown out. I began falling with the plane, a ball of fire, not far away. Blood poured over my face and pain came into my head as the loose parts of the aircraft swished round me to earth. I must have pulled my parachute ripcord subconsciously, for I found myself floating down.

I remember the shock I got as I looked down and saw my legs, encased in flying boots apparently dangling helplessly under me. I thought they must be broken. Actually, my flying boots had been blown nearly off and were hanging by the laces, half empty of legs.

I could only have been 1,000 feet or so up when I pulled my ripcord. The shock of hitting the ground stunned me. On recovering, I found myself in a sandy field full of fresh, young corn. The softness of the earth had saved me from more serious injury and I was able to scrape soil over my parachute to hide it from the Germans. My legs felt numb and my head was still bleeding as I looked up and saw the bombers I had come out with, flying back to base. That was the worst feeling of all. Some distance away, I saw my aircraft blazing like a huge bonfire and in the far distance the flames from the target shot up into the night sky.

I knew I had to get moving as soon as possible. I plunged across the field away from the plane and found a marshy woodland. Near it was a little road, which seemed to lead to a village.

A man who was in the garden of the first house I came to. I shouted to him but, evidently in terror of the Germans, he went inside. With a sinking heart, I heard him bar the door.

Further in the village I heard the sound of voices: those of women and children. They were evidently talking about the plane. I went up to them and explained in French who I was. They too were afraid and told me of the German troops nearby.

They argued among themselves, all evidently stricken by panic, except one brave old woman who took me into her cottage and gave me a glass of schnapps. Possibly it saved my life, for by then I was exhausted from loss of blood and, I suppose, secondary shock. She explained that she dare not let me stay though she gave me an old jacket that would disguise me. I took off my battledress and put it on inside my shirt, with the old jacket outside. When she saw the open wound in my head, she took up a handful of dust and dabbed it on the wound to stop the bleeding. Handing me the bottle of schnapps with a blessing she pointed in the direction of Spain: 500 miles (800 kilometres) away.

The drink revived me and I was able to walk for two hours, very warily in case of hunting Germans. My legs and ankles then began to swell and I had to sit down frequently.

On coming to a small village, I knew I could go no farther. My first thought was to creep into the ever-open chapel and lie down in one of the pews. But the Germans had caused it to be locked, so I slept in the graveyard behind a tombstone. I awoke in two hours, cold but refreshed.

With the compass and the map on my handkerchief, I set my course for Troyes, though I intended to bypass it to the south.

I walked until 11 in the morning but again I had to rest. After crossing the main road north of Troyes, I met a ploughman in a field and asked him where I could get water. He smiled and said 'go into the wood'. I needed water not only to drink but to clean myself for my face and clothes were caked with blood.

I went well into the wood and came across three young Frenchmen who, on seeing me, drew their revolvers. I opened my jacket and showed them my battledress.

They turned out to be '*refracteurs*': men who had escaped from the forced labour contingents, which were sent to Germany. They looked after me for a week. It was beautiful weather and the rest and food did a lot to restore my health and spirits. One day they brought their 'boss' out.

He arranged to introduce me to a Resistance unit, which, he said, might get me away in an aircraft. I remember the way they all kept saying, 'perhaps tomorrow' and on the next day, 'perhaps tomorrow' but nothing ever happened until they took me to a house near Troyes where I had a bath, a sit-down meal and the never-to-be-forgotten luxury of a bed with clean, cool sheets.

That night an ammunition truck in the local railway siding was blown up by the Resistance and Germans swooped on the village, hunting them. A German guard was posted on the door of the house in which I was hiding upstairs. My protector was more afraid for me than for himself, although he might have been shot had I been discovered. By some means he managed to get a car from Troyes and smuggled me out of the back door, over two back gardens. Having eluded the German guard, I crept into the car and was driven to the house of my helper's brother. I remember the good wine he gave me, though I was only there two hours. Having put my battledress into a sack, I changed into fresh civilian clothes and went in the car by night to another house.

These people had a gramophone with only two records, one of which was 'Lili Marlene' sung by a German male voice choir. I played it continuously until the people came rushing in to say the Germans had begun to search the houses in the streets. They smuggled me to another house in the village, where the people were very friendly. But clearly, there were still some lurking suspicions about me. It appeared the Germans had caught a lot of the Resistance by disguising spies as stranded Royal Air Force airmen. Apparently, my liking for the 'Lili Marlene' record had not lessened their doubts. Two Frenchmen came to question me closely, with a view to sending me to a Resistance unit. They asked for my identity discs, which I hadn't got. I told them where I had left them, sewn in my battledress but, after they went to the place, they reported there was no sack of Royal Air Force clothing there. I am afraid I strengthened what suspicions they had by speaking only French but I did this because I found that their English was much worse than my French.

They reported that I looked like a German, spoke English with an accent and obviously used French because I could not speak much English. The whole trouble was that I had no proof that I had dropped from a plane; nobody had seen me come down.

A young Frenchman with a loaded revolver was ordered to guard me. He watched me for three days, sleeping in the same bed as me and keeping his revolver in bed with him. He was most hostile and often tried to catch me out by speaking to me in German. About 0400 one morning, I was awakened and told to get ready. Another rough-looking Frenchman was waiting at the door, outside of which stood three bicycles. We rode off from Troyes, with a French guard in front, myself in the middle and a French guard with a revolver behind. This guard left me after some distance and handed his revolver to his companion, who took up the rear position,

We cycled 12 kilometres, then shouldered our cycles over some fields, beyond which was a valley with well-wooded slopes rising away from it for miles. I thought this might be the end, a lonely place where my guard might shoot me in the back and leave me. But a moment later I was surrounded by a company of men armed with machine guns and Stens (British light automatic weapons).

The chief advanced towards me with his very long-barrelled pistol. Neither he nor his companions took any pains to hide their hostility towards me. They numbered ten in all. With five in front of me and five behind me, I was marched into the woods to a most cleverly chosen and skilfully constructed hideout.

It was a big lean-to in the side of a hill, concealed by over-arching trees. Sitting around the fire was the most villainous looking crowd of brigands that I have ever seen and with them an ugly fat young woman. She turned out to be an Englishwoman, a most bloodthirsty communist, who had come up from Spain dressed in a German soldier's uniform. I also saw a tree with a rope hanging over a stout branch. At the end of the rope was a noose.

All of the men were armed with knives and revolvers. Judging from their hostile attitude and questions, they really thought I was another spy. One spoke excellent English and it was he who finally established my identity. He asked what aircraft I was flying and where I had crashed. He ferreted out my life history, where I lived, what I did for a living and whether I was married. I began to think he was an Englishman dropped to organise the Maquis (one of the French Resistance movements). He asked about my service in the Royal Air Force, too, like how long I had served and where I had trained. When I came to describe my training unit in the USA and the people I had known, his attitude changed.

'I was there, too,' he said. 'And at the same time as you, only on a different course. Yes, I was a fighter pilot. I was shot down and dragged by these people from my aircraft'. Then he turned to his companions and said 'he's all right. You can take down the rope.'

Now that my identity was proven, I was accepted as new member of the Resistance. The camp was run as a military establishment and its 40 members were well armed with light machine guns, German revolvers, knives and hand-grenades. My fighter companion, Neville Mutter, who had been a Typhoon pilot and I were, however left to decide for ourselves what part we should take in the raids. But we could see that much was expected of us.

***

When we raided a camp of the Lavalites (French Fascist collaborators) and destroyed its equipment we found a quantity of British army boots, which were obviously relics of the Dunkirk evacuation. However, our most prized capture was a fat pig belonging to a French collaborator. We needed the meat, especially as the pig weighed about ten stones and the Frenchman needed a lesson.

We had been out all that night raiding a large store for cheese, wine and other victuals and felt just ready for that pig when we set out at about 5 in the morning, with four of us in the back and two in the front of a little Renault van that we had captured. The driver was a half-mad old Frenchman suffering from high blood pressure and too much wine, so we were in luck even to arrive at the place where the pig lived in a suburb of Troyes.

All armed with revolvers, we crept out and rang the bell. The concierge came out and asked what we wanted. We said, 'the pig'. She said, 'on what authority?' One of the Frenchmen pushed his revolver into her ribs, so she rushed into the house, got the key and opened the gate leading to the sty.

Then the fun began. We daren't use our revolvers for fear of raising the alarm. The drunken Frenchman said the best way was to pickaxe the pig. At the first swing, which missed, the pig began to squeal loudly. The more wildly the Frenchman swung, the louder the pig squealed. The windows of the neighbouring houses were raised; women screamed and men shouted and the pig successfully dodged every blow. Then someone suggested we pat its head while the mad Frenchman took aim. But still the pig evaded him. By this time the whole village was aroused. So, we each got hold of one leg of the pig and, with another pulling its ears and another pushing its rear, we got it into the van. The pig finally met its end by a revolver bullet when we got back to our hideout.

***

But there was tragedy as well as humour in the life, for the Chief could afford no mercy to those who disobeyed instructions. Some of the men went down one day to get a sheep and told the old shepherd, who was nearly 90, to say nothing about our visit. After they had gone, we learned he had gone straight to the mayor and given a description of them. The next day they shot him.

***

Our local intelligence service was good. A register was kept of all those who had collaborated with the Germans and another of all those willing to join us when the time came. The night before D Day, we crept to the village from our hideout and tuned in to the BBC Overseas Service. We heard the news that everyone had been hoping for: that the invasion was about to begin.

A midnight message was sent out by a squad of runners to inform friends within a radius of 15 to 20 miles around the town of Troyes to come in and join us. We had heard previously, with joy, that the Allies planned to drop 15,000 paratroops in our neighbourhood to take the Germans from the rear.

On D-Day plus one, our ex-Foreign Legion Chief who had survived two interrogations by the Gestapo, mustered his forces. With all those who had come in, we now numbered between 100 and 150 with many armed with Sten guns dropped at various times from the air or acquired from friends.

In high hopes of the paratroop landing, we began to train our new members in Sten-gunning at once. We found, however, that our woodland hideout was too small, so we moved our headquarters to a hamlet on the opposite hillside, which was backed by deep pine woods. Here we took possession of the barns and outbuildings of four or five farms.

***

It was in the evening of D-Day plus two, while we were sitting with bowls of soup on our knees, that a nine-year-old boy ran up from the village with news that spoiled our appetites. He said that the Germans were forming up to attack us. From his description, we gathered they had armoured cars, mortars and heavy machine guns. Two men were sent in the Renault van to reconnoitre. They never came back. We learned that they met the full force of a machine gun burst at point blank range. The mad old Frenchman with high blood pressure had got drunk and had run around the town of Troyes shouting wildly about 'the bandits'. That was how the Germans came to know about us.

The rest of us never finished our soup. Mortar shells began dropping in upon us and our recruits, new to the ordeal of fire, ran as fast as they could into the woods behind us. The Germans had taken up a position on the same hillside, only higher up and 150 yards further along. From that position they had tactical advantage. The Chief wanted to stay and fight but yielded to the decision of a council of war, which decided to leave a rear-guard of ten, of which the fighter pilot and I were members. The rest doubled off into the five-mile-deep woods. We followed soon afterwards in the lashing D-Day rains, which had come down upon us. We ran most of the night and at dawn threw ourselves down under the tall bracken and slept for two hours.

Living only on wild strawberries and soaked to the skin, we kept hidden until evening, when we started off again,

The Chief decided to make for a farm he knew would give us shelter and food. We then numbered about 50: a bedraggled and hungry band which would not have frightened any Germans had we come upon them. The farmer gave us a barn in the middle of a field. He killed two sheep and we had stewed mutton. We had to stay in the barn all day. By this time we realised that the landing of 15,000 paratroops had been only a rumour.

***

By this time, too, the fighter pilot and I had decided to leave our French friends; they were going too slowly for us. So we explained to them that we would try to get back to the hide-out, where there were two bicycles if the Germans hadn't taken them.

Our parting with these brave Frenchmen touched us deeply. They respected our decision but were afraid we should be captured. 'You might', they said 'even be captured by unscrupulous Frenchmen.'

Travelling by night, we soon rediscovered our former hiding place, which was only 20 miles away, as well as the two bicycles. One had a badly bent frame and kept pulling to the left. We took it in turns on this one but became very sore trying to keep it straight.

We had a third companion: an English youth brought up in France, whom the Chief had sent with us. The boy was to take us to his relatives, who would help us on our way to Normandy. We collected a bicycle for him and the three of us, unwashed, unshaven and unkempt, trundled along the roads, looking for all the world like three escaped criminals. But the Germans were too pre-occupied with their own troubles and we passed all their convoys that day, safely.

After sleeping in a field, we set off down a long straight road with a big house alongside it. This, we saw to be a German HQ. I cannot describe our feelings as we came up to the place with its alert-looking German guards. They just stared into space and let us go by.

***

The next day, the boy left us in hiding, while he went to find his uncle. He was very frightened but came back in the evening and brought with him a young university student who questioned us.

He then took us to the uncle's house and we found ourselves the guest of a very fine family.

***

After five days, the boy's uncle told us he had arranged for us to go to Paris. We walked back some miles to a tiny village railway station where a train stopped and an old man got out, greeting us like old friends. We boarded the train and he looked after us until we arrived in Paris. There, he took us to a rough, cheap lodging house in Clichy, a low quarter of the city. He said he would get us out of France but we were to stay there two days. Eight days passed and nothing happened, except that a strange woman brought us a pack of cards.

Then the Gestapo raided the place. They must have seen the old man coming and going and suspected him.

Somebody rushed upstairs to warn us. We found a back window at the far end of a corridor and bundled out of it into a courtyard and over a wall into another street. We saw a lady standing at the corner of the street. Much to our surprise, she beckoned to us, so we joined her and all walked off quickly together. She took us down to a Paris underground station where we boarded a train. Speaking English with an American accent, she explained that she and her friends had known about the raid but could not warn us. She was a friend of the man who had been looking after us. We stayed with her five days. Then she explained she had to go into the country because her daughter was getting married. She contacted someone who took charge of us and brought us to a place in Auber-Villiers near Paris, which turned out to be a Communist Resistance Group. We disliked them from the start. They were taking full advantage of supplies and arms dropped from the air but were burying them against the time they could use them for Communist purposes in France.

We asked to be moved and were able to speak on the telephone to the lady who had met us in Clichy. It was as if we were two little boys instead of two Royal Air Force pilots when she said most kindly, 'I will come and collect you and bring you home.'

So, she took us to a comfortable flat, which was occupied by a countess, who had been guardian of the Comte de Paris when he was a child. We were fitted out in smart suits and told, 'Now is the time. You are going home.'

Apparently, the plan was to take us about 95 miles south of Paris where we were to be picked up by an aeroplane. If this failed, a force of the Resistance was to attack an aerodrome. While they attacked, we were to come in from the other side and try to start a Junkers 88 nightfighter and fly away. It sounded all right until we came to think of it and then it looked silly. But we wanted to get out and thought anything was worth trying.

The plan went in stages. We had to wear a distinguishing sign such as a yellow handkerchief or a yellow pencil showing in our breast pockets. It was similar to the method used by the Scarlet Pimpernel. None of the people we met knew what his job would be when he was warned. All he got was the code word and a message, 'Be at such-and-such a corner at such a time. You have a mission.'

***

Up to this point Tom Blackham's terrifying odyssey through enemy territory had worked well. There was one piece of information, of which he was thankfully spared. The one member of his crew who is known to have survived the shooting down was himself killed by the German army. He was Stewart Godfrey, Joe Shuttleworth's particular friend, who had travelled up to Hoylake to visit him in convalescence.

He had been hidden by Madame Deguilley of Romilly sur Seine and then joined a Resistance group. They were ambushed on 24 June 1944 and Stewart Godfrey was killed. He has no known grave.

20

Jacques Desoubrie – A Man for Evil Times

Jacques shaved himself that morning.

> *'Ouch! These razor blades are like some medieval torture'.*
> *'Bloody war! You couldn't even buy half decent razor blades anymore!'*

But then, he smiled at his face in the mirror. The war and Adolf Hitler and the *Sicherheitsdienst* [or SD, the Security Service of the SS] – the sinister body which administered terror in the occupied territories – had been very good for him.

***

Life for Jacques had not always been favourable. Jacques Desoubrie was some 22 years old. He was the illegitimate child of a Belgian doctor, in a world where illegitimacy signified a social death knell. At birth, he was rendered 'untouchable'. The father had abandoned the mother and the mother, in turn, had abandoned Jacques. He was left as a boy, youth and man bereft of parents and roots, not to mention a sense of right or wrong, true north, or any kind of moral compass.

The hard knocks of life on the street in grubby Belgian backwaters had quite eloquently educated him as to the mysteries of life.

When Jacques was 18 years old, however, the Nazis had invaded Belgium and taken the country in just a few days. Many Belgians, although by no means all, saw this as a disaster. For Jacques and the marginalised flotsam and jetsam of society, it presented a once-in-a-lifetime, heaven sent opportunity. He loved the certainty expressed by the Nazi doctrine. He loved their smart, well-tailored uniforms; their daily military bands; their message of racial superiority; their style; and their clear message of invincibility.

Adolf Hitler, once a drifter himself, had proven to be a role model of the highest quality for the young Jacques, who was also a drifter. National Socialism gave Jacques Desoubrie what he had always craved: his true north. He rapidly became a true believer in the cause of National Socialism. But how could he best serve the cause and, if possible, himself?

He had earned a modest but reasonable living as an electrician. By all accounts, he spoke English very well. His preferred route into National Socialism would doubtlessly have been via the ranks of the frontline soldiers: the feared Waffen SS.

Young men in Belgium were rallying to Hitler's flag in surprisingly large numbers. Many had distinguished themselves in the service of the Third Reich. In relation to one highly decorated Belgian SS officer, Leon de Grelle, Hitler is reputed to have said, 'If I had a son, I would want him to be just like you.

Nazism and Belgium had a certain attraction for each other. The SS *Langemarck* division took in volunteers of Flemish origin and SS *Wallonien* took in French speaking Belgians.

Desoubrie's birthplace of Luingne straddled the border between the Flemish and French speaking parts of Belgium. He could have volunteered for either. Unfortunately, he was too short and, when it came down to it, not of a military disposition. Still, in times of war and with a desire to serve the cause, he found other opportunities.

His chosen way of contributing to National Socialism was via the Sicherheitsdienst or 'SD', which was the SS's intelligence body. Life, as Jacques had learned on those grubby back streets, was about profit, survival of the fittest and betrayal. Betrayal was vital for the overworked and under-resourced officers of the SD, with their grey-green uniforms with the chilling death's head insignia on the uniform headwear.

Jacques Desoubrie and the SD were made for each other. If Desoubrie could betray someone to them and the SD believed that the person was guilty, then he got paid a sum equal to more than two weeks of wages for an electrician. It was all for just a few minutes work. *It was wonderful!*

***

Moving south to France, where he was not known, he had begun his work. Firstly, he wormed his way into a Resistance group called *Vérité Française.* They were about a hundred strong.

Desoubrie betrayed them all – every man and woman. His newly found SD masters were pleased with him. The money came rolling in.

Desoubrie then infiltrated the *Le Gualès* network. They were 50 strong. Desoubrie once again betrayed every last man and every last woman.

In the early 1940s, jobbing electricians did not typically have bank accounts. Rather, cash sufficed for their meagre wages and meagre needs. However, his wholesale betrayals had elevated Jacques Desoubrie several notches up the scale of affluence. He needed a bank account now to keep all the money. His mattress was no longer commodious for all those hundreds or thousands of Franc notes.

Within a short time, the SD became even more delighted with his work. Now, the men in the grey-green uniforms had moved him to Paris, together with documents in an assumed name. He had used his contacts from elsewhere to enter 'The Comet Line', which organised for shot-down Royal Air Force crews to be sent back to England.

***

Jacques looked at himself in the mirror again. He really had to admit it. Life was good. He was living in France with piles of money from his extra-curricular activities. It was a France of shortages, rationing, surveillance and terror, but as an SD 'voluntary helper', he was in a privileged position.

The clothes, perfume and stockings that he was able to buy endeared him to more than one female Parisienne. This opened the way to a whole range of female privileges that were available to him in return.

The SD had also given him an identity card, which rendered him immune to the 'stop and search' activities of Wehrmacht and Milice, the fascist French political police. It got him into German cinemas, clubs and even those military brothels that were reserved for officers. The Polish and Ukrainian service providers offered a stimulating value for money.

Life could be good, Jacques knew, but he also understood that he had to be careful. If he made a mistake, the men of the Maquis would interrogate him in a not-especially-gentle manner and his body would be dumped at a crossroads, ripped apart by bullets and decorated with a placard reading 'Traiteur'.

He needed to concentrate. What name was he using with this group? There had been so many groups and so many names that he could barely remember any longer who he claimed to be. 'Pierre Boulain', 'Jean Masson' and 'Jacques Leman' were all names that he had used at one time or another. His favourite name, however, was 'Captain Jacques'. He would use that one on this assignment.

***

First, he had to meet his SD controller in a wood outside of Paris.

'Heil Hitler!' said the man from the security services.

He called himself Ullman, but whether that was his real name, only he and the Lord above knew. He and Desoubrie could not be seen together, meaning the meeting had, necessarily, to be short.

'Heil Hitler, Herr Sturmführer [Captain],' said Desoubrie as he came smartly to attention, clicking heels in the best German fashion.

'There is a packet for you, Jacques, for your delivery of two weeks ago. Please feel free if you want to count it.'

Jacques smiled.

'No need to do that, I am sure, Herr Sturmführer. The Germans are honourable people. Just one question though. Where do you take these people when I pass them over to you? I have often wondered.'

'You understand that we cannot tell you that, Jacques. If you fell into the hands of the Maquis, they would get it out of you. Too dangerous, *mein Junge,* too dangerous!'

Desoubrie shrugged.

'Now, coming to business, why did you ask to see me today?'

'Yes, Herr Sturmführer. There is an RAF pilot who was shot down near Troyes some weeks ago. He is called Blackham and he is a Lancaster pilot. He was hiding out for a couple of weeks in Clichy then with our aristocratic friends. The Resistance leaders want to send him down the Comet Line and back to England – no doubt so that he can return in his bomber and kill more people.'

His handler looked pensive for a moment. 'How about the people who hid him? You should get them in as well. I am sure that our people can make them sing like birds.'

'I would recommend against that, Herr Sturmführer. Your people and the Gestapo in Clichy have them under surveillance. If they are allowed to carry on, they will deliver so many more British and American fliers to us.'

'And so much more money to finance presents for your expensive girlfriends, Jacques,' said the Sturmführer, with the slightest trace of irony. Desoubrie shrugged.

'If we bring in the other people, we will lose the opportunity for more arrests of these terrorists,' said Jacques, summoning up all possible expression of innocence. He could be quite persuasive.

'Very well, Jacques. Leave the others alone – at least, for the moment. Just one question though. I'm curious how you get away with making these people trust you?'

'It's very simple, Herr Sturmführer. I wear glasses and a tweed jacket – everyone trusts a man in a tweed jacket – and my pièce de résistance is that I tell them I am Swiss and my Gestapo friend tells them he is Canadian.'

'Swiss? Your accent is from a backstreet in Belgium.'

'We might know that, Herr Sturmführer, but the British are bad at languages and they really can't tell the difference.'

'Idiots! Right, Jacques, now this is what we have to do...'

21

Tom Blackham's Memoir – Capture and Buchenwald

At this point Tom was at last hopeful of making a 'home run' to Britain. His odyssey over three months had been life-threatening, frustratingly slow and with the odds against him at every single moment. He had met many people. Some sympathetic to his plight. Some were unsympathetic but all of them bound by a common desire: send him home to take further part in the war effort and help defeat the evil which the Nazis had visited on the world. His memoir continues.

***

So, we were conducted blindly from contact to contact until we were put in charge of a tall, grey-haired Canadian who spoke in English. At last, we thought, we have met someone who will do something and we were right.

He took us to a flat where a big man with a typically Teutonic square head and bull neck (Desoubrie) told us, in case we mistook him, that he was a Swiss. He then began to talk in French with a strong German accent. He said 'Your plans have been changed. We shall now get you to Spain. You will stay here for the night.'

The next night we were conducted by the so-called Swiss and the Canadian across Paris. I was walking with the Canadian. He asked me about the RAF: what I had been doing and my hopes for the future. I remember the relish with which I described the raids I had been in, the bombs I had dropped and how I finished up with 'Yes, the RAF are doing a wonderful job.'

'Yes,' said the Canadian. 'I hate the German swines, too.'

We were approaching the Place de la Concorde. My fighter pilot friend was with the big Swiss.

Suddenly I heard a scuffle and looking round, I saw six men with revolvers attacking him. They handcuffed him and then six more men jumped out of a car that drove up and surrounded me. I remember noticing that we were on one of the bridges.

I looked at the Canadian. He sneered as he slipped his hand into his breast pocket and showed me his Gestapo warrant. It was unbelievable. With the sight of that warrant all hope left me. It looked like the torture chamber and death for both of us. The shock of such a betrayal knocked all resistance out of me; it would have been useless anyway. My remark to him is better left unwritten.

We were pushed roughly into a taxi. A revolver was thrust so far into my ribs that I could only breathe with great pain.

'Who are you?' I asked.

'We will ask the questions. You will answer,' was the reply.

But they knew exactly who we were, although we had nothing with which to prove our identity.

***

At Gestapo HQ we were pushed out of the car and up through a barbed wire avenue. Inside the building I saw a spiral iron staircase and looking up met the grinning faces of three big Germans. They were in shirt sleeves. At the top of three flights, they grabbed us and dragged us into a room, in which was a table with a typewriter and a photograph of Hitler.

They asked us who we had been working for and who were our friends. We told them nothing.

'It doesn't matter,' they said. 'You'll be shot in the morning because we know all we want to know.'

***

We were then taken in a van to the famous Fresnes prison, where we were searched and stripped naked.

When our clothes were returned, we were put in separate dungeon cells, which contained only piles of lice-ridden straw.

About four o'clock in the morning my cell door was opened, and I was kicked by the guard into the corridor. Waiting there was a crowd of 40 young Frenchmen. One told me he had been burned on the soles of his feet and then made to run on them. Others had had their faces recently smashed and beaten. They had all been tortured. I discovered they were young Bretons who had risen before the Allies arrived and large numbers of their band had been killed.

We were all marched into the courtyard of the prison and lined up. My fighter pilot friend and I stood side by side. Fifty yards away, I could see in the dim morning light three Germans behind a heavy machine gun, its barrel pointing at us.

That machine gun was never fired. The Nazis were master craftsmen in mind torture. They left us standing in line for several hours. All the time the three Germans were preparing the gun and every moment we expected to hear the order given for them to shoot.

Instead, we were eventually hustled off to the prison dungeons, stripped of our clothing and put under cold showers. Some of the group were very feeble and one old Frenchman next to me was on the point of collapse. I spoke to him and was hit over the head by the Nazi guard. He hit me with a filthy broom. The wound it made festered, and my throat afterwards swelled so that I could only eat and speak with much pain.

Each one of us was then put into a cage-like steel locker with no room even to raise an arm. After leaving us there for some time, we were 'gently' interrogated about our Resistance comrades. We told nothing and after one or two more questionings at intervals I was separated from my fighter pilot friend and other prisoners and put into a cell by myself.

Throughout the night I could hear men and women screaming as they were tortured. From there I was moved to another cell – all part of a ceremony to make me talk – with a little Frenchman who had been horribly tortured. He had been whipped with knotted thongs and the knots had broken two of his ribs. It was agony for him to breathe.

I was there for two weeks, living on weak sauerkraut soup and sleeping on filthy lice-infested straw. The lice, however, proved to be a useful diversion as we spent much time betting each other how many of them we could catch in a given time.

Neither of us received any medical attention but by this time my throat had healed quite unexpectedly. Our next move was to the covered quadrangle of the prison, where we were all assembled with 50–60 SS guards armed with every type of weapon.

A big SS warrant officer then got up and told us we were being taken across Paris to a train. Any prisoner making the slightest suspicious movement would, he said, be shot out of hand in front of his companions.

***

Twenty-seater buses arrived, and each double seat was occupied by one prisoner and one armed guard with a tommy gun and hand grenades. At the station we were driven into covered cattle trucks, 90 prisoners to a truck. One had to fight hard even to move an arm up to one's face. The women had separate trucks. No rations were issued but the French Red Cross were allowed to put biscuits and jam in each truck.

It was a very long train. Very few of the people in it knew why they were being taken away. Some of the women had been dragged from their husbands' sides in bed: others had been taken from among their children. But none knew of what they were accused.

The trucks were locked. There was barbed wire over the ventilators and a drag of heavy barbed wire was arranged behind the train to catch any that might manage to get out between the rails.

The date was August 15th, 1944. Verey lights (signal shells) flickered in the sky to the west and south and the distant sound of artillery reached us. It was the Allies driving on to Paris. The Germans were, we now realised, evacuating the prison. They were only five days ahead of the occupation, as the British and Americans entered Paris on August 20th.

Our train jerked itself out of the station and we began to think of ways to escape. With friends coming up and already so near we felt it was well worthwhile. We pulled three boards out of the side of our truck ... but then the train stopped. We found afterwards that it stopped frequently for the guards to inspect it. When the guards saw what we had done they ordered us out on the embankment. They stripped us naked and told us that if so much as a hand was seen outside the truck they would stop the train and throw hand grenades in among us until we were all dead.

At the next surprise stop, a Frenchman who pulled himself up by the ventilator to get a little air had his hand shattered by a revolver bullet. The guards were crack revolver shots. Even when the train was moving they would take pot shots along it just to frighten us. The shot Frenchman was hauled out from among us and ordered to walk down the embankment. As he walked he was shot between the shoulder blades and rolled away out of sight.

We were in that truck for five days without receiving any food at all from the Germans and we were still naked. At Saarbrücken, our large canister was refilled with water. I suppose it was another sinister stroke of irony by the Germans to give us these canisters. Each truck now had two: one for relieving ourselves and another in the opposite corner for drinking water. They were canisters dropped by Halifaxes and contained food and supplies for the Resistance.

Finally, the train stopped in one of the main sidings at Buchenwald, which had been to so many earlier arrivals their last glimpse of the outside world. We thought that our guards up to now had been vile and inhumane, but they were mild compared with the Buchenwald guards who met us. They knocked or dragged us out of the trucks and delighted in punching and kicking us as we fell to the ground.

We were given back our clothes and marched from the railway station through SS Headquarters into the actual concentration 'Lager'. For about six hours we stood under the scorching sun waiting to have our hair shaved off and have a shower. We were given no water and no food and none of the prisoners was allowed near us.

Every time an SS man came along, we had to stand to attention and take our hats off. All our personal belongings and valuables were confiscated. We then had to stand naked whilst other prisoners cropped us from top to toe: even the hairs on our insteps. The clippers were very blunt and I had no fewer than ten cuts on my body when I was finished. All prisoners had to go through this process. I helped one French priest who was almost dying. He could hardly stand up. He received no attention and died two days later.

After this we were crushed into a large shower room. A rumour went around that the showers were used as gas chambers – that gas came from them instead of water – but we were relieved to see that water, not gas, came out. After a few moments we were hustled off and given one little napkin between four men to dry ourselves. We then went across the road, where we were given a cotton shirt and cotton trousers – nothing else.

'Shall I,' I thought as I put on this uniform, 'die in this evil place or am I destined to escape the fate of most who enter Buchenwald?'

***

Tom's own account of his story now switches to other voices to give a wider perspective of his trials.

22

Buchenwald, 'Trust No-one' and 'DIKAL'

The prisoners, including Tom, were traumatised after five days without food, but the more aware of them may have noticed two small but significant details.

Firstly, above the main gate were the words *'Jedem das Seine'* ['people get what they deserve'], written in wrought iron. Oddly enough, the sign was so positioned above the gate such that it was only readable from the inside of the camp, not the outside. In the odd world of Nazi logic and symbology, the question needed to be asked: was this significant in some way?

The second detail was worse. It was in the form of a plain clothed official, not a man who screamed or who drew attention to himself. This man, a Gestapo functionary, handed over a parcel of files to an SS officer. The SS officer duly signed a form. They would see this officer again. He was Sturmbannführer [Major] Max Schobert, second in command of the concentration camp. He believed his attendance at 300 executions was a world record.

There was something on those file covers, which would have brought despair and desolation to the RAF men, had they seen it. It was a simple stamp marked 'NNRU': *'Nacht und Nebel – Rückkehr Unerwünscht'* ['night and fog – return not wanted']. The Nazi 'night and fog' policy meant a quite junior official could decide that inconvenient people be made to simply disappear with no trace or explanation, or even a notification of death. In practice, this stamp meant that all of these men were to be murdered at Buchenwald and disappear 'up the chimney'. The files would go after them. After their murder, there would be no record of their disappearance, incarceration, or even their existence.

Each of the two Nazi functionaries gave a smart 'Heil Hitler!' salute. The plain clothes man then went off into the camp for a well-earned rest and delicious cup of Ersatzkaffee. The airmen were shoved, bullied and screamed into a building, which proved to house a large reception area.

Here, they met their kapos for the first time. Kapos were the prison guards, who ran the camp on a day-to-day level. Like other inmates, they wore the blue and white striped pyjamas and a blue and white striped beret. On the pyjamas was sewn a red triangle. Across the red triangle was a tape with a number on it. Tom would learn that this signified a political prisoner – probably a communist. He learned to recognise kapos from the armband which they wore, which was black with the word *'Lagerschutz'* [camp police]. He also learned to avoid them: any contact at all with a kapo was a life-threatening experience.

The SS made a generous offer to the prisoners who were selected as kapos: keep other prisoners in line and you will get some additional days – or even weeks – more of life. The more brutal you are, the longer you live. Don't worry if they die; they are going to die anyway. If a kapo was not brutal enough, he or she would be shot without warning, sent 'up the chimney' immediately and a suitably desperate replacement found.

The kapos held a roll call, striking out the names of some men who had been shot during the journey, buried and already forgotten.

'Form a queue,' one of them screamed.

A man who was slow in forming a queue was hit with a heavy wooden truncheon, which the kapos carried. Tom and the others complied.

***

In the next room, more prisoners awaited them with large buckets of white liquid. They painted this on their stomachs and scrotum. Tom made a sharp intake of breath at the intense pain and stinging. The man who painted him did not respond. He was not sympathetic; he was not enjoying a bit of harmless sadism; he was not taking pride in a job well done. His eyes merely gave a vacant stare and an occasional blink that showed he was, give or take, still alive. As with the barber, he simply appeared to be a bag of human bones. He was clinically alive but nothing beyond that. Whatever the man had been in his previous life – schoolteacher, office clerk, or road digger – he was now doing what he was told to cling precariously to life. His own death would be some weeks, or possibly days, from now.

* * *

Tom passed to the next room. A kapo asked his name, gave him a camp identity disc to wear around his neck and checked his name on a list. The kapo then grabbed all the men's RAF identity discs. This did not apply to Tom, as his identity disc was lost along with his uniform in Troyes. Others were to protest strongly.

'Hey, you can't take that. That shows I'm in the Royal Air Force.'

'*Nix Soldat—zivil,*' ['Not a soldier – civilian.'] said the kapo, with a malicious smile.

Tom and the other prisoners were, for some reason, no longer to be regarded as Royal Air Force officers. They were now just stateless, nameless and prospectless '*Ka-Tzetniks':* inmates of the concentration camp system.

When Tom had recovered enough to think about it, he wondered why the Royal Air Force men had been given civilian clothes rather than the blue and white striped pyjamas that all the others wore. It also occurred to him that they did not wear any of the badges that told what kind of prisoner you were.

The kapos also did not give them any footwear.

Even despite the life-threatening terror, he had to admit that they did all look rather comical with their shaven heads and ill-fitting, shabby clothes. The kapos did not find it funny though. They also had that vacant, unseeing, unfeeling look and expected to be dead soon enough.

***

A small man with an intriguing badge beckoned Tom and the others around him to follow him. This man's badge had a strange version of a star of David. It consisted of an upward pointing yellow triangle and downward pointing black triangle.

They would discover that this denoted a *'Jüdischer Rasseschänder'* [a Jewish racial offender], which meant that he was a Jew who had had a non-Jewish girlfriend. The girl, herself, was probably in the camp brothel. If she was lucky, she was dead.

The man whispered as they passed along a wide passageway.

'The camp is run by communists – the ones with the red triangle. Don't let them know you are officers, or they will make your life hell.' He re-assumed the standard vacant look.

He led them out into the central compound. Now, Tom could see the full extent of the camp. It was immense and seemed to be the size of the enormous Hampden Park football ground in Glasgow. The perimeter was marked by high barbed wire fences. Guard towers, placed at 100 metre intervals, looked down on the central compound. In the towers, he could see SS guards with heavy machine guns – the same type that he had seen used in executions at Fresnes. Inside the barbed wire fence was a second, lower fence, clearly marked as carrying a high voltage electrical current.

'The electric fence is useful,' said the guide. 'If you jump on to it, you will be dead in a couple of seconds. We see about half a dozen of those a day.'

Inside the compound were huts, low and spaced with commendable Teutonic accuracy. These were the living quarters into one of which the man was presumably guiding them. Presiding over the compound was a central, large concrete tower, which was the main observation point for the SS guards to keep watch over the compound. However, this also held some rooms, though their use was not generally known, at least not for the present.

On the large parade ground in the centre of the camp, a military band in resplendent red uniforms with gold braid played *Die Wacht am Rhein* ['The Watch on the Rhein']. The more avid filmgoers would have recognised the music as that sung by German officers in the film, *Casablanca.* This was not a time for idle reflection. This, to Tom's surprise, proved to be the band of the Jugoslavian Royal Guard.

Of a building on the right, Tom asked, 'What on earth is that on the right?'

'That is the zoo,' said the man.

'A zoo? What the hell is a zoo doing in place like this?'

The man did not answer. Later, the Royal Air Force men would discover that this was a small area, which contained a bear and an eagle. Each day, the guards would throw a Jewish prisoner to the bear. The bear would kill the man and eat him and the eagle would pick the bones. For the SS guards, this afforded an endless source of innocent entertainment. The floor of the area was strewn with bear droppings and human bones.

To the left was a gibbet with some half dozen nooses hanging down. Two bodies swung in the air. Beyond the gibbet was the squat, dark menacing building, which was the camp's crematorium. Flames and smoke poured out of the chimney.

'It operates 24 hours a day,' said the man.

The smell of burned flesh filled the air and mixed with the stench of excrement on the ground. All around them were men dressed in the blue and white pyjamas, sleep-walking their way through the compound as though they did not know where they were and were really not bothered any more. Apathy, emaciation and hopelessness were the order of the day until their imminent death.

'How long before we look like that?' said someone.

'This place is not all bad,' said the guide. 'Over there is the Goethe oak. You have heard of Goethe?'

'Of course, he's the greatest German writer. Didn't he write *Faust?*'

'That's right. Well, he used to live just outside what is now the camp. He used to wander through the forests here and according to legend, he used to sit under that oak tree and write.'

'I wonder what he would have thought of this.'

'Well, Faust goes to hell and even Faust's hell isn't this bad.'

Tom noticed something very marked. Wherever the kapos roamed around the compound, men would studiously move away and get as far away from them as possible. Those that were unfortunate enough to come close to the guards studiously removed their camp regulation berets and bowed obsequiously and ingratiatingly low in front of them.

'If you don't bow in front of them,' said the guide, 'they will beat you with a pick handle until you cannot stand. Then, they take you to the camp infirmary.'

'What, there's actually an infirmary here?'

'There is actually an infirmary. Many people go into it, but no-one ever comes out. They do experiments in there. Honestly, you do not want to know what the experiments are like. The hospital is Block 46, with the 'guinea pig block' next door. Just keep away from them.'

Tom decided not to press the man for further details.

'Here we are!' said the man at last. 'This is the Little Camp.'

The Little Camp had originally been a stabling area for some 50 horses in the days of the Prussian cavalry. It was now converted to hold prisoners, as the main compound was stuffed to overflowing. The Little Camp now held 2000 people. There was no shelter or sanitation. Some dozen appeared to be sleeping, or dead.

'Where do we sleep?' asked a man with a marked New Zealand accent. 'Here,' said the man.

'But there is no hut here and no accommodation.'

'That is correct,' said the man. 'But the most important thing is to trust no-one.' He turned to go. 'Trust no-one,' he repeated, very pointedly.

Then, he left. They never saw him again.

Tom had seen that man with the New Zealand accent before. On the railway station before leaving Paris, he had tried to make some point or other to an SS officer. The SS officer had knocked him to the ground and pointed his service revolver at the man's head. They had all thought he was going to pull the trigger but, for some reason, he did not. Whoever this man was, he certainly had some courage.

So, this open area was where the 169 allied airmen were to live among some two or three thousand others, eat and sleep without shelter, blankets, or any other form of refuge from the elements.

'We'll see about that,' said the man with the New Zealand accent, who someone mentioned was called Phil Lamason, a Squadron Leader.

***

Lamason found an SS *Scharführer* [sergeant] and demanded to see the commandant. To his surprise, the man replied '*Ja, komm mit*' ['Yes, come with me.']. Lamason was somewhat surprised at the positive response. Maybe it would not all be so bad after all.

Lamason now had a problem: he did not speak German. It turned out that an American prisoner, Sergeant Scharf, spoke fluent German.

The Scharführer led them back across the camp. As they crossed the grounds, Lamason saw children with heavy iron balls chained to their ankles. He was horrified.

The Scharführer laughed. *'Zigeunerkinder!'* he said, helpfully.

'They're gypsy children,' said Scharf.

The Scharführer led Lamason and Scharf to the administration block where they had all been processed and to a large office on the outer side of it.

'Bleibt da stehen!' Lamason got the gist: *wait there.*

***

Lamason and Scharf were shown into the commandant's office. The first thing which he saw was the inevitable heroic portrait of Adolf Hitler.

The commandant was Oberführer [Colonel] Hermann Pister. He was a very cold man, whose tendencies to sadism had been honed by his position of untrammelled power over life and death. He had had the good fortune to come to the attention of Heinrich Himmler. The leader of the SS saw in Pister just that lack of humanity, decency, or pity, which was perfect for his organisation. Himmler recognised talent when he saw it. Pister had found his metier and rapidly rose through the ranks of the SS Camp Guard hierarchy to be commandant of Buchenwald – one of the biggest and most industrially productive concentration camps in Germany.

'*Ja?*' Pister asked Lamason.

'Herr Kommandant, I am Squadron Leader Lamason of the Royal Air Force, equal to a major in the Luftwaffe. I represent 169 allied airmen. We were all shot down and taken into captivity in a fair fight. I demand that we be released from this place and be put into a prisoner of war camp, in accordance with the Geneva Conventions and under the protection of the Red Cross.'

Pister called in his adjutant, Sturmbannführer [Major] Max Schobert. Lamason had seen him before. This proved to be the man who had taken the files from the Gestapo official when they arrived.

'Is that correct, Schobert? Are these men *Soldaten* [soldiers], rather than the usual Jewish and other miscellaneous scum that we have here?'

'I have had a look at their papers, Herr Oberführer. They do indeed seem to be allied airmen. However, they have been sent to us by the Sicherheitsdienst and there is nothing that we can do about it.'

'I demand that we be sent to a proper prisoner of war camp and released from this hell hole.'

'I do appreciate your point of view, Herr Squadron Leader, but it seems that there is little I can do about it. I am afraid you are rather – how would you put it? – stuck here. *Abtreten!*' ['Dismissed!']

That was the end of it. This was an environment where the slightest disobedience could result in a bullet in the back of the neck.

Lamason and Scharf then noticed something on Pister's desk that chilled them to their very soul. It was something which revolted them. It told them the nature of the place in which they had found themselves.

After Lamason held left the room and the door was safely closed, Schobert had shown Pister one of the files. He pointed to an innocuous looking stamp surmounted by a German eagle. The letters on the stamp were 'NNRU'.

'DIKAL?' Schobert asked Pister.

Pister nodded. 'DIKAL! Stamp the files immediately.'

'DIKAL' meant *'darf in kein anderes Lager'* ['not to be sent to another camp'].

In the well-administered world of Nazi atrocity, 'DIKAL' was the code word that translated into 'execution with no trace left'. It was now Pister's job to systematically murder all of the airmen in any manner that he saw fit. The main goal was to make sure that there was no evidence that they had even been in the camp. After they were murdered, the files, with their 'DIKAL' stamp, would follow their bodies into the crematorium oven.

Schobert duly stamped all 169 of the files with the code for the death sentence. One of the groups, for which he was responsible, took delight in long-drawn-out and sadistic murders. The only question was when and how. Pister had dozens of other people to kill first.

***

The SS Scharführer took Lamason and Scharf back to the Little Camp. Lamason now had to arrange his thoughts. What he and Scharf had seen on Pister's desk was a shrunken human head, fulfilling the role of paperweight.

Firstly, Lamason had to ask himself whether he had really seen that. There was no question: he had.

The second question was whether they should tell the others.

'Look, Scharf, you saw that thing on the Kommandant's desk. We should keep that to ourselves. If we tell the others what we have seen, it will just make them even more bloody despondent.'

'Very well, sir.'

This was the first of three secrets which Phil Lamason would keep to himself. However, it was not to be the most dramatic!

23

Tom Meets Dodkin

The Little Camp was surrounded by three electric fences. There were also three rings of SS guards and Alsatian dogs that prowled about the perimeter at night.

The day began at 0430, when the airmen stood to attention for two to four hours while the prisoners were counted. One British non-commissioned officer was smacked across the face for standing in the British fashion, with his fists clenched at his side.

One third of a litre of coffee substitute was then issued. It was cold because it had to be collected by a party of men at 0300. It came down in barrels and if any was spilled, the men responsible were beaten by the kapos. Alternatively, the kapos might just beat someone anyway.

The most terrible daily ordeal was having to stand in line for so long, while so many of them had dysentery. Any who tried to relieve themselves were beaten almost senseless.

At 1100, the inmates of the Little Camp received half a litre of 'soup', which was often just grass and water and one eighth of a loaf of bread, with a small piece of margarine substitute. It was tragic to see men fighting like wild animals to scrape the bottom of the food barrels. The strong beat the weak underfoot and the weak often died; nobody seemed to mind. It was quite common to see two or three dead prisoners lying where they had died. The bodies were picked up later and burned.

At this time, the Russians were very kind to the Royal Air Force men. At the risk of their own lives the Russians brought bread and clogs. The Russians were treated on a more lenient scale but the British and American airmen were given the same appalling treatment as Jews.

***

The Human Experimental Block was the most sinister place in Buchenwald. Young SS doctors injected people experimentally with drugs and germs and when the victims died, they preserved their heads or cured their skins if there was anything peculiar about them. The men saw heads of people preserved just as they had died.

All this time, many were suffering intensely from festering wounds caused by the lice that had bitten them in Fresnes Prison. With no medicine and no nutritious food, the wounds would not heal and many had to stuff the holes in their flesh up with paper to soak up the matter. Tom had a cut that was the size of a half crown (2cm) and two inches (5cm) deep.

***

One very wet night after standing for six hours, the airmen were crowded into a hut with 900 Jews and gypsies. The prisoners were running with lice, which swarmed all over them and drove them almost mad, much to the guards' amusement.

Typhus broke out in the camp and some men had the dreaded louse in their clothes. The prisoner sanitary attendants tried to help, but the whole of Buchenwald was terribly overcrowded and the sanitary conditions were appalling, so there was not much that they could do.

Many men started to sleep in the latrines, because it was more convenient if they had typhus or dysentery.

***

One day, Tom saw 500 Jews who had been forced to work in a synthetic petrol factory near Leipzig. They had been horribly burned when the factory had been bombed by the Americans. They were sent to Buchenwald to await transport for the Auschwitz extermination camp.

They were terrified when they were marched from Buchenwald to the railway station and forced into cattle trucks. Although the trucks were designed for 40 people or eight horses, 120 Jews were crammed into each. Those who couldn't march were piled on carts, which were drawn by fellow prisoners.

Many were close to death. Those who had the strength struggled feebly to get their heads up from under the pile of half dead bodies, but the others died there as they lay. When the cart got to the train, the limp bodies were picked up by the guards and flung into the cattle truck.

A Pole who tried to escape was hanged in the middle of a square formed by the prisoners. He took five minutes to die.

***

A vehicle like a pantechnicon arrived one day and into it were crowded 250 little gypsy boys, aged six to sixteen. The back of the van was closed and sealed. They were then gassed by connecting the exhaust pipe to the interior of the van.

***

One American officer went mad. He was taken to the 'hospital' and tied down to his wooden plank. He died some days later.

***

Lamason, however, preferred not to be psychologically destroyed.

'Right, chaps! Up you get! It's morning parade time. Do I have a warrant officer here?'

'Warrant officer here, sir. 408 Squadron, Royal Canadian Air Force. Linton on Ouse.'

'Linton on Ouse? God! I had to put down there once. Bloody freezing it was!'

'That's the place, sir.'

'Right, warrant officer. Bring the parade to attention.'

'Par-ade! Par-ade! Atten-shun!'

The ragbag parade of exhausted, sick, worn out men stepped back into their role as a disciplined military unit.

As Senior British Officer, Squadron Leader Lamason addressed the men. 'Gentlemen, we have ourselves in a very fine fix indeed. The goons have completely violated the Geneva Conventions and are treating us as common thieves and criminals. However, we are soldiers. From this time on, we will also conduct ourselves as our training has taught us and as our countries would expect from us. We will march as a unit to roll call and we will follow all reasonable commands as a single unit.'

'Understood, sir.'

Lamason then gave his initial orders to the group.

'Do not provoke or have anything to do with the SS guards. As we have seen on the train, they are unpredictable and trigger happy. Do not attempt to go on voyages of discovery around the camp; we have no idea what obscure rules we may fall foul of. I will, as we find out how this place works, make further representation to the authorities to get us out of here.'

Lamason then organised the parade into groups by nationality. He appointed a commanding officer for each group. Lamason appointed Tom Blackham for the British contingent and also found suitable commanding officers for the American, Canadian and Australian and New Zealand groups. The sole West Indian was included in the British group.

'Warrant officer, dismiss the parade.'

'Par-ade! Parade, dismiss!'

The other prisoners looked at them in astonishment. Lamason's address had almost jolted the pyjama-clad lost souls out of their apathy.

The SS guards looked on disapprovingly. Someone taking an initiative in the camp was a threat to their programme of destroying humanity. Doubtlessly, reports would be lodged with higher authority.

***

Breakfast appeared on a trolley. The trolley was pushed by one of the pyjama-clad lost souls who hardly seemed to know where he was, what day it was, or even who he was.

Breakfast consisted of one litre of thin sauerkraut soup per day and, at the special interval of twice a day, one loaf of bread between six men. SS nutrition experts had calculated this diet to kill a man of average size and health in three months. Food was an expense in the concentration camp empire. People came free of charge and were eminently replaceable.

Lamason ordered two teams of three men each to do a surreptitious 'recce' around the camp and report back in half an hour with details of what they had seen. 'For God's sake, don't upset the guards or they'll probably shoot you.'

***

Very early on during their time at Buchenwald and possibly on this first reconnoitre, Tom Blackham was to meet a remarkable and intriguing man. He was not dressed in the regulation blue and white pyjamas with classification badges, but in cast-off civilian clothes, as were the Royal Air Force men. He was of medium height and build and with the regulation shaved head. Still, his gait was not the shuffling shambles of the lost souls – that is what Tom noticed first. This man was still very much alive.

Tom and the other men on the recce looked at him with a blend of curiosity and intrigue as he approached.

'Excuse me, old chap. Are you the Senior British Officer?'

'No, I'm Tom Blackham, Flight Lieutenant, Royal Air Force.

And who might you be?'

Tom had already detected his accent, which said 'English private school'. He had heard it often enough among Royal Air Force Officers.

'I am Squadron Leader Kenneth Dodkin, 138 Squadron.' 'What? You're British? Christ! What are you doing here?'

Instinct took over. Tom and all of them had spent time in France where informers were rife, where few could be trusted and where a simple wrong admission meant death. All of them had been betrayed. This man needed to convince him that he was who he said he was. Similarly, he knew that he had to persuade Dodkin.

'No, don't answer that. Tell you what. Let's go for a walk.'

'Certainly,' agreed Dodkin.

As they walked, Tom asked, 'So, how long have you been here?'

'About six weeks as far as I can tell, but one loses touch. I imagine that you want some sort of assurance that I am who I say I am.'

'I would say that that cuts both ways,' Tom said, remembering that admonition to 'trust no-one!' 'How on earth did you know we were British?'

'Oh, word gets around pretty quickly. I think it was the Russians that knew about you – God knows how. Anyway, in those civvies [civilian clothes], you stand out like the proverbial sore thumb.'

***

Dodkin took Tom to hut 17.

'Be it ever so humble and all that,' said Dodkin. 'I'm afraid the domestic staff have got the day off, so you'll need to take us as you find us.'

The inside of the hut was dark and gloomy and the stench of unwashed bodies and faecal matter made Tom want to retch. The hut had been built for a hundred men, but perhaps 400 were stuffed into it. The bunks were three-high and reached to the ceiling. Each bunk had, perhaps, two feet of headroom. Some bunks held three men; some held four. In some bunks, men lay sleeping, if they were not already dead. It was disgusting.

Dodkin introduced Tom to two men. They were colonels from the Russian army.

'*Der Blockältester kommt!*' ['The Block Elder is coming!'] shouted a voice.

Everyone in the hut tried to look as innocent as they possibly could. The Blockältester was the kapo who was appointed leader of the hut. They were trusted by the SS and, in reciprocation, would pass on any information, titbit, or even suspicion they had. This might secure them an extra week or two of life.

'*Er ist weg.*' ['He's gone.']

The emergence of this very unusual Brit called for the Senior British Officer's presence. Tom sent someone to find him.

'Look, while we're waiting for him, can you just tell us what this place is?'

'Well, it is certainly a slave labour camp, as you can see over at the Gustloff works.'

'Has anyone asked you to do any slave labour?'

'No, not so far. I don't know what that means, I must say.'

'And why are we left in civvy clothing, when everyone else is in these pyjamas with the classification code and number on them?' Dodkin shrugged his shoulders,

Lamason appeared with his usual brisk and breezy walk.

'Pleased to meet you, old boy,' Dodkin said, as he introduced himself.

Tom would have noticed a certain reserve on behalf of Lamason. This was, without doubt, due to the 'trust no one' admonition.

Some five minutes later and outside in the Little Camp, the remainder of the group were amazed to see Dodkin, the Russians and Lamason return with a collection of blankets, warm clothes and wooden clogs for the men to wear. Together with Lamason, they organised a foraging party to round up enough bric à brac to start erecting some primitive tents. In the midst of hell, this was a considerable win.

Dodkin also brought another man with him. This was Alfred Balachowski, an entomologist who had worked with the Resistance and been betrayed to the Gestapo. Due to his medical skills, he was not condemned to death, but was instead employed in hut 46 to work on the development of a vaccine against typhus.

Lamason addressed Dodkin in his customary clipped and direct style. 'Look, old chap. All of this largesse is very kind and all that, but it doesn't actually tell us who you are or which side you are on.'

At this point, Lamason was guarding his second great secret in Buchenwald.

By one of those strange coincidences in life, Phil Lamason actually knew Squadron Leader Kenneth Dodkin of 138 Squadron quite well. He also knew that this was not him. He really had to wonder at what was going on. When he talked to this man, he had a commendable grasp of the detail of Dodkin's life. He knew things like the names of pubs around Dodkin's home station of Royal Air Force Tempsford near Cambridge. He appeared to know common acquaintances. The man even had some of Dodkin's mannerisms. To all appearances, he was Kenneth Dodkin, alive in some surrealistic parallel universe.

But there was another side to all of this. Lamason knew that 138 Squadron and Royal Air Force Tempsford, although nominally under Bomber Command, were involved in things that were not to be talked about or asked about. That, at least, gave the man the benefit of the doubt.

Lamason played along without betraying his misgivings to anyone, least of all to Dodkin. Nevertheless, it was prudent to remind the national commanding officers that they should trust no one 'just on principle, you understand'.

Lamason also sought the advice of Christopher Burney, another Englishman who had, for some bizarre reason, washed up in Buchenwald. Lamason had already found out that Burney was not Royal Air Force but had found an intriguing reason to trust him. Lamason's survival antenna had been energised at the kindness of the Russians in providing building materials and clogs. This was odd. Buchenwald was a place in which kindness was unknown, unimagined and even unasked for. Lamason felt that there had to be an angle behind the Russians' unexpected philanthropy. There most certainly was such an angle.

Burney had put to the Russians that Buchenwald was likely to be liberated by the British or Americans. Their co-operation with the Royal Air Force personnel could go very much in their favour on the day when those other uniforms burst into the camp. This simple but effective diplomatic move told Lamason that despite the instruction to 'trust no-one' Burney was to be trusted.

Burney's story was that he had been picked up by the Gestapo whilst working for some clandestine organisation in France and kept in solitary confinement for 15 months in Fresnes prison to make him talk. Lamason believed that as well. Burney also confirmed to Lamason that Dodkin inhabited that secret world, which was not to be asked about. Burney agreed to pump Dodkin for whatever information he would part with.

Burney was of the opinion that Dodkin was 'on our side' and could be trusted. Despite all the subterfuge, Dodkin and Tom Blackham became good friends in Buchenwald. It is therefore probable that Lamason also asked Blackham to pump Dodkin for information.

Dodkin was not slow to catch on that he was under evaluation. He showed Tom his wrists.

'How about this, then?'

His wrists showed livid red and purple scars. Those scars could not be faked – they had to be earned in a Sicherheitsdienst torture chamber. When Tom talked to him further, it was clear that Dodkin had been taken, as he had himself, first to the avenue that was sealed off by barbed wire and then to a building with a spiral staircase made of iron.

Something else was clear: the SD had moved Tom on very quickly, whereas they had held Dodkin for quite a long time and tortured him appallingly. That said that while Tom was a small fish, Dodkin was a big fish, or at least the Germans thought so.

'Well,' said Dodkin, 'I cannot imagine the locals have been terribly good at etiquette, so let me welcome you to the world of "*Ka-Tzetniks*".'

'The world of what?' Tom laughed.

'My German is not terribly good old boy, but 'KZ', or 'Ka-Tzet', as the Germans have it, it is short for 'concentration camp'. So, 'Ka-Tzetniks' are we lucky few who inhabit the concentration camps. You will notice that the inmates wear striped pyjamas and have a colour coded symbol with their 'Ka-Tzetnik' number. Yellow triangles are Jews, red triangles are political prisoners. Oh and purple triangles are Jehovah's Witnesses. Purple is the colour of repentance apparently. Good to see the goons have a sense of humour.'

'Well, we haven't got a colour coded symbol,' said Lamason. 'And neither have you. What's more, we are all dressed in civvies. We all wonder what the significance of that is.'

'No idea at all, old boy. It seems to mean that we are 'off the books', in some way.'

Whatever it meant was bound to have a sinister connotation. Neither man needed to say it.

Dodkin explained about the camp. 'Right, Tom. Well, as we were saying earlier, this appears to be primarily a slave labour camp, although there are some people here for short stays as 'education prisoners'. Over there is the Gustloff works, which makes armaments for the Luftwaffe. There are Luftwaffe people going in and out all the time. They make anti-aircraft guns there and they are desperate for as many as they can get.'

'Nice to know we're appreciated,' said Tom with a smile. 'How many would you say are in the camp in total, Dodkin?'

'I would guess about the same as a Cup Final crowd at Wembley – about 100,000.' Then, Dodkin added, 'Whatever else happens, though, it is best to keep your heads down. Attracting attention is not good in this place. By the way, you chaps know that Paris has fallen, do you?'

'No,' said Tom. 'No-one tells us anything.'

'It finally fell last week. There was no fighting – the German general just declared the city open and our chaps moved in. The Free French got to head the parade down the Champs Élysées, which was a nice touch. Adolf must have been fuming!'

'Christ,' said Tom. 'They got us out just as the first allied forces were moving on Paris. We could hear the guns in the distance.'

'Any idea about the eastern front?'

'Yes,' said Dodkin. 'The Russians have occupied Romania and Romania has dropped out of the war. The Japanese are in full flight in India. All in all, the other side have only got one option: cease fire and ask for the best terms available.'

'If any,' added a voice.

'Where do you get your information from, if I might ask?'

'Alfred Balachowski,' said Dodkin. 'You've already met him. He is a scientist. The Germans are forcing him to work on an experimental programme to find a vaccine for typhus. I would trust him with my life. If you are going to trust me, you are going to trust him. He listens to the BBC radio, which is strictly a death sentence if you are caught. The SS are dependent on him for typhus research, so blind eyes are turned, if you get the drift. Oh, and they're also dependent on him for real news – no one believes what the German propaganda radio tells them anymore.'

When the men returned from further 'recces', Lamason, Tom and the other commanding officers took further debriefs from them.

'We found some very strange places, sir. There is something very odd about hut 2.'

'There most definitely is something extremely odd about hut 2,' added Dodkin. 'That is the pathology hut. Just keep away from it.'

'What do they do there?' asked one of the men.

'Well, if you really want to know, it is where they make lampshades out of prisoners' tattoos. They have shrunken heads in there of Russian prisoners of war and tanned human skin that they make wallets out of. Oh, and down in the basement, they are making soap from human fat. Avoid hut 2, old man – avoid it! Oh, and Phil, if any of your men have tattoos, tell them to hide them from the guards. They might finish up as lampshades.

'Christ almighty. Is there any kind of depravity that these people are not capable of?'

'Oddly enough, there are limits,' Dodkin replied brightly. 'There was a chap here a while ago – one of the guard non-commissioned officers, called Sommer apparently. His speciality was to single out priests and crucify them upside down, which he thought was massively funny. He was removed from the job, however.'

'Was he punished?'

'Don't believe so. They just transferred him somewhere else.'

∗∗∗

Dodkin and Tom Blackham were beginning to trust each other and got on well. Blackham was in for perhaps the greatest surprise of his life.

Lamason, Tom and the other commanding officers now had two immediate problems. Firstly, they had to organise the men either into one of the improvised huts or transfer them into one of the existing but horribly overcrowded huts. Any hut, no matter how bad, would be better than sleeping in the open air on cobblestones.

They also had to make a final decision as to whether they could trust Dodkin. Tom's instinct said 'yes', but he was faced with the difficulty of recognising reality enmeshed in a crazed, dreamlike universe, where things could happen that were not merely bad, but the products of perfectly legal, unhinged minds.

Lamason came to see Tom. 'Tom, you're obviously getting on with Dodkin. I'd be indebted if you could you just get him to open up just a bit more. I would like to think he is who he says he is, but we've all met Captain Jacques and after encounters with that gentleman, trust comes slowly and with great effort.'

***

Dodkin, for his part, seemed to be perfectly happy to chat on any subject. Over the next few days, several of the Flight Lieutenants engaged him in idle and innocent conversation. Reports came back to Lamason that Dodkin had lived in France. Not only that, but he spoke French that was so perfect that any Frenchmen would take him for French. The rumour was that Dodkin had apparently fled France after the German invasion and gone to England. He had been educated in an English private school, but Lamason and Tom knew that already from his accent. But did that make him English or French? If he fled France and was French, why did he sound like an Englishman? All of this triggered a dim memory in Tom's mind. What was it? It was something he had heard when he was with the Resistance.

'He may call himself Squadron Leader,' said one of the information gatherers. 'But he says he is in 138 Squadron. If I remember, they fly Halifaxes. In my opinion, he can't tell an aileron from a mid-upper turret.'

'Don't worry about that too much,' said Lamason. 'He told me as much himself.'

'Well, if he isn't from Bomber Command, how does he come to be on-the-run in occupied France?'

'I don't know,' said Lamason. 'But don't let's damn him out of hand at this stage.'

'He seems to be an expert in ladies' dresses,' reported another of the gentle interrogators. 'He said they had made dresses for Vivien Leigh, Marlene Dietrich and Greta Garbo. If he is involved in ladies' clothes, do you suppose he is a homosexualist?'

'No idea,' said Lamason. 'But what about the war?'

'Well,' said another of the interrogators, 'he may not know much about the Royal Air Force, but he knows an awful lot about the Resistance. He is usually very open when he talks, but when he gets onto that subject, he suddenly clams shut. He appears to have made several trips to different parts of France and to have had some sort of organising role. He also seems to have used different names. He especially seems to know about the teams that go around murdering Germans.'

This tweaked Tom's curiosity even more. 'Sir, I would like to try something on Dodkin. Can I have the next go at him please?'

'Certainly, Tom. Report back when you've got something.'

***

'Ah, Tom!' said Dodkin with a knowing grin, as they strolled in a casual manner around the compound.

'You've come to pump me for information like your other chappies?'

They both laughed.

'Perfectly understandable, old boy. Quite tickety-boo.'

'OK, Dodkin. I just wondered if you knew of a guy called Shelley?'

Dodkin looked Tom pointedly in the eyes and laughed the laugh of a man found out. Tom had scored a hit.

'You know him?'

Dodkin suppressed a laugh. 'I am him, you silly bugger. I'm Shelley.'

This was an astonishing revelation, but wasn't it dangerous to admit it in this place?

'Oh, don't worry. The Huns know that I'm Shelley, so if you have any stool pigeons in your ranks, they won't get any medals for unmasking me.'

'You're the guy who organised the Resistance? I was with the Resistance for some weeks and they talked of you as a leader all the time.'

'Well, among others, there was Jean Moulin as well and Guingouin and several other people.'

Tom must have been extremely pleased to have found Shelley – the man that hardened Resistance men spoke of with awe. At least he understood why Squadron Leader Dodkin knew nothing about the air force. He wasn't in it. Precisely, who Dodkin worked for had to remain a mystery, which Tom would have understood perfectly.

***

Later that day, Tom reported back to Lamason.

'Did he bite on that poet's name that you mentioned, Tom? What was it? Byron?'

'It was Shelley. And yes, he is Shelley. As soon as I asked him, he bit immediately. He said "Yes, I am Shelley and the Germans know that, so I can tell you".'

'What the heck does that mean?'

'What it means sir, is quite incredible. The Resistance people spoke of him, although I don't think any had actually met him. It means that he is the guy who went to see Churchill...'

'What? Winston Churchill?'

'He went to see Winston Churchill to ask for more aircraft, weapons and so forth to help the French resistance and Churchill backed him.'

'How do you know this?'

'One of the Resistance men at Troyes knew about him. He said he was a brilliant organiser. He is totally fearless and very resourceful. What's more, his reputation is that he is capable of almost anything. He was betrayed by an informer for money.'

'Was he betrayed by that Captain Jacques creature who betrayed most of us?'

'No, I asked him that. It was someone else. There seem to be a lot of traitors in France.'

***

Blackham was to become a close friend of Dodkin, or Shelley, or whoever he was, at Buchenwald. His memoir also pays special tribute to Doctor Balachowski.

24

Dodkin's Madcap Plan

They were to discover that Dodkin indeed was resourceful. He was the rare kind of man who appears capable of dreaming up the most outrageous plans and then persuading people to help him carry them out.

Tom was destined to know some of this, but not all of it. That would be the subject of Lamason's third secret.

After some ten days in the camp, Dodkin asked Lamason for a meeting with himself and the national commanding officers. They were to meet in a corner of the Little Camp, away from the guard towers and appear to be doing nothing very much. Tom Blackham would have been included in the group.

'Right, Dodkin. Here we are! What are we here for?' said Lamason, in his brisk and businesslike manner.

'I have a plan for an escape and I think we can do it,' said Dodkin, with his usual upbeat confidence.

There was little to lose. They might as well hear him out.

'Stage 1, we fight our way out: the Russians have some weapons and will come in with us. Stage 2, once we are outside, there is nothing very much to stop us getting a short distance away. Stage 3, working parties tell us that eight miles away, there is a small airfield called Nohra. It is something of a Luftwaffe backwater and is poorly guarded. Stage 4, we have enough pilots and navigators to pinch some aircraft and fly them westwards until we are over allied lines.'

'How do we get past the guards?'

'We shoot our way out. We will have surprise on our side. In the middle of the night, the guards will not be able to use the heavy machine guns for fear of hitting their own men.'

'How do we get to Nohra?'

'We steal some vehicles; hot-wire them, if necessary.'

'There is one thing that we do need to worry about,' said Lamason. 'There is one of the American chaps with us, Sergeant Scharf. I have seen him speak to the guards in German. I am concerned that he may be a plant.'

'We can always work around him.'

'And if we fail?' someone is bound to have asked.

'It hardly seems to matter. I doubt if any of us are going to survive this anyway.'

It did not matter who had said this. The sense of their imminent murder did not need elaboration. Every one of the Royal Air Force men in that hell-on-earth understood that reality and understood it well.

***

Dodkin, Lamason and the commanding officers began detailed planning immediately.

The first task was to find out where the allied lines were. Balachowski was able to provide that information easily from his secret radio. Most of Belgium was now in allied hands. If they could fly as far as Hitler's Siegfried Line, on the border between Belgium and the Reich, then they were home. Navigators estimated it was 600 kilometres: the equivalent distance from London to Glasgow. Heck! That was a long haul in broad daylight with the Luftwaffe after you! But, if they stayed put, they were going to die.

The proposition was one of risk versus one of certainty.

'Well, you chaps, is this thing on?' asked Lamason to his coterie of national commanding officers.

'Might as well,' was the consensus.

There was nothing to lose. If they failed, then death would be painful, but quick, as opposed to agonising and long and drawn out. The prospect of dying in some spirit of defiance and dignity held an undeniable appeal.

342

***

The next thing was to plot the easiest route to the outside. That was across the main compound and though the administration block.

However, they would need teams armed with crow-bars to break down doors.

Dodkin brought the Russians in to find out what weaponry they could offer.

***

During the afternoon of 9 September, however, events took place that were to have a devastating effect on morale.

It had all started innocently enough. The camp loudspeaker boomed out and gave an apparently innocuous order.

'*Achtung! Achtung! Achtung!* ['Attention! Attention! Attention!'] The following men from hut 17 are to report immediately to the guard tower.'

It gave the names of 16 men, two of whom – Hubble and Kane – were close friends of Dodkin. It seems that no-one thought very much of this order.

'Probably some sort of identity check,' was the received wisdom.

However, that night, the named men did not return. Nor did they return the day afterwards.

Lamason and Blackham found Dodkin in a state of grief on the following day. The Polish network had got word via Balachowski to Dodkin that the men had been taken into the guard tower and, one by one, beaten until they were almost – but not quite – senseless. Then, still conscious, they were put into torture bins. These were brick structures, in which a man could not stand up or lie down. They were carefully constructed so that over time, the stress into which the body was forced caused immense pain. They had been left there for hours.

'What the hell for? We had all this interrogation stuff with the Sicherheitsdienst,' Dodkin had said to Balachowski.

'This was not for intelligence gathering,' said Balachowski. 'This was for fun.' Now they knew what those mysterious rooms in the guard tower were used for.

Worse was to follow. At Major Schobert's command, when the men were taken out of the torture bins, they were taken in the dead of night to a cellar next to the crematorium. Inside the cellar, they were hung with wire nooses on hooks so that they took hours to die. They were put into the furnaces when they were dead.

'Well,' added Balachowski, 'They were dead if they were lucky.'

***

The implications of this were clear. This was going to be the fate of all of them. It was merely a matter of how many men could be hanged on hooks for hours per day in that cellar. Balachowski confirmed that he had heard some of SS officers discussing this.

'Come on, old man,' said Lamason to Dodkin. 'What about your Russian chums? Is there anything about the firearms that they are supposed to have squirreled away?'

The Russians had not come up with the goods. Dodkin could not say with any certainty that they ever had any weapons. Without weapons, any attempt at escape was simply suicide.

***

Now, every few days, they heard the dreaded announcement.

'*Achtung! Achtung! Achtung!* ['Attention! Attention! Attention!'] The following prisoners from hut number 21 must present themselves immediately to the guard tower.'

Each time, they knew the fear of God. But each time, it was not for Lamason's men. How long would it be?

***

A few days later, Lamason found Blackham.

'Tom, have you heard the news about Dodkin?'

'No? What's happened?'

'He has come down with typhus and gone to hut 46. Poor bugger. He'll be dead in a couple of days.'

'Christ, can we visit him?'

'Balachowski says not. If we go into hut 46, the SS will want to kill us straight away because we could be typhus carriers. He says he will give our best wishes to him, though.'

'Christ, Phil. That is a loss. It is a real loss. I did like his madcap scheme though.'

'We are going to have to do something though, Tom. If they call us to the guard tower, we know what will happen. We have to organise a last stand. Even if we go down in a hail of machine gun bullets, it will be quicker than the alternative and we will maintain some dignity as well.'

'Right, sir. I cannot see that we have more than a couple of weeks left. Let's get our heads together on a last stand. If possible, we should try and take a few of the buggers with us. One thing we have on our side is surprise.'

And so saying, Lamason, Blackham and the flight lieutenants began work on a plan for a last stand, which would be activated when they heard those dreadful words *Achtung! Achtung!* and their names were read out.

***

Over the next few days, more men were called to the guard tower. On each occasion, the men were never seen again. The crematorium chimney continued to belch out greasy, black smoke 24 hours a day. The stench of burned human flesh was ever present.

Morale plummeted. There was no way out and Dodkin, with his bout of typhus, was luckier than most. After some days, logic said that he must already be dead.

They did not see Balachowski, either. No-one knew what had happened to him.

25

Alarm! Alarm!

On the afternoon of 15 October, the air raid sirens blared out across the camp.

'Alarm! Alarm!' shouted the guards over the camp loudspeakers.

The SS guards and civilian administrators ran in desperation for the air raid shelters. There were, obviously, no shelters for the prisoners, who would just have to take their chances. A quick death through bombing was, in any case, highly preferably to the horrors of the guard tower, typhus, or, especially, the 'zoo'.

'Is there a chance of escape?' Blackham must have wondered.

However, the guards in the sentry boxes remained at their posts. Enough guards stayed in the compounds to shoot anyone who might have had ambitions of escape.

The loudspeaker also blared out an order that all prisoners were to stay in their huts or be shot immediately. This brought out a wry smile in the Little Camp, where there were no huts to stay inside.

Then, Blackham saw them. High in the sky at about 15,000 feet (4,600 metres), there were the dark green shapes of the massive American B17s.

'There they are, Phil! Isn't that wonderful? That is the most joyful sight I've seen since I got shot down. Come on you, beauties! Flatten this whole bloody place and send these bastards to hell.'

'God, Tom, would you look at that? We're here in the middle of Germany and they have got fighter escorts. I never once had a fighter escort in 45 operations.'

'Me neither! The fighters must be the new Mustangs that we've heard so much about. When I was on the run in France, I palled-up with a guy called Neville Mutters who flew them. He said the Mustangs were the next generation of fighters beyond the Spitfires and some of them had long range tanks for operations over Germany. But look at those formations. They are perfect! They have actually got from England to here without losing a single aircraft. What does that tell you?'

'It tells me the Luftwaffe is out of the sky.'

They smiled at each other. Their own situation may be dire, but the situation for the Herrenvolk was not looking too bright either. Each man must have experienced a quiet satisfaction, knowing he had played a part in that.

The pure white condensation trails behind the B17s left livid white slash marks across the celestial blue autumnal sky.

'Yep! It means the Hun can hardly get an aircraft into the air to have a go at a sitting target like that.'

The B17s drew closer. Would they head for the Gustloff factory, or go somewhere else? Could they be heading for the chemical works at Jena, or the munitions factories at Leipzig?

'Christ, Phil. I think they're coming here, you know! How many of them do you reckon there are?'

'400, I should think, or 500.'

The white condensation trails were now heading straight for the camp.

'I am going to enjoy this so much.'

'Wonder if we'll survive it.'

'Who cares?' They shrugged their shoulders and smiled again.

The aircraft were too high to see if bomb doors were open, but small black dots began to drop from the underbellies. Those were bombs. They watched as the first dots plunged rapidly through the air, heading vaguely towards the camp, but they fell short. They exploded with a massive boom. Debris from the explosion spattered across the camp.

'Five hundred pounders, I should say,' said Blackham. 'That's the trouble with the B17. A Lancaster can carry 14,000-pound (6350-kg) of bombs, but the B17 struggles with 5000. God, I wish they could drop some of our 4000-pound cookies on this place.'

More bombs fell. The explosions were coming closer and closer to the camp.

'Get down!'

Bombs fell on the parade ground and then, bullseye! A stick of bombs hit the Gustloff factory, sending debris hundreds of feet into the air. Cheering broke out from the Royal Air Force ranks. It was joyful, it was heartfelt, it was triumphant.

'Come on, you Yanks! Plaster the bloody place!'

If the entire situation was not so life-threatening, the men who took part in that exhilarating display would have said it was almost like a football match. Some huts had been hit by bombs. The SS barracks was hit too, which raised the biggest cheer of all.

'*Halt das verfluchte maul!*' ['Shut your damned mouth!'] screamed a terrified SS guard from the tower.

'What are you going to do, you German bastard? Shoot us and put us out of our misery?'

More bombs dropped. More debris went up into the air. More debris – and bodies and body parts –

dropped across the parade ground, the huts and the Little Camp.

The factory was on fire now. Thick brown smoke came from its broken roof, flames leapt into the air and glass shattered. The flames roared into the air, sparked by hundreds of small incendiary bombs.

The camp's fire-service was overwhelmed and could do little to put the fires out. Fire appliances from outside the camp arrived, but it was no good. The factory had lost its roof, the walls were smashed and the machinery inside must have been pulverised.

The ever-present smell of human death from the crematorium chimney was overcome by the acrid stench of burning German war effort.

And how the Royal Air Force men cheered!

***

After a terrific ten minutes of dropping death and destruction onto Hitler's Thousand Year Reich, the dark green armada of B17s and Mustangs turned slowly south east, then south, then westwards and back to Blighty.

'Give my love to England, you Yanks!' shouted a voice.

'Have a pint for me down the Dog and Duck!'

The roaring of the aircraft receded but the roaring of the fires in the factory kept going.

The fires burned all afternoon, all evening and all night. The crematorium operators had taken shelter wherever they could. The crematorium, for once, was cold. Unfortunately, the crematorium had not been hit.

Morale among the Royal Air Force men was now back high. They might not survive but, oh boy! They had seen the enemy given a very bloody nose. Their euphoria was tempered by the dead bodies of pyjama-clad prisoners strewn around the camp.

'You can't even feel sorry for them. Their suffering's over.'

***

To everyone's dismay, the squat crematorium chimney began to belch out its evil miasma once again the next day and resumed its 24-hour shifts. Firstly, they burned the dozens of dead from the air raid. Then, they resumed burning all the other dead from the daily death toll.

Tom must, at about this time, have thought, 'Dodkin finished up going through that bloody chimney. May he rest in peace.'

***

A couple of days later, one of the Royal Air Force men came to Lamason.

'There's an interesting thing happening, sir. Might be worth having a look at. It's some sort of deputation looking over the bomb damage.'

'Well, I wasn't doing an awful lot else. Let's have a shufty.'

Several of the Royal Air Force men strolled over to where the Gustloff works, still smouldering in some parts, was being inspected.

'Look at those uniforms, Phil! They're not SS. They're dark blue, a bit like ours. What are they?'

'Those are Luftwaffe uniforms, I think. It's odd, when you come to think of it, because those are the buggers that shot me down, but I've never actually seen one of their chaps in uniform in the flesh, so to speak.'

The Luftwaffe deputation was clearly there to assess the bomb damage and the impact on the production of aircraft armaments. It looked considerable. Most of the factory was out of action, but some few machine shops still struggled to carry out operations. The rail spur was a devil's jumble of twisted rail lines, upended locomotives and rolling stock, which meant that finished weapons could not be moved out, nor could new materials be brought in.

Balachowski had told them that the factory was making a range of armaments. As the Luftwaffe had sent people here, it presumably meant that they were manufacturing machine guns for fighter aircraft or flak guns for anti-aircraft batteries. If the fighters and batteries did not have guns, they could not harass British and American bombers.

'How on earth did our side even know there was a plant here?' asked one airman.

'Never mind that,' said Lamason. 'Let's just keep an eye on those blokes in the blue uniforms.'

'Have you got an idea, Phil?'

'Not sure yet, but let's see what pans out. Oh, do something for me, if you would. Go and find Sergeant Scharf, the American chap who speaks German.'

***

After a half hour or so, the Luftwaffe deputation finished the inspection.

Kommandant Pister escorted them over to the main camp. Lamason watched as the camp gates opened into the compound, where the Royal Air Force men stood waiting.

The SS guards ushered the Luftwaffe officers through and into the main compound. The guards gave a smart 'Heil Hitler!' salute. The Luftwaffe men returned it, pointedly, with a military salute.

Lamason gathered around him as many men as he could, which amounted to several dozen. On Lamason's order, they sauntered casually, but on a carefully thought-out collision course with the Luftwaffe men.

They speeded up their saunter, timing their movement to reach the Luftwaffe men before the outnumbered guards could stop them. They sauntered faster and faster. The guards began to notice them but had not yet had time to react.

'Now!' shouted Lamason.

On Lamason's command, one of the airmen, Sergeant Scharf, ran towards the Luftwaffe men. The SS guards screamed 'Halt!' but were not going to shoot without the Kommandant's order.

The guards ran forward. As they did so, a dozen men ran between them and the Luftwaffe deputation. The guards cursed them, but the Kommandant did not want to commit murder in front of people who could report it on the outside. In Nazi Germany, what went on in 'those places' was kept secret from a largely unsuspecting civilian population.

More guards ran forward to intercept the American but, on Lamason's command, another dozen ran forward to hold the guards back.

The Luftwaffe deputation were taken aback at this unusual turn of events and were quite speechless when the American ran up to them.

'Please help us! We are allied airmen who were shot down on military operations and are in the hands of the SS. They are going to kill us all horribly. Please help us and get us into a proper prisoner of war camp.'

The senior Luftwaffe man was quite astonished.

'What nationalities are you?'

'American, British, Canadian, Australian, New Zealand and others, but we were all on operations. We should be covered by the Geneva Conventions and should not be in the hands of these SS butchers.'

The Luftwaffe man looked to the Kommandant. The Kommandant looked embarrassed and menacing. He nodded and tried to say something light-hearted to the senior Luftwaffe officer, though his face-saving quip appeared to fail. The Luftwaffe officer looked uncomfortable. He did not accept Pister's gambit, and this was quite clear.

The Senior Luftwaffe officer spoke to the American.

'It is no secret that the Luftwaffe and the SS do not generally get on well, but I will see what I can do for you. I am unable to make any promises.'

'Thank you. If you get us out of here, you will save our lives.

You will uphold the honour of German soldiers.'

The prisoners looked defiantly at the Kommandant, who remained incandescently impassive. The Luftwaffe deputation looked blank with amazement. There was no doubt that the Luftwaffe men felt that serving airmen should not be in these places.

***

After the Luftwaffe men had left, there came the inevitable question.

'Think it will work, sir?' asked Blackham to Lamason.

'Don't know, Tom. It's all we've got.'

There were no reprisals from the SS for having made the appeal.

'Why would they bother with reprisals?' said Blackham. 'We're slated for death anyway.'

26

Dodkin Survives

Squadron Leader Kenneth Harold William Dodkin – the real one, not the man in the camp – was alive and living in England's green and pleasant land. He had been taken off operations in 1940 after being wounded in action. After he was invalided out, some men in plain clothes had approached him and asked for a most unusual favour.

'Shelley' was thus briefed in detail to take over Dodkin's identity. Dodkin was happy to share his identity, as it would mask the real name of the man who was taking it.

Shelley had been quite happy to share his pseudonym with Tom Blackham. It is most unlikely that he would share his real name, or the top-secret organisation for which he worked. Had he told Tom Blackham the name of the organisation, he would not have recognised it.

Shelley's real name was Forest Frederick Edward Yeo-Thomas. He saw himself as British, although his family had lived in France since 1855. At the outbreak of the war, he was 38 years old and a director of Molyneux, a prestigious fashion house. He had been recruited into the organisation known as the Special Operations Executive.

The Special Operations Executive had approached Kenneth Dodkin to share his identity with Yeo-Thomas, along with a false family history to go with it. This was so that, if captured, his real identity would not lead to the Gestapo arresting every member of the Molyneux fashion house and, indeed, everyone that he knew in Paris. When Yeo-Thomas became Dodkin, it was a move to protect some hundreds of quite innocent people.

The Germans knew all about 'Shelley' and what he had done. This was not secret. Yeo-Thomas' real name was most definitely secret.

***

It was clear to the fake Dodkin in Buchenwald Concentration Camp that he was unlikely to survive. He very much wanted to live, but also someone needed to survive to tell the soon-to-be victorious allied powers what the Germans had been up to in 'these places'.

He needed a stratagem. His ingenious plan seems to come from a psychological stew of logic, intuition and – who knows?-divine inspiration. Perhaps it is the just the outcome of the adage that 'necessity is the mother of invention'.

Dodkin worked with his good friend Balachowski, who was forced by the SS to work on a vaccine against typhus in hut 46, the 'guinea pig block'.

Dodkin asked Balachowski to arrange a meeting with Sturmbannführer [Major] Erwin Ding-Schuler, head of the typhus experiments. This man also had the prestige of being a personal friend of Heinrich Himmler. Ding-Schuler was another medical practitioner brought into the concentration camp system and given an SS rank. Although a psychopathic and sadistic murderer, Ding-Schuler was not a career SS man.

'Germany is losing the war,' Dodkin put to Ding-Schuler. 'If the allies catch you after what you have been doing, you will hang.'

Ding-Schuler listened attentively but could not disagree.

'What I propose is that you save the lives of some men, on the understanding that they will testify on your behalf in the inevitable military court. It could make the difference between kicking on the end of a rope and a prison sentence. There is a clear alternative. When the war is over, you could try to disappear. It is a simple question of which alternative offers you the lower risk.'

Ding-Schuler was quiet again, he asked, 'And how would you propose to achieve this?'

Inwardly, Dodkin felt a note of triumph. Ding-Schuler could see some merit in the idea. Dodkin was offering him a lifeline and Ding-Schuler was biting on it.

Dodkin told him the plan. Ding-Schuler said he would consider it and get back to him.

***

A couple of days later, Ding-Schuler summoned Dodkin to his office. He got straight to the point.

'These are the terms. I will let this plan go ahead for three men, of which you must be one. As you are trusting me, I will trust you, but I will expect you to speak on my behalf.'

'You have my word.'

'There is another condition. You must arrange the complicity of Dietzsch, the kapo of hut 46. It is of the essence that you do it separately. Dietzsch must not know of my part in this plot.'

The reason for this was evident: if Ding-Schuler was known to be collaborating with a prisoner, then he himself would soon be dead. Also, if Dietzsch knew of Ding-Schuler's collaboration, he could betray it to the camp's commandant and receive a valuable reward, such as a few more weeks of life.

Ding-Schuler's condition raised a dangerous roadblock for Dodkin. Artur Dietzsch was known to be a sadistic thug who very much enjoyed his work – which, in essence was to kill people slowly. He was graded as a 'Funktionshäftling' or 'trusty'.

He had lived in various concentration camps for 20 years, as a reward for his earlier communist sympathies. His time in these camps had stripped him of humanity. By now, he was a sinister individual. His eyes have been described as 'grey and cold and hard' and that his 'shaven skull glistened like a paving stone'.

Another complicating factor was that Dietzsch spoke no English or French and Dodkin spoke little German. The approach had to be made via Balachowski and Kogon, who was Ding-Schuler's secretary. Balachowski reported back quickly that Dietzsch had immediately – and surprisingly – agreed to take part in the plan. His motivation was by no means clear, but the circumstances dictated that there was no chance of a deep discussion about it. All they could do was trust Dietzsch and hope he would not betray them.

***

Under Balachowski's supervision, Dietzsch gave Dodkin an injection which, some hours later, would induce a high fever that would resemble the symptoms of typhus.

Dodkin returned to his block, knowing that he could take two others with him. It is unclear how he made his choices, but the two who he chose were Harry Pueleve, an Englishman (despite the name) and

Stephane Hessel, a German. Dodkin told them that they had been chosen for escape.

The next part of the plan was that he would disappear the next day. Then, a few days later, each would receive word from Balachowski that all was well and they too should go to hut 46. There, they would also be given an injection to bring on the faked symptoms of typhus. This would be their passport out.

The time delay was a clever device to make sure that Dietzsch did not double cross him and kill him. If Dietz did indeed betray Dodkin, then no word would come from Balachowski.

***

Two hours later, Dodkin reported to the Blockältester that he had a fever and felt unwell.

A Czech doctor found his temperature was 40.7. He was taken immediately to block 46.

What he found in block 46 surprised him greatly. He was shown into a private room. It was clean. There were proper beds. Even the beds were clean and not a sea of bug-infested filth, which was the case in the rest of the camp. There was a washroom with baths. At one end, was a padlocked door, which led to the mortuary. On the opposite side of a central corridor was a large ward with some 20 patients, all of whom were going to die in the next few days.

364

The medical orderlies were male and wore the regulation blue and white striped pyjama-like uniforms. The badge on their jacket was an inverted green triangle. This signified that they were career criminals, with, presumably, no medical experience of any kind.

Nevertheless, they took away Dodkin's filthy rags and burned them. They gave him a bath. It was his first bath in six months. Despite the fever, it felt so wonderfully luxurious. They put him into white nightshirt and lay him down in the clean bed. It was utter, utter luxury!

***

Dodkin's symptoms worsened rapidly. His teeth were now chattering uncontrollably and his limbs were trembling violently.

The orderlies called for Dietzsch.

'Typhus!' pronounced Dietzsch. 'Wrap cold wet sheets around him to bring the fever down.'

The orderlies did so and went off duty. When they had left, Dietzsch returned to give him a booster injection.

When the orderlies returned the next day, they found the fever had returned. Dietzsch ordered more cold sheet treatment. The orderlies now clearly believed that Dodkin was stricken with typhus.

Dodkin received a brief and perfunctory visit from Kogon, Ding-Schuler's secretary. He brought a pencil and paper. Dodkin wrote on the paper, 'OK to come now'. To this, he added a code word. It was a summons for Pueleve and Hessel to join him.

Pueleve and Hessel went through the same routine as had Dodkin. As far as the orderlies were concerned, they too had typhus and were doomed for an early death.

***

It was now time to activate the next part of the plan. Ding-Schuler immediately transferred the orderlies onto other duties far from hut 46. He brought in two new ones, who did not know who was in the hut.

Before the new orderlies could arrive, Ding-Schuler moved Dodkin, Pueleve and Hessel rapidly to a room upstairs, which was formerly used as a bedroom. Ding-Schuler told them to remain quiet, make no noise and at all costs, not be seen. In a place like Buchenwald, they could well imagine the consequence of non-compliance.

The room, in which they found themselves, was sparse and functional. Still, after the privations of the prison block from which they had come, the three hopeful escapers found the accommodation congenial beyond imagination. They found playing-cards there and played bridge and a variant of Ludo, which they called 'Silly Buggers'.

Dietzsch, the murderous kapo and psychopath of a hundred murders, proved to have a kind side to him. He brought them books to read and, sometimes, cigarettes. Perhaps there was just a semblance of residual humanity still smouldering in his ruined psyche.

Despite the considerable upgrade, there remained one extremely unpleasant aspect to the new luxury accommodation. It overlooked the Little Camp, where the airmen were still sleeping on cobblestones and with little shelter after a month. Dodkin could also see Jews in the Little Camp, who had been left there with no food or sustenance to starve to death. He could also see the Jews being marched out in the morning for slave labour, to repair the enormous damage to the Gustloff armament works. At night, they would stagger back, carrying their dead. There was another hut which he could see, where Jewish inmates were packed in so tightly that no one could sit down or lie down. Each day, several died standing up.

***

They had now to wait for the next part of the plot to unfold. Now, they needed three people – preferably two Frenchmen and a German – to die.

Ding-Schuler found just the men to play their unwitting part: Maurice Choquet, Marcel Seigneur and Michel Boitel. They had contracted typhus and were going to die. They were all French, but desperate men cannot afford to be fussy.

Ding-Schuler had them transferred to block 46, 'in order to prevent an epidemic'. They waited patiently for the men to die. All three put up a tremendous fight. It was beyond frustrating! They would not die and instead, for some unfathomable reason, clung irritatingly to the torments and purgatory of their existence.

***

Matters turned sharply for the worse.

Over the loudspeakers came that chilling and terrifying order once again: 'The following prisoners from Block 17 should present themselves to the tower immediately...'

One of them was Puelevé, but Puelevé was not present in his hut where he should have been. To make matters even worse, Ding-Schuler had made a trip into Weimar on his motorbike and was not present either to arrange a quick solution to this new and potentially deadly situation.

The solution needed to come from Dietzsch. It was comforting that Dietzsch was now so implicated in the plot that to betray it would, in effect, bring about his own suicide.

He approached Kommandant Pister.

'Herr Kommandant, the prisoner Pueleveé is in the typhus hospital and on the point of death. He is physically unable to even walk to the tower.'

'Very well, Dietzsch, then I will send two men and a stretcher to carry him to the tower.'

Whether Pauleveé was or was not dying of typhus, Pister still intended that he would suffer the endless death agonies that he had prescribed for him. This gave Dietzsch an immediate problem. When the stretcher bearers arrived, they would see easily enough that Pauleveé was not suffering from typhus and then questions – life-threatening ones – would be asked.

Dashing back to hut 46, Dietzsch gave Pauleveé a booster injection to bring on the symptoms of typhus. This would take time.

Within a half hour, a stretcher party, supervised by a Scharführer [SS sergeant], was knocking on the door.

'You're going to have to think of something quickly,' said Dodkin.

Pauleveé had no symptoms at all. Dietzsch had to be resourceful.

He went to the door. 'Herr Scharführer, I cannot release this man to you without the express order of Sturmbannführer Doktor Ding-Schuler.'

'The Kommandant's order has precedence over the Sturmbannführer's,' said the unimpressed Scharführer.

'My order is to bring him back on the stretcher to the tower.'

The stretcher party departed back to the Kommandant's office for further orders.

***

Before they could return, Ding-Schuler roared up on his motorcycle to see that the Kommandant had now sent an ambulance to convey Paulevé to the tower. Ding-Schuler powered his motorcycle quickly over to the Kommandant's office.

'It is inhumane to execute a man who is about to die from typhus,' pleaded Ding-Schuler.

At this point, the plot was starting to unravel. It seemed very odd to the Kommandant that this man was starting to use laughable words like 'inhumane'. Erwin Ding-Schuler had committed hundreds of sadistic but quite legal murders under the guise of medical experiments. He was always perfectly happy in his murderous work and had previously been quite unencumbered with notions of philanthropy or human decency.

'We are not here to practise benevolence,' insisted Pister, in that irritated voice that superiors display when forced with a subordinate who questions completely reasonable instructions. 'Orders are orders! We are here to follow orders. Bring him to the tower.'

Ding-Schuler was becoming positively sweaty and prickly under the silver death's head motive on his grey-green uniform. He needed to think quickly. He could see one final gambit before the entire plot fell apart. It was to be a 'do or die' moment.

'There is one rather tricky consideration,' he said. He said it dispassionately, deliberately and thoughtfully, as the sweat trickled inside his uniform jacket. 'If we bring this man through the camp, it is completely possible that he will spread typhus through the entire prison and SS population. More to the point any such outbreak could quite easily prevent the Gustloff factory from reopening. It is my view, as a medical practitioner, that such a dangerous journey has the potential to wipe out a large proportion – if not all – of the camp.'

Pister hesitated. An inner sense of prudence reminded him forcibly that Ding-Schuler was a personal friend of Heinrich Himmler, the head of the SS. If such an outbreak did occur, then Pister would be held responsible for ignoring Ding-Schuler's advice. Pister did not know what the consequences would be. He was, however, quite sure that he would not like them.

'Well, have him shot inside hut 46.'

'I have just the man to do it. Herr Kommandant. Heil Hitler!' Ding-Schuler breathed an imperceptible but deeply felt sigh of relief.

'Heil Hitler, Herr Sturmbannführer. Abtreten!' ['Dismissed!'] said Pister, with the hang-dog air of a man who knew that he had been bested.

***

The plot was back in business.

Back at hut 46, Ding-Schuler gave the job to a Scharführer called Wilhelm (surname not known). During his time in Buchenwald, Wilhelm had earned a reputation for a certain connoisseurship in the fields of cruelty and murder. *'Jawohl, Herr Sturmbannführer. Zum befehl.'* ['Certainly, sir. At your command.']

As it happened, Wilhelm also had earned himself a reputation for extreme drunkenness. Ding-Schuler thoughtfully offered the man a generous glass of Schnapps to fortify him for his task.

'Noch einmal?' ['One more?'] he asked Wilhelm.

'Gerne!' ['I'd love to!'] said Wilhelm.

Then Wilhelm accepted another glass, then another and another, until the bottle was empty and Wilhelm could barely stand, focus his eyes, or even stay awake. Ding-Schuler steered Wilhelm into the hospital ward, where the first of the three men destined for the swap had just died. The body in the bed was that of Seigneur.

'This one,' said Ding-Schuler, as the other inmates in the ward looked on in abject horror.

Wilhelm took out his service revolver and fired a number of shots. Whether the bullets went into the corpse, the bed, the wall, the ceiling, or the other prisoners is not recorded by history. Paulevé became Seigneur.

***

The next morning, Wilhelm staggered to the Kommandant's office in a state of extreme hangover, reporting that he had personally murdered Paulevé.

'*Gut gemacht! Abtreten!*' ['Well done! Dismissed!'] said Pister.

Now, they had to wait for the other two Frenchmen – Choquet and Boitel – to die. Ding-Schuler suggested that this could be achieved quite easily. He could just have them shot. However, Dodkin, Hessel and Paulevé (happily recovered) would not hear of it. The SS man was going to be heavily dependent on their testament at a trial in the semi-distant future, so agreed that, on balance, shooting them might not be the best solution. Further murders would not play well for him in a courtroom.

During this waiting period, Dodkin had asked Balachowski to bring him a visitor under terms of the greatest secrecy: Lamason. This was to be Lamason's third great secret in Buchenwald. Because of the extreme sensitivity of the situation, Lamason could not reveal even to Tom Blackham that Dodkin was still alive and on the verge of an escape.

'Look, Lamason, I don't know if this stunt is going to work but when and if you get sent on to a prisoner of war camp, when and if you get back to England, would you tell people what happened to us?'

'Quite honestly, Dodkin, I don't even know if they will pass us on to a prisoner of war camp. This place is hell on earth. We Royal Air Force types could just as easily disappear up the chimney as much as the other thousands and no-one would be any the wiser. I suppose you don't want me to mention to anyone else that you're still alive. I mean, I know you were friendly with Tom Blackham.'

'Absolutely not, old man – much too dangerous. There's a war on. A secret shared with anyone is a secret compromised. We cannot compromise on this.'

'Good luck, then.'

They shook hands. Lamason would not tell Blackham.

***

On 13 October, Choquet died. Dodkin assumed the identity of Choquet because their height was similar. Choquet was cremated as Dodkin. Blackham would most certainly have heard of this. It is probable that Lamason would take responsibility as Senior British

Officer to break the news to Blackham. He would also take responsibility not to tell the whole truth.

On 18 October, Boitel died and he was sent to the crematorium as Hessel. So now, Seigneur, Choquet and Boitel had died and Dodkin, Hessel and Paulevé slotted into their places.

It was roughly at this time that Pister signed the order to take the Royal Air Force men in batches and shoot them. The date of execution was to be 24 October.

Ding-Schuler also told Dodkin that the Kommandant had signed an order for him to be shot as well.

'Just as well I don't exist,' said Dodkin.

'Quite so,' said Ding-Schuler, with a bland smile.

Dodkin must have thought how very odd it was that he had finished up in a plot on the same side as an SS man. The problem now was quite straightforward. What could Ding-Schuler do with the miraculously resurrected Seigneur, Choquet and Boitel? Being a well-educated person, Ding-Schuler was to formulate an elegant but effective solution.

Ding-Schuler had camp administration officials post 'Seigneur'(Paulevé) and 'Boitel' (Hessel) to an aircraft factory at Schönbeck in Mecklenburg Vorpommern, far from Buchenwald. He organised for 'Choquet' (Dodkin) to go to a subcamp of Buchenwald, a work camp at Gleina.

All three were to wait there in their false identities, until they were liberated by American forces in the April of 1945.

27

The Luftwaffe Returns to Buchenwald

For three days after the United States Air Force raid, nothing happened. The Royal Air Force men, plus their American interpreter Sharf, had made a good attempt at asking the Luftwaffe to help them, but so far, nothing had come of it.

Time was running out. So was hope.

On the fourth day, someone called out to Lamason that the Kommandant's adjutant, SS Sturmbannführer Max Schobert, had entered the Little Camp, together with a bodyguard. German officers could never be too complacent when surrounded by desperate men.

He was heading towards the primitive humpy which Lamason called home.

'*Guten morgen, Herr Major,*' ['Good morning, Major'] said Schobert. 'It seems that you have some visitors. You are to come with me immediately.'

The people standing around Lamason felt the worst. They had learned that 'going with the SS' usually betokened some new depth of horror and depravity.

'Really, Herr Sturmbannführer? And who might these visitors be?'

'You may not ask questions but accompany me as I have requested.'

'Best of luck, Phil.'

They watched Lamason disappear with Schobert, Scharf as interpreter and the bodyguard.

'Think we'll see him again?'

'Let's just hope.'

***

A half hour later, word went around the Little Camp. 'He's coming back!'

Lamason walked across the main camp, looking rather pleased with himself.

'Right, chaps. Please find every one of our men and tell them to come here. I have something to tell you all of the greatest importance. Do it quickly, come on! Sharp's the word! On the double!'

Ten minutes later, he was surrounded by the majority of the 169. Some dozen could not attend, as their medical condition was worsening and they were unable to be taken from their primitive beds on the cobblestones.

'Gentlemen, we do, indeed, have visitors. There is a deputation from the Luftwaffe. It seems that our plea to help us has been taken seriously. There are three *Oberleutnants* [Flying Officers] who are here to ask you questions. If you can persuade them that you are indeed Royal Air Force men, then they will try to effect our transfer to a proper prisoner of war camp.'

'Sir, we are all told to give only our name, rank and number. How are we to persuade them?'

'In these circumstances I will take responsibility as Senior British Officer. The war is drawing to a close. If every one of you was to tell these chappies everything that you know, it is not going to change the course of the war by the slightest amount. Whatever they ask you, just answer the questions and maybe we'll get the hell out of here. We'll go in rank order. That is, I will submit myself for interrogation first, followed by the commanding officers, flight lieutenants and so on. Wish me luck, chaps – here I go.'

***

Upon Lamason's return, he said, 'Not too bad!' It then became the turn of Blackham as senior officer of the British prisoners.

He walked over the main camp to the administration block – the same one where they had been processed upon arrival some weeks ago. Weeks? It felt like decades.

An SS Scharführer ushered him into a small office. Behind a table sat a Luftwaffe officer. This man looked like what Blackham would have expected a German officer to look like. His uniform was immaculate and his posture was recognisably military. His speech was, in the jargon of the day, *'echt preussisch'* [real Prussian].

He introduced himself and his rank. Tom could see by the look in the man's eye a mixture of pity at his debilitated condition and revulsion at his personal hygiene. He had not had a bath or shower since arriving at the camp all those weeks ago.

He also saw a look of sympathy in the man's eyes. He had never seen that in an SS man.

'Please have a seat. Can I have your name, rank and number please?'

'Thomas Blackham, Flight Lieutenant.' The man wrote it down.

'Thank you, *Herr Hauptmann* [Flight Lieutenant]. Your crewposition?'

'Pilot.'

'Your squadron and home station?'

'50 Squadron, based at Skellingthorpe.'

'What aircraft did you fly?'

'Lancaster Mark III.'

'What was your target when you were shot down?'

'Mailly le Camp, near Paris.'

'What date were you shot down?'

'3 May – no, the morning of 4 May.'

'Where and what time were you shot down?'

'South of Paris, near Troyes. It was about 0230 in the morning.'

'What was the squadron number of the aircraft?'

'I'm pretty sure it was VN-T and the serial number, I think, was LM480, but that is as far as I can remember. We flew in different aircraft, but I think that was the one.'

'Thank you, Herr Hauptmann. I have no further questions. We can easily check this against our records. Please send another one of your men in here.'

'Thanks a lot for trying to help us. The SS people in here are utter beasts.'

'Thank you, Herr Hauptmann. I have lived in Germany since the beginning of the present regime. You do not need to tell me.

We are all quite conversant with all of this. We'll try and get you out.'

***

A week later, the adjutant Schobert appeared again in the Little Camp.

'Well, Herr Lamason – or should I say, 'Herr Major', it appears you are very lucky. There are trucks to take you to the rail head, where a train is waiting to move you to a prisoner of war camp.'

'Thank you for the information.'

There could be no bonhomie with this man. He was responsible for thousands upon thousands of needless deaths.

At the railhead, there were some five railway vans waiting for them. As previously, the numbers '40/8' were on the side again: 40 men or eight horses. This time, there were only 30 to a truck. They could actually lie down! What luxury!

The Luftwaffe had also given them some buckets of clean water to drink, some empty buckets for sanitary purposes and even some bread for the journey.

In the event, only some 157 of the 169 were able to make the journey. Twelve were left behind as being too sick to be moved. They had no chance of survival. Their fate is not known.

It was now 19 October. Oberführer Pister had signed an order to have them killed five days later.

28

From 'Ka-Tzetnik' to 'Kriegie'!

The five goods vans with the Royal Air Force personnel were shunted, clanked, shuffled and buffered onto a goods train at Weimar.

It went slowly eastwards. The train journey would take two days and two nights. As against this, there were compensations. At least there were only 30 men to a truck, which was less than the regulation 40. They could all lie down and sleep. At least they had water to drink. At least the Luftwaffe gave them some food, if not much. At least the trucks were not watched over by SS guards, who would chop them down with Schmeisser machine guns as a matter of casual routine. Even so, no one felt like escaping.

The vans were shunted from train to train and the journey went on and on. After leaving Weimar, the train passed through Naumburg.

'Hey, I've been on Naumburg,' one or two men are bound to have said.

'We dropped an awful lot of bombs for very little damage,' was the consensus.

***

Hours later, the train passed through Leipzig.

'Hey! I've been on Leipzig,' several enthusiastic voices are bound to have said, including Tom Blackham. 'What a bloody mess we made of it!'

What had been a fine medieval city was now just a smouldering blackened ruin, with smashed factories and streets of uninhabitable workers' houses. This was excellent for morale.

***

Even more hours later, the train passed through Dresden.

'Not a bloody mark on it! It hasn't been touched! Nice looking town, though.'

This was bad for morale.

Chatter inevitably turned to 'shop'. Which were the better and worse aircraft: Lancasters, Halifaxes, or Stirlings?

Which were the good (and bad) Royal Air Force stations? Everyone reckoned Waddington was the best. By comparison, some of the stations in Lincolnshire were so bad that they used to organise rat hunts, so that the airmen could keep warm during especially cold winters. These were recalled with great nostalgia.

They discussed the pros and cons of Boulton Paul versus Frazer Nash gun turrets.

Which were the worst targets to fly over? Berlin and Happy Valley (Essen) were always seen as the worst, but Hamburg, Bremen and Dortmund next in the pecking orders of threats to life and liberty. 'Not sure about Hamburg,' one man is bound to have said. 'There was nothing left of it last time I flew over'.

Then, there was the inevitable question as to how chaps had been shot down. Some people had theories about aircraft with upward firing machine guns. Some did not believe it. Some said it was a proven theory.

How had chaps been dealt with on station if they had been declared 'LMF' (lacks moral fibre)? This was the worst thing that could happen to a Royal Air Force man, certainly worse than risking their life over Berlin or Happy Valley. They did need to reflect, however, that Buchenwald was uniquely worse than 'LMF'.

It must have gone through Tom Blackham's mind that his late friend, Dodkin could not have taken part in one of these 'shop' sessions. Only the men who flew would have the background and the detailed experience. Yet, Dodkin was masquerading as a Squadron Leader. Just who was he and who did he work for? Poor sod. He was dead now – at least, as far as Tom knew, he was.

***

On the journey, Tom saw troop trains by the dozen, or even by the hundred, moving men, guns and vehicles eastwards in the direction of the Red Army. In the other direction, they only saw a couple of hospital trains, full of men who were shot to pieces and barely alive. It was clear that of the German soldiers moving eastwards, few – if any – would see home again.

There were other points of extreme interest during the otherwise interminable rail journey. For example, from the train, the Royal Air Force men saw another phenomenon of the times.

There was just the start of a trickle of refugees starting to move from east to west, to get away from the Russians. There were odd family units of old men and women with pathetic belongings on horse-drawn carts, trudging hopefully, fearfully and desperately away from the feared Ivans.

It was also clear as they passed through farming country that there were only women, old men and young boys to be seen. There were few men of between 18 and 40 to be seen, or at least very few with a complete set of arms and legs. The picture was become clearer. The picture was that Germany was losing the war heavily.

***

The train stopped.

'Anyone know where we are?'

'The station sign says 'Sagan'.'

'Ever heard of it, you navigators?'

'Nope.'

'It looks like we've arrived, anyway. There's a reception committee on the platform.'

'What colour are the uniforms?'

'Blue – a bit like ours.'

'Luftwaffe!' said someone. 'Thank God for that. At least it's not the bloody SS.'

Blackham noticed that the reception committee on the platform was not unlike the SS reception committees they had seen previously, except that the guards looked bored, rather than having that psychotic SS stare, which proclaimed an inner compulsion to commit legalised murder.

Their escort formed them up into a single column and marched them through the town. Boys in brown-shirted Hitler Youth uniforms threw stones at them.

Haut mal ab!' ['Bugger off!'] shouted a guard and the nasty little boys went away, dejected.

***

They passed into a thick forest and, after half an hour's walk through the darkness of the trees, came upon a clearing.

It was a prisoner of war camp. Outwardly, this was similar to Buchenwald, with high barbed wire walls, guard towers and searchlights on poles. One immediately noticeable difference was that German marching music was not blaring out of the loudspeakers. Another noticeable feature was the absence of the smell of defecation, mortification and death. There was no chimney belching out black smoke.

The inmates of the camp wore a mixture of blue-grey Royal Air Force and dark blue Fleet Air Arm uniforms. Some wore the dark brown of the South African Air Force. The inmates looked thin, gaunt and rather world weary, but did not have the concentration camp emaciation or 'thousand yard stare' of perpetual horror. One or two smoked cigarettes as they watched the new boys march, or rather, shamble across the parade ground, past rows of long, low huts to the camp hospital.

They were checked by the Medical Officer. He declared them all as showing signs of severe malnourishment and covered in lice. Their clothes were taken away to be burned. Someone produced a mixture of spare Royal Air Force and other assorted uniforms, which they put on after showers and delousing. A pilot might be wearing a navigator's tunic and an RAF wireless

388

operator might be wearing a Fleet Air Arm uniform, but no-one worried too much.

A Royal Air Force man was deputed to guide them across the compound to a large building at the far end of the camp. They may well have considered that the man who had fulfilled a similar function in Buchenwald was probably now dead. The large building proved to be the theatre.

Theatre? Blackham looked instinctively for the gibbet with its dangling bodies and the crematorium permanently belching black smoke. But it was definitely true! There was no smell of death, human faeces, or burned corpses. Things were looking up.

The camp adjutant ushered them into the theatre, invited them to find a seat and then called them to attention as the Senior British Officer, Group Captain Wilson of the Royal Australian Air Force, addressed them.

'At ease, gentlemen. Well, it looks as though something remarkable has happened. My opposite number, Colonel Braune, the Kommandant of this camp, tells me that some of his Luftwaffe colleagues have had you chappies sprung from Buchenwald concentration camp.'

He looked around for confirmation. Blackham thought, 'That accent reminds me of Joe Shuttleworth. I wonder where he is now. Lucky sod!'

'I can see that you all have had a dashed bad show of it from the condition you are in. The German Medical Officer has said to me you will all need building up and monitoring as to your condition. You are now in the hands of the Luftwaffe at Stalag Luft III. There are some things with which I must acquaint you.

'Firstly, you can expect reasonable treatment here, but food is short. Even so, I have spoken with the senior German officers here. You will all be on double rations for one month to bring you back to health. I can assure you that the Luftwaffe are not like the SS and they do not like the SS any more than we do.

'Secondly, you will go from here and the adjutant will find accommodation for you in the huts. We're getting a bit overcrowded as more and more chaps are being shot down, but you should all at least have a bunk.

'Thirdly, I understand that most of you have been shot down and were on the run with the French Resistance. Is that correct?'

'Yes, sir,' said a chorus of voices.

'Well, in that case your home stations and your families will by now have had official notification that you are missing and probably dead. In fact, your families have probably received a short letter signed by King George VI, giving his Imperial condolences. They will be distraught. I will send your details to the International Red Cross through the Luftwaffe to correct this. You can also send a letter to them, confirming that you are alive and well, though Christ knows when it will arrive.

'Please do not write in your letters that you have been mistreated by the SS. Everything that you write will be looked at by censors, both in Germany and the UK. Just say you are alive and well. You can also say something disarming, such as 'We have plenty of fags.' Your lettergram will have the words *Kriegsgefangenenlager* [Prisoner of War Camp] Luft III' on it, which will be your return address. You cannot say where you are, or the censor will take a dim view and your letter will not get through.'

'Very good, sir,' said several men.

'Finally, I have to acquaint you all with something that happened here. Some seven months ago, 76 airmen escaped down a tunnel and got out of the camp. It caused the most almighty stink, as the Jerries used thousands of troops trying to find them.'

There were cries of 'Bloody good show!' Group Captain Wilson waited for the euphoria to die down.

'Of these 76, some 50 were shot in cold blood by the Gestapo. In the months after the escape, we had urns full of ashes being sent here by the dozen for final disposal. The boxes were marked with the place of each execution. Some had got to Danzig, some had got to Breslau, some got to Hirschberg in Thüringen and some got over the border into France. The backwash of all of this is a state of tension between prisoners in the camp and the guards. The prisoners have said some dashed, insulting things to the guards. The guards then said similar things to the prisoners. It has culminated in guards in the towers taking pot shots at prisoners. I emphasise that these were warning shots and not shots to kill. Nevertheless, one of the shots over in the south compound hit an American sergeant in the mouth and he died instantly.'

He looked around for effect.

'Now, because of this, I want you all to be aware that I have expressly forbidden any further 'goon baiting'. Teasing the guards was a merry pastime practised here since the camp was set up two years ago. Now, it is not funny and is likely to get more people shot.

'By the same token, all of you are forbidden to tell anyone in this camp that you have been in a Nazi concentration camp. If this knowledge were to leak out, it is likely to exacerbate the situation between the prisoners and the guards. This, in turn, raises the high chance of bullets flying.'

Again, he looked around for effect.

'Is that clear to everyone?'

'Yes, sir!' they affirmed in chorus.

'You all need to be aware that some guards will try to bait you. There are one or two nasty characters who will ask how your wives are enjoying their black

American boyfriends. You will need to think of something witty to counter this and make them go away. If you fall for the bait, you will be in a fight and that means ten days in the cooler. If you reply in kind and say that the German Fräuleins are buttering themselves up for the Russians, the guards are likely to throw a dicky fit and shoot you. Don't do it. You must all understand that the Germans are extremely worried about what the Russians are going to do when they eventually arrive here.'

'Very well, sir.'

'I wish you all to know that in the aftermath of the big escape here, we have orders from London that no-one is to attempt further escapes. The war is clearly coming to a close now and your orders are to sit it out until the war is over.

'Is there any chance that the Russians might liberate us, sir?'

'That is a good question, but the situation is problematic. We have reports just in today of massacres by the Russians as they pass into German territory. There has a report today in East Prussia at Nemmersdorf. It is utterly ghastly, with naked women crucified on barn doors. We do not know what will happen if the Russians get to us before any other troops. The Polish chaps here have suffered appallingly at the hands of the Russians and are extremely worried that this rumour may well be true.

'Now, the adjutant will allocate you to huts and you can start to settle in. I have made provision for you all to receive a Red Cross parcel and that will also help to start to put a little meat on those very spare looking bones. Thank you, adjutant. Dismiss the men if you would.'

***

So it was that Tom Blackham ceased to be a 'Ka-Tzetnik' and became a Kriegsgefangener (prisoner of war): Kriegie for short. He looked at his new dog-tag: 78380. At least there was going to be some record of him – unlike at Buchenwald, where his existence was scheduled to terminate.

Stalag Luft III was, indeed, to be a brave new world.

'How the heck does London get orders into here?' Blackham must have thought. 'How the heck do they know about that place in East Prussia?'

The latter was more understandable. Royal Air Force wireless operators were able to make primitive but useful radios out of very little.

There was more. Shortly after arrival, an officer wearing the uniform of a lieutenant commander of the Fleet Air Arm came knocking on the hut door. 'Morning, chaps. I'm John Casson. We're just casting for a new play, *The Wind and the Rain* by Merton Hodge. Have any of you types trodden the boards before?'

Blackham's accent would have attracted his immediate attention.

'Oh, this is heaven sent! The play takes place in Edinburgh and you have a Scottish accent.'

'I'm afraid I'm not an actor.' This was surreal. Only a few weeks ago, he had been subjected to vile torture by the Gestapo and Sicherheitsdienst. Now, he was being solicited to take part in a play about students in Edinburgh.

'Oh, yes, you're one of the new lot, who look rather emaciated. The Senior British Officer asked me to leave you alone, so I suppose I better had. Dashed frustrating, though, with that accent of yours.'

After he had left, one of the long-standing inmates is bound to have said, 'Do you know who that was?'

'No – just a rather keen theatrical type.'

'He's the son of Dame Sybil Thorndike.'

'Good heavens! No wonder he's theatrical.'

'Poor old Casson's had a bad time of it. You heard about the escape of all of those types getting out?'

'Yes.'

'Well, Casson is friends with Hauptmann Pieber. He's German, but a really decent sort. Pieber had warned him privately that any escape was likely to be met with very harsh reprisals. Casson had tried to stop the escape and it all got very bloody. In the event, everyone now thinks that Casson was right all along and that he's rather a good sort.'

John Casson was significant in another way. He was an operative of a shadowy organisation, which was at least as secret as the Special Operations Executive. Casson worked for MI9. He was in touch with controllers in London by coded messages. He had sent a lot of useful information back to London. It was he who had received the message 'no more escapes', which he had passed on to Group Captain Wilson. The means of communication between London and prisoners of war would not be known during the hostilities, nor for many years afterwards.

***

Tom Blackham settled down to life in a Luftwaffe prisoner of war camp. He would find that it was markedly different from Buchenwald.

Stalag Luft III was approximately the same physical size as that terrible place, but held some 10,000 inmates, as opposed to 100,000. There was no forced labour, daily executions, or any of the other horrors which he had seen at Buchenwald. The guards were not psychopathic thugs. Some were men too old or unfit for active service. Some were men who had been wounded in action, who were as yet unfit to return. On the whole, the guards were happy to be at Stalag Luft III, as it meant that they were not on the eastern front, being shot to pieces.

Among the inmates, life was surprisingly favourable. In addition to Casson's theatre, there were classes in languages: French, German and Afrikaans. There were lessons in engineering, law and history. There was an active chess club, along with bridge and some more exotic card games that the non-British men showed them how to play. There were two camp newspapers in production in the British north and east compounds. Goodness only knew what the Americans had in the south and west compounds!

They talked 'shop' and lots of it, but here, the talk was of escape and the escapers. Over in the east compound, three men – Williams, Codner and Philpott – had escaped by means of a wooden horse. This was a piece of gym equipment, which was carried each day to the same place by the wire. As the horse was carried out, it contained the three men. While the horse was being vaulted over all day long, the three were working underneath, tunnelling their way out. They had actually got home to England, which was a huge boost to morale in the camp.

As exotic as the wooden horse escape was, it was nowhere near as exotic as Dodkin's plan to storm the gates at Buchenwald. Poor sod! Poor, poor bloody sod!

The north compound, where Blackham was situated, was where the huge escape had happened. Men spoke in hushed terms of Squadron Leader Roger Bushell. The escape was his brainchild. He had the concept and the managerial ability to run a project of 600 men. He had displayed the leadership qualities to inspire every one of them. Bushell's intention was to get 200 men out. He had had three tunnels surveyed and designed by a mining expert. He had formed a tunnelling team; a team to get rid of the excavated dirt; a team to make civilian clothes; a team to make false documents; a team to watch the guards and report on their activities; a team to make maps; and a team to make compasses. Bushell was known to have been murdered by the Gestapo.

The men spoke in hushed terms also of Squadron Leader Harry Day, who was one of the escapers. His preposterous disguise was that of an Irishman – a colonel in the Royal Enniskillen Dragoon Guards – complete with that regiment's distinctive bottle green trousers. His cover story was that he was travelling under guard to Berlin where, as a loyal Irishman, he was going to betray secrets of the hated English to the Wehrmacht High Command. He was under escort from an impeccably dressed 'German soldier', equipped with a perfect replica of a German standard issue rifle, a Karabiner 98 – perfect in every detail, except that it was carved out of wood. Day was not on the list of those executed, nor had he been returned. They did not know what had happened to him, though they would have been fascinated to know the truth. The Gestapo had sent Day to Sachsenhausen Concentration Camp, from where he had also tunnelled out, been caught, brought back and held, chained to the floor, in one of the many condemned cells. For some reason, he was not executed.

The men talked with hilarity of Corporal Griese, also known as Rubberneck, whose job it had been to find and thwart escape attempts. Griese had been quite sure that an escape plot was being hatched, but he could never track it down. Logic told him that it started from hut 104, which was correct, but even though Griese pulled the hut apart several times, he never found the entry to the tunnel. It was under the stove. After the escape, Griese had disappeared. Other guards thought that he had been sent to the Russian front, which, in effect, was a death sentence.

Blackham would have also noted the tones of sympathy for the previous Kommandant, Colonel von Lindeiner. He had always been fair with the prisoners and tried to make their life as comfortable as possible. The prisoners knew that the SS wanted to take over the camp and also knew what that meant: firing squads until no one was left alive. Blackham would have pondered that SS firing squads were at the benign end of the scale. They were capable of much more than that. But Von Lindeiner had fought the SS off and protected his charges. After the escape, Von Lindeiner was removed from office and court martialled.

***

Behind all of the dramatic and barely believable stories, there was one reality which never went away. This reality led to the second most frequent topic of conversation: food.

There was never enough to go around. Men who might have entered the camp in 1941 at 80 kilograms now might weigh 65 kilograms.

It was true that the Red Cross delivered hundreds of food parcels each week, but the food distribution process was finding it difficult to keep up with demand.

***

Over in the Eastern Compound, there had been the most fearful stink.

'Honestly, Tom. I know that you new chaps are not going to believe this story.'

'Well, try us.'

'Well, there was a Squadron Leader over there who had no legs.'

Tom had had to put up with one phoney Squadron Leader, poor dead Dodkin and was not inclined to believe a story about a second one.

'No, you're right. I don't believe it.'

'Well, he was and you have my word of honour on it.' 'Please, go on with your cock and bull story.'

'Well, this chap was called Douglas Bader. He was a Squadron Leader in 242 Squadron, based at Duxford. Well, he had been no end of a problem to the camp administration and a more bloody-minded wallah than I have ever met in my life. Well, the Kommandant decided to transfer him to some kind of special camp, at a place called Colditz.'

'Oh Christ. Not a concentration camp, is it?'

'Don't think so, but not a holiday camp either. Anyway, Bader refused to go. This caused a contretemps between the guards and the Kriegies. Hauptmann Pieber came to sort it out and Bader was absolutely bloody to him. Anyway, Pieber came back with a guard of six men. It was going to get nasty, you could see it. As it happened, Harry Day got wind of it. He had been Bader's commanding officer at 20 Squadron earlier in the war, so he requested permission from Kommandant Von Lindeiner to go from the North Compound to the East Compound to see if he could help.'

'And did he?'

'Well, he did persuade Bader to toe the line. When Bader came out of the hut where he was holed up, the escort of six guards were standing there. Bader barked an order at them-'*Achtung! Stillstanden!*' ['Attention!'] They snapped smartly to attention and Bader walked up and down the line...'

'Even though he had no legs?'

'That's right – actually, he had a set of tins legs. Anyway, old Bader went ahead and did a formal inspection of their kit. He told one guard his rifle was filthy. The Kriegies were in fits of laughter and even Pieber could not help himself. Anyway, they marched him off to a truck and everyone sang, 'For He's a Jolly Good Fellow'. And now he's over at Colditz, which I think is over Leipzig way.'

To Tom's utter astonishment, the story turned out to be true.

***

Tom Blackham had been in the camp some six weeks.

On 4 December, they were summoned to the parade ground. They were astonished to find that the Luftwaffe Kommandant, Colonel Braune had organised a memorial service for the murdered Royal Air Force men. The previous Kommandant, Colonel von Lindeiner, had commissioned a memorial to them, which he had paid for out of his own money. Not all Germans were psychopathic butchers.

The memorial, built by Luftwaffe volunteers, was now finished and stood just outside of the camp. Group Captain Wilson, as Senior British officer, took one officer from each of the 13 nations whose men had been murdered outside the camp on parole, to visit the dedication.

Two German military padres – one Protestant and one Catholic – presided over a memorial service. A Luftwaffe guard of honour fired a volley over the memorial. A Luftwaffe bugler played the 'Last Post' from the parade ground in the North Compound. It was one of the strangest, but also most moving, ceremonies of World War II.

***

As the Christmas of 1944 approached, a number of dynamics changed visibly in the camp.

After the joint Luftwaffe and Royal Air Force memorial ceremony, the enmity between Kriegies and guards gradually thawed. At first, there was a slightly formal mutual respect. Then, gradually, friendships began to blossom.

The guards began to ask questions such as, 'Do the British treat their prisoners well?' and 'What are the most important items to take into prison?'

***

As January wore on, they could hear the sound of thunder.

'Russian artillery!' said someone.

It was! It was a moot point whether the Russians would joyfully liberate them (as the more socialist British thought) or joyfully murder them (as the Poles thought).

***

Outwardly, camp life carried on as normal.

One of the great features was skating. A skating rink had been formed in the centre of the parade ground. Skating took place to the sounds of Johann Strauss waltzes, played over the camp loudspeakers. Some of the Canadian Kriegies had shown them how to make delicious ice cream from snow, cocoa powder and condensed milk.

However, there was a reminder that it was not a holiday camp; it was a prisoner of war camp. All was not well.

The guards tipped off the prisoners that the SS were again trying to take over the camp. Group Captain Wilson re-introduced full military discipline, which had grown lax over the previous year.

Wilson began to organise Resistance groups. He knew that they could not win in a fight with the SS, but at least they could go down fighting. If they were going to go down, they would take one or two of the blighters with them. The Kriegies would not have firearms, but many thought it possible that the guards would help them.

The prisoners of war also made clubs made from table legs and weapons from the carpenters' tools from the theatre. These had been accepted by John Casson to build his theatre 'on parole'. Casson had solemnly undertaken that these tools could not be used for escape purposes and this undertaking had been steadfastly honoured by all of the Royal Air Force men. However, there was no undertaking that said they could not be used to shuffle off the mortal coil of an SS thug.

The revelation of another part of the Resistance plan led to Tom Blackham's utter amazement. There was actually another tunnel – 'George' – that was complete and ready for operation. It led from the camp to the outside. George had been abandoned after the 'no escape' order but could be recommissioned quickly in case of an emergency.

The officer in charge of the Red Cross parcels had climbed to the top of the silo where they were kept. When he returned, he reported seeing refugees. There were now thousands of them, pouring from the east and heading for the west. Blackham is bound to have remarked, 'And when we got here, a few weeks ago, it was just a trickle!'

The guards were now talking openly of deserting. That was not good news for the Kriegies. If the guards absconded, the SS might well arrive to fill the void. Tom Blackham and the other 157 Buchenwald alumni were painfully clear on what that would entail. The SS would simply shoot the lot of them.

Over at Sachsenhausen Concentration Camp, where Squadron Leader Day was being kept, the Kommandant, *Standartenführer* [Colonel] Anton Kaindl was making arrangements for the 30,000 inmates to be taken to a Baltic port, loaded onto ships and for the ships to be sunk in the sea. Tom Blackham did not know this. He would not have been surprised.

Rumours flew around in large numbers. The guards were now openly asking the prisoners for the latest news. They did not trust the Nazi propaganda radio and knew that the prisoners could, somehow or other, receive BBC broadcasts. A BBC news bulletin confirmed that the Russians had advanced 160 kilometres in just five days. An advance Russian tank unit was over the Oder river at Steinau, north of Breslau. Worryingly, this was just 60 kilometres from Sagan. That was in line with the far-off thunder that they had heard. That, in turn, meant that the arrival of Russian troops was now not only inevitable, but imminent.

Group Captain Wilson increased the pace of the Resistance preparations. He ordered slit trenches to be constructed. He ordered more primitive but deadly weapons to be constructed. Wilson formed specially selected men into Commando units. They would storm the guard towers, seize machine guns and kill as many guards as possible prior to a mass break out.

He also ordered the production of hundreds of wooden sleighs. Kommandant Braune had informed him that as the Russians came closer, it was probable that he would be ordered to move the prisoners westwards and that would otherwise mean going on foot in temperatures of-5 Celsius during the day and-20 during the night. The means of transport would be critical.

***

At 2100 on 27 January came the bombshell: 'Be ready to move out'.

There was no insurrection or mass breakout. The camp was being abandoned. They were to pack up their belongings and be ready to go in 30 minutes. For Blackham and many others, the ordeal was not yet over. Nevertheless, there was an urgent need for a quick and effective organisation. There was little time to think.

The first principle was to take the minimum of clothing: just enough to keep warm.

The second principle was to take as much food as possible. Each man was allowed two food parcels. The food was important, but the cigarettes, chocolate and soap would be vital for bargaining with the civilian population. Cigarettes were something that the prisoners had plenty of. Those were really worth taking with you!

The third principle was to take something of value. Many of the men had written diaries in the camp, even though this was forbidden. Given what had happened with the escape, they did not want to leave those diaries behind. Those diaries would be vital evidence when and if, they ever made it to freedom.

Most of the guards were given two days of 'hard rations' and taken out of the camp to be sent eastwards to the front line. There was no great expectation as to their survival. The few left, who were mainly the older ones, would supervise the evacuation. The Kommandant let it be known that orders from Berlin said that anyone attempting to escape would be shot without warning.

John Casson was fuming. He received the order in the middle of the dress rehearsal for *The Wind and the Rain* and now the production was being ditched. *Was there no end to the depredations of this awful bloody war?*

29

The Long March Westwards and 'Doon ra Watter'

The march started on 27 January. It would last some 12 exhausting, nerve racking, debilitating weeks.

Would they ever arrive at their destination? Where was their destination? Would they be attacked by rogue SS troops, known to be operating without any command structure but with weapons and the malice to use them?

The weeks were tedious as they had marched from one camp or farm or random place to another.

Food was firstly scarce, then rare, then it ran out. The Kriegies had an ace up their sleeve: cigarettes! The official German currency, the Reichsmark, was now worthless. Cigarettes were now the means of barter and exchange. From their Red Cross parcels, they had thousands, or maybe even tens of thousands. It was one of those ironies of fate that in their hour of need, of great threat and plummeting morale, they were, ironically, quite rich.

***

Three days later, the ocean liner *Wilhelm Gustloff* was torpedoed by a Russian submarine. It was grossly overloaded with 9000 desperate refugees, military troops, civilians and anyone who could bribe their way on board, trying to escape the wrath and bestiality of the oncoming Russian army.

In the freezing Baltic waters, all 9000 died – six times as many as on the *Titanic.* It remains the greatest maritime disaster in history.

When Tom Blackham heard the news, he would have recognised the name. It was the name on the slave labour factory, whose bombing at Buchenwald had led to their improbable rescue by the Luftwaffe.

***

Some eight weeks later, on 23 March, they heard via the wireless operators' homemade radios that allied troops had crossed the Rhein river and were on German soil. So, it seemed clear that the war would end and allied forces would rescue them. That, at least, was the theory.

Sometimes, the column of prisoners moved on foot, sometimes by train and sometimes by truck. The route was from Sagan to Spremberg, to Magdeburg, to Braunschweig, where Tom had done his first raid flying 'second dicky'.

Hitler had said that if he became chancellor in ten years, you would not recognise Germany. Tom was to find this was quite true. There was hardly a large building still standing in any German town of note. The country was ceasing to function. The population was in penury.

They went on to Hannover and finally to Tarnstedt near Bremen. There was still no sign of allied forces. It was over a month since the Rhein crossing and still no sign of help. Would this ordeal never end?

***

'Does anyone actually know where we are going?'

The question was asked every day. The Senior British Officer did not know. The guards did not know. The Kommandant, when he appeared, did not know either. The column just kept on marching west-ish and north-ish, in the vague direction of Lübeck.

Despite the hopelessness of their situation, they still had advantages. They were resourceful. This body of men had been in prison for up to four years. Their expertise in foraging, conniving, bargaining and, if required, thieving were all at a high level of development. Whilst none of them was putting weight on, none of them starved either.

As the warmer spring weather came, the need for shelter became less acute. Although they were underfed, miserable and frustrated, they were the winners in the war, which was about to end. Despite the privations, frustrations and inconveniences, winning a war is a wonderful boost for morale.

***

At last, they came to two large estates. Navigators had reported to Group Captain Wilson that the column was still heading in a north westerly direction, somewhere between Hamburg and Lübeck.

Trenthorst and Wulmenau were two large country properties, which belonged to Mr Raemsma, who bred prime Frisian cattle. Looking at these well-ordered, prosperous businesses, it was as if they had walked out of wartime dystopia into a dreamlike, well-heeled paradise.

Group Captain Wilson went to see him. Raemsma proved delighted to help and showed every sign of being grateful of the opportunity. Well, that was interesting! What Mr Raemsma would get out of it was clear: invaluable bargaining chips with the soon-to-be-occupying forces. It even offered the possibility of distancing himself from the previous Nazi overlords who, of course, he had never liked.

Mr Raemsma and Wilson agreed how the impromptu invasion of ragged airmen would be organised. Group Captain Wilson paraded the prisoners.

Standing orders allowed the men onto some parts of the estate, but other parts were off limits. Airmen had to keep away from the 167 prize milking cows,

412

even if they knew how to milk them. There was to be no thieving, damage, or delinquency of any kind. There was to be no baiting of farm workers, 'just like the order for no goon-baiting, chaps.' The prisoners were not to interfere with the operation of the farm.

Other than that, they could make themselves comfortable in barns. Water was also plentiful for washing clothes and for brewing tea. Fair barter was quite in order.

***

The Kriegies were surprised to find able bodied men working the farm. These proved to be Polish *'Zwangsarbeiter'* [forced labourers]. Initially, they gave off an air of menacing resentment, although this evaporated when they discovered that the blue uniforms were Royal Air Force and not Luftwaffe. The notion of dropping high explosive bombs on Germany was very well received among them and cordial relations began at once.

A joke circulated that was told by the Poles to the Royal Air Force men.

'A polish soldier has a German to his left and a Russian to his right. He only has two bullets. What does he do?'

'No idea,' replied the bemused airmen.

'He shoots the German first and the Russian second. Do you know why?'

'No idea.'

'Because business comes before pleasure.'

Brews of tea, cigarettes and sharing of the remnants of Red Cross parcels began immediately with the Poles.

***

Later that afternoon, the farm manager, who the Poles identified as a confirmed Nazi, tried to impose a whole raft of unreasonable restrictions on the prisoners.

At Wilson's request, Mr Raemsma appeared and harangued the farm manager sharply in German.

'*Der Krieg ist verloren!*' ['The war is lost!'] were the last words of the tirade.

'*Verloren?*' asked the farm manager, displaying the body language of a man given sudden and unexpected bad news.

'*Verloren!*' confirmed Mr Raesma, firmly and finally.

Apparently, this farm manager had the distinction of being the last person in Germany to know that the war was lost and that Germany had lost it.

***

Tom would have been involved in the foraging parties, which Wilson immediately set up. These searched through local woods for firewood, any other material to make temporary shelters. After their experiences at Buchenwald, this was child's play. The Poles went off joyously to enact terrible revenge on some of the local populace, who really had it coming.

In the distance, they could hear the crackle of small arms fire and the booming of artillery. They had been on the road for weeks. Surely to God, Adolf would end it all?

Three days later, Adolf Hitler came to the same conclusion. He considerately blew his brains out.

Still, there was no relief! Was this all just one endless bloody nightmare?

***

On the following day and without ceremony, a large, dirty and battered battle tank roared past the farm in a cloud of blue petrol fumes.

It slowed, paused for a moment, then stopped and reversed. The tank commander took a curious and prolonged look in through the gate. The huge, armoured vehicle then roared and clanked its way slowly and massively into the large courtyard outside of the estate at Wulmenau.

Tom and the other Kriegies would have looked at it and wondered just what this meant. The tank bore a garish yellow divisional badge with the symbol of a black bull. How did the Germans have the petrol (or diesel) to run tanks?

A lean figure vaulted out of the turret. This was a figure wearing a black beret and khaki drill shirt. Then, it struck them.

'The Black Bull – it's the eleventh armoured division!' shouted a voice.

The Kriegies roared with gloriously un-British abandon. Tom and the others saw what they thought they would never see. *It was a British Cromwell tank!* They swarmed over the tank and pulled out the crew – shook their hands, slapped their backs and jumped up and down.

After a half hour of jubilation, Group Captain Wilson cajoled them, pleaded with them and finally ordered them, for goodness' sake, to put a sock in it. They listened in silence as the tank commander, a captain, gave his position on the radio and said the words, 'I've just found a couple of thousand of Royal Air Force prisoners.'

They cheered again. They listened in silence as the tank commander said that he had been sent forward to take possession of Lübeck. 'I understand there's not too much left of Lübeck, but my orders are to take possession of whatever is left.'

This provided an opportunity for Mr Raemsma, who had nothing to do with the Nazis, had never been a member of the party and did not support them in any way whatsoever. He was able to demonstrate his good character again as he pointed out the road to

Artienburg, where there was a bridge over the River Elbe. Well, at least, it was there was two days ago.

Those around the tank listened in silence again while the captain told Group Captain Wilson that they had heard, a couple of weeks previously, about some kind of concentration camp to the south of there. There were 60,000 people in it and it was worst place than anyone could ever imagine. 'It's called

Belsen and they've got a camera crew down there, but you're going to hear more of it.'

After the inevitable cup of tea, the tank roared and clanked its way to Artienburg. It got to Lübeck later that afternoon when the mayor formally surrendered the town. There was no fighting now. Everyone just wanted the whole sorry mess finished for once and for all.

***

Tom Blackham and the others watched as the Luftwaffe Kommandant surrendered formally to Group Captain Wilson. Colonel Von Braune had been a decent captor and it was possible to feel sympathy at a personal level.

The guards, such as were left, surrendered their arms – or, at least, any rifles which had not already been thrown away for being too darned heavy to carry. The rank and file were grateful it was all over and they were still alive.

Group Captain Wilson designated a barn as the armoury. This proved to be a good decision. Units of the German *Landwehr* [Home Guard] appeared. Heck! There was not one of them under 50, but they were well equipped with rifles and bazooka-line Panzerfausts. They were grateful as well – firstly that it was all over and secondly that they were still alive.

Shortly after this, a unit of *Allgemeine* [General] SS appeared. They were hard-line, true believers of the late Führer and lavishly equipped with high powered machine guns. Their attitude was surly and insulting. The Royal Air Force men were now armed with small arms from the Landwehr. If there was going to be a firefight, the Allgemeine SS were mightily outnumbered. Once their firearms were locked in the barn, they calmed down.

The men were startled to hear a mighty crash. It proved to be a number of Kriegies, who had taken Panzerfausts and were using trees as target practice. A round from a single Panzerfaust could destroy a tank, let alone an oak tree. Group Captain Wilson put a stop to this.

A more refined pleasure was the game of 'search the German'. As prisoners of war, they had all been searched so many hundreds of times that it was a source of great pleasure to slam a German SS man against a wall and go through his pockets. Strip searches proved to be even more fun. It remained unclear whether anyone had actually ordered this. It probably just seemed like a good idea at the time.

***

The next day, a British scout car appeared. A lieutenant from the 11th Armoured passed on orders: all Royal Air Force prisoners of war were to remain where they were until transport could be found for them. All of the German prisoners of war were to wait there for further orders.

The officer in the scout car asked Group Captain Wilson to point out any guards who had not behaved well. Several prisoners immediately pointed out one particular guard. This man had needlessly shot and killed a prisoner during the march. The officer ordered the man into the scout car and prepared to depart.

'Don't you want evidence for a court martial?' asked Wilson.

'Don't worry, sir. It's all in hand,' the driver, a sergeant, reassured him.

The scout car roared off.

'Well, they'll need some sort of evidence,' said Wilson.

'I don't think that bloke will make it back to divisional HQ, if you get the drift, sir.'

'Oh! I see.'

***

There were other things to get on with. Matters, which had been rather calm since the arrival a few days, now began to liven up. The Polish forced labourers appeared again at the farm, with pickaxe handles, scythes and other implements of revenge.

'Where is the farm manager?'

No one knew. He was there last night. Then, someone believed they heard a farm tractor early in the morning.

'I noticed it because I had never heard a tractor going that fast. God knows where he got the petrol from.'

It transpired that some Royal Air Force men had tipped off the farm manager that the Poles had every intention of killing him and his family and would greatly enjoy doing so. He had disappeared, very quickly, together with his family. The Poles looked cheated.

***

British infantry now arrived in force and took possession of the area. Tom would have seen British soldiers stopping civilians in the street and taking their watches, valuables and, particularly, cigarettes. He thought we would have been better than that.

Landwehr and SS prisoners were taken off somewhere in trucks. It was possible to feel sorry for the Landwehr – they were just old geezers pressed into uniform. For the SS, no retribution was harsh enough.

That was it, then! There was nothing to do but lie in the spring sun and sunbathe. Food could be found upon bartering with the locals. There were no more guards or weapons or SS or Nazis.

It was all over. It was bloody well all over.

***

A day later, the colonel in charge of the prisoners of war appeared with some medical staff. More rations appeared in the form of trucks loaded with bread, cans of beef and vegetables.

Things were moving now.

***

A day later, a massive convoy of trucks appeared. Tom, eventually, loaded onto one of them.

'What date is it?' he may well have asked the driver.

'It's 3 May, mate. Erm, I mean sir.'

Tom would have laughed at that. It was the anniversary of the date on which he had taken off for the raid on Mailly le Camp. He had been away exactly a year.

***

After the liberation, he was taken for a medical examination, allowed a shower, given a new uniform and scheduled for a trip back to Blighty.

Fittingly, Bomber Command were given the task of repatriating prisoners of war and even more fittingly, it was to be in a Lancaster bomber.

He had done 27 operations in those wonderful aircraft. He knew this would be his last trip in one of those glorious machines, of which he was mightily glad. Nevertheless, the purring of those Merlin engines was still something to set the blood on fire. He would never forget that.

And as he boarded a Lancaster for the last time, he is bound to have thought, 'They say that Lancasters just look right. They do! They flippin' well do!

***

A week later Tom Blackham was homeward bound at last on a train from Glasgow Central to Gourock. From there, the ferry would take him home to Dunoon. There were several joys in this. He was still alive. He would see his family again. The war was won and he was on the winning side.

He must have given a thought to the crew who had gone down over Mailly: Walton, Stephenson, Jones, Godfrey, Wilkins, Ridd and Dixon. One had survived, but he did not know which one and probably never would. Nor would they know what became of him.

He would have thought too of Lamason and that poor bastard Dodkin, dead of typhus. If he was to read Yeo-Thomas' biography, *The White Rabbit,* ten years later, he would have found out the truth. There was, however, nothing to link the Yeo-Thomas of the story with the Dodkin that he knew.

Then, there was Joe Shuttleworth. Where was he now?

***

There was a supreme irony in this.

The start of Joe's journey back to Australia had started by going '*doon ra watter*' [down the water] at Greenock.

The end of Tom's journey from Germany had ended by going '*doon ra watter*' to Gourock.

They were 30 minutes' walk from each other. Tom and Joe had crossed paths very closely, though had missed each other by some weeks. They were not destined to meet again.

But Tom must often have thought of Joe, as Joe thought often of Tom.

APPENDIX 1

MacRobertson Air Race Results, October 1934

Official Finishing Order

Aircraft type	Identity	Race No.	Crew	Country of origin	Notes
DH.88 Comet 'Grosvenor House'	G-ACSS	34	C. W. A. Scott, Tom Campbell Black	Britain	Elapsed time 71 h 0 min Outright Winner
Douglas DC-2 'Uiver'	PH-AJU	44	K.D. Parmentier, J.J. Moll, B. Prins, C. van Brugge (died on board the attacked BOAC flight 777 in 1943)	Netherlands	Elapsed time 90 h 13 min Winner on handicap
Boeing 247D 'Warner Bros. Comet'	NR257Y	5	Roscoe Turner, Clyde Edward Pangborn, Reeder Nichols	United States	Elapsed time 92 h 55 min
DH.88 Comet	G-ACSR	19	O. Cathcart Jones, K.F. Waller	Britain	Elapsed time 108 h 13 min
Miles M.2F Hawk Major	ZK-ADJ	2	S/Ldr. M. McGregor, H.C. Walker	New Zealand	Elapsed time 7 d 14 h Fastest single-engined
Airspeed AS.5 Courier	G-ACJL	14	S/Ldr. D. Stodart, Sgt. Pilot K. Stodart	Britain	Elapsed time 9 d 18 h
DH.80 Puss Moth 'My Hildergarde'	VH-UQO	16	C.J. 'Jimmy' Melrose	Australia	Elapsed time 10 d 16 h Second on handicap
Desoutter Mk.II	OY-DOD	7	Lt. M. Hansen, D. Jensen	Denmark	Arrived 31 October
DH.89 Dragon Rapide 'Tainui'	ZK-ACO	60	J.D. Hewitt, C.E. Kay, F. Stewart	New Zealand	Arrived 3 November

Not classified

Aircraft type	Identity	Race No.	Crew	Country of origin	Notes
Miles M.3 Falcon	G-ACTM	31	H.L. Brook, Miss E. Lay (passenger)	Britain	Arrived 20 November
Fairey IIIF	G-AABY	15	F/O C.G. Davies, Lt.Cdr. C.N. Hill	Britain	Arrived 24 November
Fairey Fox I	G-ACXO	35	Ray Parer, G. Hemsworth	Australia	Withdrew from race at Paris. Eventually reached Melbourne 13 February 1935
Lambert Monocoupe 145 Baby Ruth	NC501W	33	J.H. Wright, J. Polando Warner	United States	Withdrew at Calcutta
DH.88 Comet 'Black Magic'	G-ACSP	63	Jim Mollison, Amy Johnson	Britain	From Karachi, Mollison lost his way and landed at Jubulpur. No high-octane fuel available, filled up with petrol. Engines 'burned out' on flight to Allahabad.
Pander S4 'Panderjager'	PH-OST	6	G.J. Geysendorffer, D.L. Asjes, P. Pronk	Netherlands	Destroyed in ground collision at Allahabad.
B.A. Eagle 'The Spirit of Wm. Shaw & Co Ltd'	G-ACVU	47	F/Lt. G. Shaw	Britain	Withdrew at Bushire
Lockheed Vega 'Puck'	G-ABGK	36	J. Woods, D.C. Bennett	Australia	Overturned on landing at Aleppo, withdrew
Airspeed AS.8 Viceroy	G-ACMU	58	T. Neville Stack, S.L. Turner	Britain	Withdrew with multiple mechanical issues at Athens
Granville R-6H 'Q.E.D.'	NX14307	46	Jacqueline Cochran, W. Smith Pratt	United States	Withdrew with malfunctioning flaps, after landing damage at Bucharest
Fairey Fox I	G-ACXX	62	H.D. Gilman, J.K. Baines	Britain	Crashed near Palazzo San Gervasio in Italy; both crew killed

APPENDIX 2

What Happened After the War?

Person	Role	After the war
Joe Shuttleworth	Central character	After Freda joined Joe in Brisbane, he settled down into family life and had a daughter, Dawn. He worked in managerial roles in an engineering company and then in services' repatriation hospitals in Brisbane and Melbourne. He was recognised with an MBE for his achievements at the Heidelberg Repatriation Hospital in Melbourne.
Tom Blackham	Central character	Tom stayed in the ranks of the Royal Air Force and attained the rank of Air Commodore. He also became equerry to Queen Elizabeth II.
Hans Krause	Shot down Tom Blackham	Hans remained in prisoner of war camp in England for some years.
Jacques Desoubrie	The man who betrayed Tom Blackham	Jacques fled to Germany after the war. He was arrested after being denounced by his ex-girlfriend and shot by firing squad in December 1949 in the fort of Montrouge, outside Paris.
Oberführer Hermann Pister	Kommandant at Buchenwald	Hermann was condemned to death at the Nuremberg Trials, but died of a heart attack before the sentence could be carried out.

Person	Role	After the war
Forest Frederick/Edward Yeo-Thomas (a.k.a. Kenneth Dodkin, 'the white rabbit' and 'Shelley')	Friend of Tom Blackham at Buchenwald	Edward gave testimony at the Nuremberg trials against 31 camp guards from Buchenwald, including the commandant, Oberführer Pister. He then returned to the fashion house of Molyneux and resumed his career.
Alfred Balachowski	Friend of 'Dodkin' and Tom Blackham at Buchenwald	Alfred survived the war and gave evidence at the Nuremberg trials. This led to the conviction of many SS personnel from the Dora and Buchenwald concentration camps.
Arthur Dietzsch	Medical orderly at Buchenwald	Arthur survived the war.
Stephane Hessel	Co-escapers with Yeo-Thomas	Stephane was recaptured and sent to a slave labour camp at Dora. He escaped during a transfer to Bergen-Belsen and survived the war to become a writer, diplomat and ambassador. His book, Time for Outrage, sold 4.5 million copies.
Harry Puelevé		Harry survived the war and went to work for Shell in South America and for other companies in Spain and the West Indies. He was deported from Egypt in 1956.
John Casson	Ran the theatre at Stalag Luft III; MI9 agent	John went back to his theatrical career and emigrated to Melbourne, Australia where Tony, his son, worked with Jeff Steel.
Wing Commander Heward	Joe and Tom's commanding officer at Skellingthorpe	Heward retired from the Royal Air Force in 1976 as Air Chief Marshal.

Person	Role	After the war
Kenneth Dodkin	The false identity for Yeo-Thomas	Emigrated to New Zealand after the war. His file was marked 'not to be opened for 70 years.'
Christopher Burney	Inmate of Buchenwald	Worked in establishing the United Nations in New York and in a commission to establish Libyan independence. Wrote the controversial 'Dungeon Democracy' about life in Buchenwald.

APPENDIX 3

Letter Received by Blackham's Mother After the War

Dear Madam,

This is to let you know that your son Tommy landed safely in France near Troyes (Champagne) when his Lancaster was hit.

His crew bailed out while he remained at his post trying to steady his engine. He believed they all had time to save themselves before he was blown out himself by the explosion. He was only slightly injured in the head and after many adventures in the Maquis reached Paris with a friend Lt. Neville Mutter who had fallen also near Troyes some days previously. I met them on the 15th. June and took charge of them for over a month. They were both such charming boys. We all got fond of them and did all we could to make them happy, but they hoped of course to get home. We put them in touch with an agent who was to insure their passage home and we thought they were safely with you since 19th. August. I have just heard with the deepest sorrow that they were betrayed and taken by the Germans, it is a great blow as they were like our own children and I share your grief with all my heart. I pray and hope you will soon have news through the Red Cross and I beg you to let us know. I did not know Lt. Mutters address, I believe his mother lived in Birmingham. He was a Fighter Pilot on Mustang III. Could you try to give the news to Mrs Mutter through the R.A.F?

With Deepest sympathy.
There was no name and address, just a Paris postmark.

Acknowledgements

The project started life with a request from Joe Shuttleworth's daughter, Dawn. She asked if I could write her father's story and research what happened to his pilot, Tom Blackham.

The project was immediately attractive. Joe, at the time, was one of very few Lancaster bomber crew members still alive. He was to pass away shortly after the manuscript was completed.

I would like to acknowledge Dawn and her husband John, for the subsequent friendship which has developed between us.

So, the first acknowledgement is to Dawn and the second to Joe, who gave a large amount of time and commitment to the project to make sure that I had his story absolutely correct. Even at the age of 90, his mind was sharp and his long-term memory excellent.

I would like to make a special acknowledgement to Andrew Dennis of the Royal Air Force Museum and Katie O'Halloran of the Royal Air Force College in Cranwell, UK, where Tom Blackham was a senior officer after the war. They collaborated to find a long-lost article that was written by Tom Blackham in 1954, which detailed his time with the French Resistance and subsequent betrayal to the SS.

I also wish to acknowledge the late Mr Tony Casson of Melbourne, Australia, son of Lieutenant Commander John Casson, who appears later in the story in Tom Blackham's time in Stalag Luft III. He had, fortunately, talked about it in detail to his son. In the research phase, Tony gave of his time to me generously and provided crucial insight into some aspects of the Great Escape, which for many years have remained hidden from other researchers looking into that astonishing event.

I particularly wish to acknowledge the United Kingdom National Archives at Kew, for the now-declassified records relating to all aspects of Royal Air Force operations in World War II. The operational records books were vital in piecing together Joe's and Tom's operational career over Hitler's Third Reich.

I would particularly like to acknowledge Bruce Marshall, whose 1952 book *The White Rabbit* gave the details of the story of Wing Commander Yeo-Thomas, who was a close friend of Tom Blackham during their appalling incarceration at Buchenwald Concentration Camp.

I must pay tribute to Allison Paterson and Denny Neave of Big Sky Publishing for their enthusiasm, encouragement and belief in the project and managerial skills in turning the project into a book. A warm acknowledgement is also due to my editor, Lorna Hudson.

I would especially like to acknowledge the following men who flew in the Royal Air Force Bomber Command. I had drawn heavily on their experience for a previous project. Between them, they gave me a vast canvas of Royal Air Force life on which to draw for this project. This ranged across operational details, nomenclature, air force life and culture and anecdotes of facts, feelings and faults.

Sergeant Frank Walshaw	44 Squadron	Wireless operator
Pilot Officer Peter Langdon	44 Squadron	Flight engineer
Pilot Officer Colin Watt DFM	44 Squadron	Pilot
Flying Officer Don Charlwood	103 Squadron	Navigator
Warrant Officer Bert Dowty	44 Squadron	Front gunner
Warrant Officer Dennis Over	106 and 227 Squadron	Rear gunner
Sergeant Charles Churchill DFM	44 Squadron	Wireless operator

Finally, I wish to pay tribute to the 185,000 men who flew in the Royal Air Force Bomber Command for their determination, modesty, courage and acceptance that their own life may have to be given to rid the world of an evil. Almost all of their stories have been lost.

At least these two were not!

Jeff Steel
Melbourne,
Australia, February 2021

Select Bibliography

Books

Bellamy,C. 2009, *Absolute War,* Pan Military Classics

Bushby, J. 1972, *Gunner's Moon,* Futura Publications, London

Carroll, T. 2004, *The Great Escape from Stalag Luft III,* Pocket Books, London,

Chorlton, M. 2012, *The RAF Pathfinders,* Countryside Books (GB)

Charlwood, D. 1956, *No Moon Tonight,* Angus & Robertson, Australia

Cheshire, L. 1955, *Bomber Pilot,* Arrow Books (UK)

Constable, T.J. & Toliver, R.F. 1986, *Das Waren die Deutschen Fliegerasse* 1939–1945, Motorverlag, Stuttgart

Cooper, A. 2013, *Air Battle of the Ruhr,* Pen and Sword Aviation, Barnsley UK

Crawley, A. 1956, *Escape from Germany,* Fontana Books, London and Glasgow

Dear, I.C.B and Foot, M.R.D. 1995, *The Oxford Companion to the Second World War,* Oxford University Press

Eriksson, P. 2017, *Alarmstart: The German Fighter Pilot's Exerience in the Second World War,* Amberley Publishing, UK

Freeman, R. 1993, *The Royal Air Force of World War Two in Colour,* Brockhampton Press, London

Falconer, J. 1998, *Bomber Command Handbook 1939-1945,* Sutton Publishing, UK

Feast, S. 1992, *The Pathfinder Companion,* Grub Street Press, London

Hastings, M. 1979, *Bomber Command,* Pan MacMillan, London

Halfpenny, B.B. 2004, *Bomber Aircrew in World War Two,* Pen and Sword Aviation, Barnsley, South Yorkshire

Irving, D. 1964, *Und Deuschlands Städte Starben Nicht,* Schweizer Druck und Verlagshaus AG, Zürich

Jacobs, P. 2020, The Twins: *The SOE's Brothers of Vengeance,* The History Press, Cheltenham, UK

Marshall, Bruce, 1952, *The White Rabbit,* Pan Books, London

Middlebrook, Martin, 1988, *The Berlin Raids,* Pen & Sword Aviation, Barnsley, UK

Murray, W. 1988, *Luftwaffe,* Grafton Publishing, London

Neillands, R. 2004, *The Bomber War,* John Murray, London

Padfield, P. 1990, Himmler, Reichsführer SS, Papermac, London

Richards, D. 2001, *RAF Bomber Command in the Second World War,* Penguin, London

Terraine, J. 2010, *The Right of the Line,* Pen and Sword Military, Barnsley, South Yorkshire

Wilson, K. 2019 *Men of Air,* Simon and Schuster

Journals

Blackham T, RAF Flying Review July/August 1954, *Escape to Hell*

UK National Archives

RAF Operational Record Books ref AIR/27/1788

Films

Lost Airmen of Buchenwald, 2011, directed by Michael Dorsey

Websites

50 and 61 Squadrons Association Website
http://www.no-50-and-no-61-squadrons-association.co.uk/veterans-album/air-com-thomas-h-blackhamdfcobe-pow/

Asisbiz Military History Website
https://www.asisbiz.com/history.html

Australian War Memorial
https://www.awm.gov.au/visit/exhibitions/stolenyears/ww2/germany/story5

France Craches
http://francecrashes39-45.net/buchenwald.php

RAF Pathfinders Archive
https://raf-pathfinders.com/

Wikipedia – 'Bombardment of Mailly-le-Camp'
https://en.wikipedia.org/wiki/Bombardment_of_Mailly-le-Camp

Wikipedia – 'Nacht und Nebel'
https://en.wikipedia.org/wiki/Nacht_und_Nebel

World War Two Today Website
http://ww2today.com/4-may-1944-heavy-raf-losses-in
-attack-on-wehrmacht-barracks

About the Authors

Jeff Steel

My interest in Hitler's war started dramatically. At age seven, with my parents, I emerged from Euston Station in London. The immediate area resembled a smoke-blackened Pompeii. 'There was a terrible war,' my parents told me. Their house in Coventry had been bombed: their sole remaining possession was a large mirror. The world had gone mad. This triggered a strong desire in me to understand the craziness.

The result of this seminal event was a lifetime of intense curiosity on all aspects of the war. As a student, I had worked in Germany on the site of the Battle of the Bulge. I found many artefacts; fortunately, none of them exploded. Throughout my professional life, I visited many World War II sites, including Pearl Harbour, Dresden and the Burma Railway. I was fortunate to not only meet and hear the stories of the men who had fought for the Allied side, but also the veterans of Stalingrad and the Siege of Leningrad.

Over time, one paramount feature distilled its way to prominence. *In the crucible of war, ordinary men do extraordinary things.*

My breakthrough in writing was to ghost-write *No Heil Hitler* for my friend Paul Cieslar, which won a prize and is now published in four countries.

This success led to other assignments, now including *Best of Times, Worst of Times.*

Joe Shuttleworth was silent about his wartime experience for most of his life. The key to the secret, extraordinary wartime adventures of this decent and undramatic man had lain hidden in his memory for six decades. I am very glad to have been granted the privilege of telling his story.

Joe Shuttleworth

Shortly after the cessation of hostilities Freda was to follow Joe to a joyful reunion in Australia. They were to remain inseparable for life. Joe retired from the uniformed aspect of military life. He joined the Repatriation Hospital in his native Queensland as a clerk. In this role he organised the medical care of survivors of World War II plus the Korean and Vietnam Wars. His diligence, administrative talent and natural intelligence took him to the top job.

In 1981 he was recognised with an MBE award for services to the repatriation of Australian servicemen and women.

In 1985 he moved to Melbourne as the Chief Executive Officer of the Heidelberg Rehabilitation Hospital in Melbourne. It is a mark of the man that it was said

440

of him that he knew every member of staff by their first name.

As with many members of the armed forces Joe was not initially keen on the process of writing this book. It was true that Joe's war may have been 'the best of times'. This was more than balanced by the loss of his comrades in the bomber crew.

It was thanks to his daughter Dawn that Joe took part in this project. She persuaded him that the course of his life had taken him through a crisis in world history and that his personal experiences should not be lost. It was profoundly sad for him to learn what became of the rest of the crew.

It was, admittedly, beyond sad for Jeff to tell him what had happened to Stewart Godfrey, his special friend, as well as of the appalling ordeal of Tom Blackham, his pilot and friend.

Joe Shuttleworth may be the last Australian serviceman to write a personal memoir about World War II.

There is one message for present and future generations that Joe wanted to come from this book. It is his personal dictum: 'In war no one wins.'

441

Also by the Author

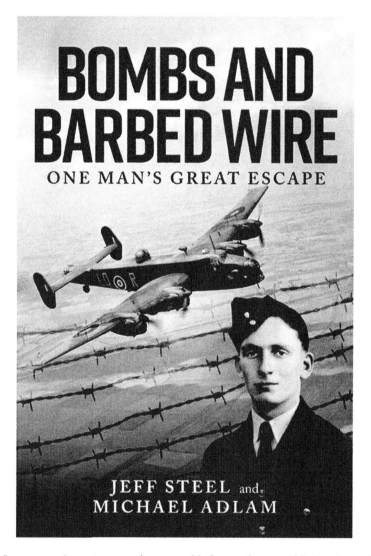

View sample pages, reviews and information on this book and other titles at www.bigskypublishing.com.au

Available now online or at all good bookstores

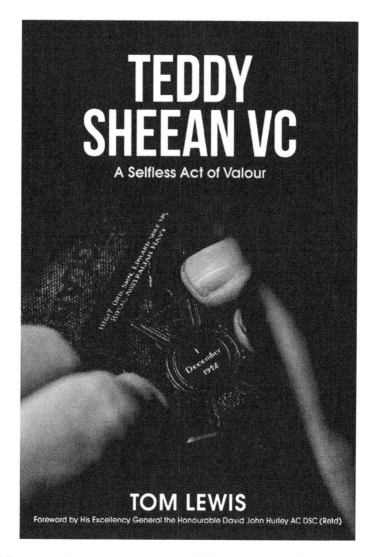

View sample pages, reviews and information on this book and other titles at www.bigskypublishing.com.au

For More Great Titles visit

www.bigskypublishing.com.au

Back Cover Material

"It was the best of times, it was the worst of times..."

Charles Dickens

Joe's love of flying and adventure led him to volunteer for active service: dropping bombs on Nazi Germany. Tom's hatred of Hitler's vile regime brought him to the same point. The war to throw Joe and Tom together. Within a few desperate seconds, a nightfighter attack would rip them apart.

Best of Times, Worst of Times tells the story of two very different men but with a single vocation: to destroy the Nazi war machine. Each described themselves as ordinary men, yet their wartime experience was extraordinary.

For Joe, fate brought the best of times. He crossed the Atlantic on the Queen Elizabeth and found the woman to whom he would be married for the rest of his life. As a gunner on a Lancaster Bomber, he enjoyed the camaraderie of a band of brothers and high status among the wartime population.

For Tom, fate decreed the worst of times. Throw out of an exploding plane, he was sentenced to death by the French resistance. He knew the horror of betrayal, survived the hands of the Nazi secret police, and

446

experienced abject fear within the Buchenwald concentration camp.

A gripping true story of war, betrayal and survival constructed from personal experience, meticulous research and eye-witness accounts.

Printed in Great Britain
by Amazon

36800625R00251